From Lowbrow to Nobrow

From Lowbrow to Nobrow

Peter Swirski

McGill-Queen's University Press
Montreal & Kingston · London · Ithaca

© McGill-Queen's University Press 2005
ISBN 0-7735-2992-6 (cloth)
ISBN 0-7735-3019-3 (paper)

Legal deposit fourth quarter 2005
Bibliothèque nationale du Québec

Printed in Canada on acid-free paper.

McGill-Queen's University Press acknowledges the support of the
Canada Council for the Arts for our publishing program. We also
acknowledge the financial support of the Government of Canada
through the Book Publishing Industry Development Program
(BPIDP) for our publishing activities.

LIBRARY AND ARCHIVES CANADA CATALOGUING
IN PUBLICATION

Swirski, Peter, 1963–
From lowbrow to nobrow / Peter Swirski.
Includes bibliographical references and index.
ISBN 0-7735-2992-6 (bnd)
ISBN 0-7735-3019-3 (pbk)
1. Popular literature – History and criticism. 2. Fiction – 20th
century – History and criticism. 3. Čapek, Karel, 1890–1938.
Válka s mloky. 4. Chandler, Raymond, 1888–1959. Playback.
5. Lem, Stanislaw. Katar. I. Title.
PN56.P55S94 2005   809.3   C2005-903570-6

Set in 10.5/14 Sabon with Compacta and Univers Condensed
Book design & typesetting by zijn digital

This book is dedicated to Rosanna

Contents

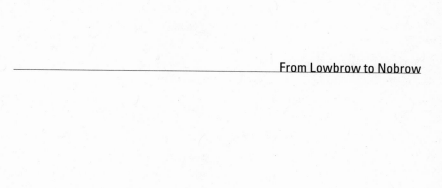

From Lowbrow to Nobrow

Introduction: Books without Frontiers

We are seeking to define and consider one central principle: that of the essential relation, the true interaction, between patterns learned and created in the mind and the patterns communicated and made active in relationships, conventions, and institutions. Culture is our name for this process and its results.

Raymond Williams, *The Long Revolution*

Being at once an aficionado of "serious" writing and a buff of pulp fiction may be the lot of many scholars and readers of literature. It has been self-diagnosed, after all, in such impeccably credentialed intellectuals as Gide, Borges or Amis. Professing the classics and, when no one is around, languishing over a dog-eared copy of a James Fenimore Cooper, James M. Cain, or Elmore Leonard may be typical symptoms of this literary-critical syndrome. One is reminded of a playful scene from Walker Percy's *The Moviegoer* in which a small-time stockbroker, Binx Bolling, maintains professional appearances by concealing the popular book he reads from the eyes of his secretary. With a studious mien, he thus buries himself in one of C.M. Doughty's adventures enclosed in a Standard and Poor binder. More than a fictional creation, Binx Bolling is each of us who has passed away hours reading sci-fi or spy-fi, watching *Prime Suspect* or *Monty Python*, or listening to Zappa or 2Pac – *mon semblable, mon frère*.

Yet, professing the institutional coverage model, many institutions and curricula appear resistant to the implications of a vast corpus of scholarship on *Trivialliteratur* or *paralittérature* in the German and French tradition, let alone such research in popular culture studies. On the inherited view of institutional education, literary studies ought to refrain from taking seriously the aesthetics of popular fiction, with the exception of folk traditions from the past dim enough to become disciplinarily legitimate. Conspicuously it beguiled even Marxist scholars, those theoretical champions of the masses. Tony Bennett, a distinguished Marxist and popular culture expert himself, pulls no punches. "Marxist critics have, for the greater part, merely mirrored bourgeois criticism, accepting its valuations and duplicating its exclusions."[1]

For better or worse, the evidence appears to support him. Even the most famous graduates of the Frankfurt School, such as Adorno, reserve space for the discussion of popular culture but in the name of values that are demonstrably elitist. Others, like Althusser, segregate by fiat the crème of "authentic art" from works of "average or mediocre level" and proceed to completely ignore the latter.[2] Nor is this atypical. If you look past the jargon-laden theory of academic manifestos such as the monumental *Marxism and the Interpretation of Culture*, critical practice is all too often at odds with the official stamp of approval bestowed on mass culture. At worst, many Marxists pause only long enough to trash popular fiction before moving on to the true and tried classics of our civilization. At best, they ignore it altogether. This is unfortunate inasmuch as literary scholarship cedes the initiative to other disciplines only too willing to take up the study of genre aesthetics. In recent years, for example, popular culture has become the subject of intense philosophical scrutiny, with Nöel Carroll in "The Nature of Mass Art" openly goading philosophers to come to grips with this "most dominant art in our times" (5).

Numerically at least, genre fiction is the nexus of modern culture, but this very popularity means that it is not art – or so goes the tacit consensus. After all, if genre literature were art, it would not appeal to so many people. These are the same people whom Plato and Burke dismissed as oxen and swine, whom Thomas Hardy patronized as mentally unquickened and who, according to D.H. Lawrence, should never learn to read and write. This is the same Lawrence who scandalized his age with heavy-duty erotica, and the same young Hardy who liberally exploited the conventions of the then most popular of genres, the sensation novel. If anything, documents Katherine Neale in "Desperate Remedies," this is one more proof of Hardy's "debt to popular fiction, and not his rejection of it" (122).

Even from a socio-cultural standpoint any demarcation of a field of study that leaves the majority of its subjects outside the gates must appear methodologically shaky. A chemist who contended that the province of chemistry is only a select group of valuable elements such as platinum or gold, would surely not be worth his NaCL. Mass appeal has always been identified with the lowest denominator. Little regard has been given to the view that novels may reach wide audiences because of their ability to identify and to satisfy a taste shared among a large number of people. Did Alex Haley's crossover blockbuster *Roots* target the lowest of the common? Did Eco in his medievalist and Latinate *The Name of the Rose*? If you answer "No," then there may be a world of semantic and cultural difference between the *lowest* and the *largest* common denominator.

Over the decades popular fiction has been the target of trenchant critiques by cultural luminaries of the calibre of Leavis, Eliot, Ortega Y Gasset, Horkheimer, Adorno, Greenberg, Baudrillard, and Bloom. Finding mostly rank commercialism and literary paucity, many fashioned scenarios of cultural doomsday, though typically without much concrete data to support them. Such absence of systematic evidence is only one reason why many perceptions pertaining to this most dominant art in our times are more wishful thinking than a viable axiological theory. Several recent studies have gone quite a way towards demystifying some of the vices with which genre literature has been saddled in the past, such as bastardizing the literary culture in general or precipitating a decline in book reading in particular.[3] Joining the debate, I propose to evaluate the socio-aesthetic merits of popular fiction through a comparative analysis with highbrow fiction. I document how thoroughly their aesthetics have interpenetrated each other, integrating early in the twentieth-century into what I identify as an abiding literary phenomenon – nobrow art.

The scale and the nature of the difficulties involved is, without doubt, immense. Like Bush's Son-of-Star-Wars fantasy, popular fiction stirs passions and controversy left and right, making if difficult to find deliberative middle ground. An aesthete of Arnoldian persuasion might even object that comparing genre literature and canonical art is mixing crab-apples and Sunkist oranges: fruitless at best, incommensurable at worst. These are important considerations, and I address them head-on in Chapters 1 and 2. But even if we can raise theoretical doubts as to whether popular and highbrow fiction differ in degree or in kind, such divisions may not hold up in practice. Graham Greene, a modern classic, began his career trying to distinguish between novels he thought of as espionage entertainment and those he thought of as art. The day he realized they were one and the same, he began to write his best fiction in the popular vein and never looked back.

THE NATURE OF LOWBROW AND NOBROW FICTION

The average critic never recognizes achievement when it happens. He explains it after it has become respectable.

Raymond Chandler

My working assumption is that popular literature expresses and reflects the aesthetic and social values of its readers. As such the decision to participate in genre literature is a matter of choice and not necessarily ideological brainwashing, cultural brow-beating, or

declining literary standards. Debating the aesthetics of genre literature demands, of course, attention both to its literary and its socio-
ideological traits, including the nature and range of its subjects, the
values it feeds back into public opinion, and the level of cultural
literacy it shapes. In Part 1 of this book, Chapters 1 through 3 ask a
series of general questions about the nature of lowbrow and nobrow
fiction and their relation to their canonized kin. This tripartite
separation of the main lines of inquiry – sociological, aesthetic, and
related to literary genres – ought to be something of an improvement over studies in which they mix freely, sometimes to the detri-
ment of the clarity of the issues under discussion.

In Chapter 1 a review of available socio-statistical data permits
me to shed light on the key, if not always fully articulated, beliefs
still underwriting many institutional curricula. As these beliefs, by
now a part of our cultural subconscious, lie behind most critiques
of mass fiction, refuting them goes towards establishing a better
model of literary culture and a clearer understanding of the forces
shaping it. In the past, getting a grip on popular fiction has occasionally been impeded by ignorance of its products. As I argue at
length, today such ignorance is not only a matter of highbrow prejudice but also the sheer inundation of print. In the days of yore,
one might have believed that literature deserving recognition would
sooner or later find its shelf in the cultural supermarket. Not so in a
system grown so large as to be on the verge of collapsing under its
own weight. As some observers have mordantly observed, dozens of
Shakespeares might be writing today under the mantle of obscurity
thrust upon them by the quantity of books in print.

Many humanities-trained academics gloss – or, at best, wax
apocalyptic – over the exponential growth of the publishing industry. Few put statistical data on the table, and fewer still acknowledge the impact of the changes this growth portends. Yet a simple
comparison suffices to make the point. A little over a century ago
the first English edition of *Books in Print* compiled by Joseph
Whitaker (of the world-famous Almanack) boasted 35,000 titles
from 135 publishers. These days the millennial edition of Whitaker's hovers a couple of breaths away from 1,000,000 titles from

over 40,000 publishers. In France, *Livres Disponibles* is inching towards 500,000 titles available for leisurely browsing. Germany, Austria, and Switzerland boast 830,066 titles and row entries plus 1,500,000 references from more than 15,000 publishers, as per *Verzeichnisses Lieferbarer Bücher*. On the other side of the Atlantic, the *American Books in Print* database tips the scales at more than 3,400,000. Sobering as they are, these numbers do not reflect the total quantity of titles available, only the titles in print in any given year. How these figures changed the relations among writers, readers, and critics, and how the entire literary system might evolve further, are some of the questions I aim to answer in Chapter 1.

Building on this statistical and comparative data, in Chapter 2 I survey and synthesize a century of popular fiction criticism in an effort to elucidate the aesthetics of popular and nobrow art. In a departure from studies that typically focus on a single genre or single historical period, I seek a broader perspective in a systematic overview of these positions and their oppositions. Copiously illustrated with case studies, Chapter 2 forms the historical and argumentative backbone of the book. It makes headroom for the comparison of highbrow and lowbrow aesthetics by spotlighting the ways in which they have always interpenetrated each other. An inventory of this kind also illuminates the socio-aesthetic determinants of canon selection, particularly since many of today's classics were unabashedly popular bestsellers in their day.[4]

In many cases, this synthetic review of historical data alone will offer a corrective to the assorted debates about the aesthetics of popular fiction. At other times I proceed by a *reductio* of their premises or by a thorough documentation of pulp fiction's "inbred" analogues with the canon. To contextualize the debate I conclude with a few words about the novel cultural environment brought about by the means of mass production and dissemination of literature. As will become apparent, some of the qualitative roots of inattention to genre fiction grow out of the quantitative changes highlighted in Chapter 1. The critical methods and educational models of yesterday no longer suffice in an era where more books have seen the light of day since 1950 than in all of history combined. As many of the arguments rehearsed in Chapter 2 bear on the issue of literary democracy in the classroom, a comparative look at highbrow and lowbrow fiction may, if nothing else, help us to adjust our curricular strategies.

Speaking of popular fiction, it would be difficult to avoid the subject of genres altogether. Bearing this in mind, Chapter 3 argues for no less than a complete rethinking of the concept of genre. My prime target here is the structuralist model, which, despite a prolonged intellectual siege, continues to influence scholars of sundry disciplinary stripes. Armed with a thought experiment about a remarkable civilization with a remarkable form of art, I raise doubts about the notion that literary genres are empirically definable and immutable. Comparing two stories about two series of macabre deaths, I further show that aesthetic properties of stories are determined not only by what's in the text, but by the text as filtered through the work's category.

The remainder of the chapter sketches a pragmatic model of a literary genre as a *game* in the game-theoretic sense. The game I have in mind behaves very much like something straight out of Lewis Carroll. Not only is it open-ended, but it has pretty flexible rules, some of which may even be made up as you go along. Put more formally, I make the case for a model of genres as gaming strategies during an interactive, interdependent, and imperfectly informed game of literary interpretation. Before this full-scale make-over, however, it is useful to set the stage with a look at some of the debates about the nature and interpretation of genre fiction. For this reason Chapter 3 begins by testing the integrity of a few philosophical arguments developed to take stock of how and why we read popular literature. Prominent among them is an intriguing paradox known in aesthetics as the paradox of junk fiction.

IN PURSUIT OF WHAT I CALL ARTERTAINMENT

Procrustes, you will remember, stretched or chopped down his guests to fit the bed he had constructed. But perhaps you have not heard the rest of the story. He measured them up before they left the next morning, and wrote a learned paper "On the Uniformity of Stature of Travellers" for the Anthropological Society of Attica.

Arthur Eddington

All together, the first three chapters form a panoramic and interdisciplinary Part 1 that is quite distinct from Part 2. Where Part 1 is synthetic, Part 2 is analytic; where Part 1 lays down the theory, Part 2 is all interpretive practice; where Part 1 seeks an overview, Part 2 seeks to understand particular novels and particular writers.

Having surveyed popular literature under diverse methodological banners, I put my theses to a test by examining a range of literary case studies. Specifically, I zero in on three popular genres – science fantasy, the hardboiled novel, and the medical thriller – and on their forays into highbrow aesthetics. Chapters 4, 5, and 6 thus investigate three authors whose books highlight the hazards and rewards of nobrow traffic between the lowbrow and the highbrow. Nobrow, in my view, is not merely a matter of crossover reception but, rather, an intentional stance whereby authors simultaneously target both extremes of the literary spectrum. Shakespeare was a popular writer at the Globe and his work was equally appreciated by the English court. But inasmuch as the highbrow-lowbrow divisions were not part of the socio-aesthetic paradigm of his times, he was not a nobrow writer. On the other hand, in contradistinction to scholars who, particularly after John Seabrook's 2000 book, identify nobrow culture as essentially a contemporary formation, my argument is that, by the first decades of the twentieth century, the popular-highbrow distinction in literature had already dissolved into nobrow art.

Chapter 4 thus introduces a modernist master, Karel Čapek, and his brilliant science fantasy, *War with the Newts* (1936), whose reception is almost as whimsical as is the novel itself. This acrobatic satire won Čapek the Nobel nomination, only to lose him the prize as fear-whipped Swedish academics backed down in alarm over Hitler's reaction. Unforgettable as it was for its contemporaries, today *War with the Newts* lies largely forgotten. Questions of cultural memory fuel my discussion of the novel as I try to account for its disappearance from the modernist canon. Part of the answer lies in its refusal to succumb to the Procrustean hatchet of ready-made aesthetic categories. Out of the formulas of the scientific romance, adventure story, and dystopia Čapek engineers a nobrow oxymoron, a hybrid of high modernism and popular art.

In Chapter 5 I investigate another genre-defying novel that fell through the cracks all the way down to the literary basement. Nowadays Raymond Chandler may be slowly gaining a toehold in the highbrow camp, thanks to such hardboiled classics as *The Big Sleep* or *Farewell, My Lovely*. Yet within his canon, if one may speak of such a thing, his last novel, *Playback* (1958), plays the unenviable role of a partly retarded cousin. Hardly anyone cares to remember it or even mention it by name, and those who do often sound like they wish they hadn't. This may be understandable insofar as Chandler's swan song is anything but a vintage Philip Marlowe caper. Yet this refusal to fit the mould is precisely what is so interesting for, even as it blends popular form, socio-philosophical content, and self-deconstructing parody, *Playback* adapts the tough-guy formula to the pursuit of an ultramodern aesthetics of irony. Too literary for the murder-mystery mainstream, too lowbrow for the literati, the book in which the author and his famous creation shake hands, trade quips, and pay a campy intertextual tribute to an entire literary school may be a nobrow winner in search of a pennant.

With Chandler taking us out of the first half of the twentieth century, Chapter 6 takes on a writer whose career flourished in the second half and continues in our millennium. Fabulists like Stanislaw Lem, who habitually tackle questions of type and magnitude that take them outside the radius of realism, may be literature's equivalent of remedial students. Known in North America – when known at all – as a science fiction ace, Lem is one of the most eclectic and unpigeonholeable writers in recent history. In a constellation of international bestsellers that runs into dozens of titles, a star of the first magnitude is his philosophical nail-biter *The Chain of Chance* (1976). A game of probabilistic chess plotted with the precision of a Cray taraflop, for a quarter century the novel was known only – if known at all – as a work of science fiction. If so, it is a peculiar kind of science fiction as, on balance, there is more future shock to be got out of "Rip Van Winkle." Indeed, calling it sci-fi is like trying to do justice to Baywatch babes by calling them viviparous mammals: technically not inaccurate, but missing the point altogether. If popular art trucks in formulas, Lem forages for them in the most unlikely places, including quantum science and laws of probability. Questions of genre and popular conventions, spawned by the interpretive ambiguity and cognitive hubris of Lem's novel, are at the forefront of Chapter 6.

No one can, of course, exhaust the interpretive and socio-cultural issues dormant in these three novels. My efforts must perforce be limited to detailing the ways in which they crisscross the literary highs and lows in pursuit of what I call artertainment. A liaison between a pedigreed Derby champ and a lowly donkey yields no more than a sterile mule; in literature, however, crossing cultural tracks often rejuvenates rather than stultifies. Mediating back and forth between the intellectual and the popular, the three works show that the only sterile thing around may be the socio-aesthetic categories that cannot accommodate them.

ACADEMIC DICTIONARY OF QUOTATIONS

The critic, one would suppose, if he is to justify his existence, should endeavour to discipline his personal prejudices and cranks ... in the common pursuit of true judgment.

T.S. Eliot

The eclectic array of novels that make up Part 2 is as much a matter of cross-cultural coverage as chronological continuity. Čapek's demise in 1938, only two years after *War With the Newts*, segues into Chandler's novelistic debut in 1939, while the latter's *Playback*, which came out only a year before his death in 1959, coincides with the early efforts from Lem. Between them, therefore, the three writers cover the entire century over which one can examine their nobrow art. Published in Europe as well as America, the three provide an even more representative illustration of the issues at hand, reflecting the fact that, in culture and business, popular fiction is a genuinely international phenomenon, transcending national, political, and linguistic frontiers. Bearing this in mind, when possible I introduce data on select European and even global trends in addition to those in the home market. The fact that much of my data comes from the United States is not only a factor of access but also of sheer size, which makes the US of A one of the global trend-setters.

The question of representation rears its Hydra-head every time one enters the thicket of popular fiction criticism and scholarship. A mosaic of positions, oppositions, suppositions, and presuppositions fills the air, reshaped and reconfigured in the critical version of "telephone." This is so much so that a comprehensive account of names and attributions would end up resembling a telephone directory. It is easy to lose one's bearings surrounded by libraries of sociological, philosophical, and lit-crit material on popular culture, or get bogged down in the rarefied nuance of this or that argument. Yet the need for a panoptic view necessitates an occasionally selective approach to individual theorists and individual variants of their theses, one in which I'm resigned to indulge for fear of turning this book into yet another academic dictionary of quotations. Taking issues at hand and not their proponents to be of consequence, I thus typically focus on the argument rather than on the source of that argument (unless it introduces a wholly new spin on the debate).

Inevitably there is a price to pay in attribution, chronology, and perhaps even nuance of thought. My hope is only that the gain outweighs the loss. What may be occasionally forsaken in bibliographic particulars is recouped, I venture, through a gain in perspective and clarity. In the day of disciplinary divisions and, consequently, limited visions, there is more, not less, need for a panoramic perspective. Although minted afresh, a number of arguments pursued in the opening sections of *From Lowbrow to Nobrow* have been previously rehearsed on both sides of the Atlantic.[5] Mapping strategic movements at the expense of tactical moves, Chapter 2, for example draws on decades of scholarship without necessarily trying to replicate the complete set of argumentative steps developed in each case. Critical synthesis and overview need not, of course, entail redundancy, only reinforcement, just like rereading a good book need not entail a waste of time but a recapture of pleasures past.

A short note on terminology. Speaking of popular fiction, sundry scholars call it genre, cult, mass, pulp, entertainment, junk, low, and lowbrow almost interchangeably. While demonstrably not equivalent, to sort these labels out properly would require a book in itself. If anything, defining and distinguishing terms such as highbrow, elite, canonical, classic, and avant-garde might take even longer, overwhelming this study even before it has begun. Social and cultural elites, for example, do not map perfectly onto consumers of high culture, and the avant-garde frequently seeks to break away from the highbrow mainstream. Similarly, highbrow fiction is occasionally popular as, indeed, is a significant part of the canon. All this is meant to flag my awareness of the difficulties surrounding these distinctions and definitions, and my qualified willingness to disregard them in the name of doing my bit for the rainforest and keeping this book down to printable proportions. In the end, I'm betting that my common sense grasp of terms like popular and highbrow (and their kin listed above) will be not too different from what everyone else understands everyone else to understand these terms to mean.

Through this book I hope to make a contribution to a more informed debate on the cultural standards of today and the cultural policies for tomorrow. Some of the evidence introduced in the pages that follow may be needed for a better comparison and understanding of popular and highbrow literatures and the ways in which they have been recombining into nobrow art from much earlier than supposed. With this goal in mind, *From Lowbrow to Nobrow* was written in a way meant to be easily read and easily understood. If it fails in this or indeed any other aspect, the *culpa* is entirely *mea*.

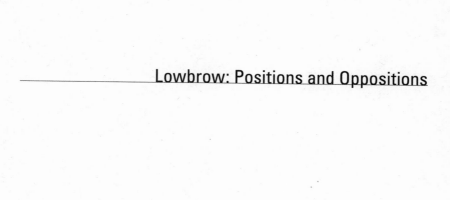

Lowbrow: Positions and Oppositions

1 Facts and Popular Fictions

Popular literature has been the object of a constant bombardment of social anxieties for over two thousand years, and nearly the whole of the critical tradition stood against it. The greater part of the reading and listening public has ignored the critics and censors for exactly the same length of time.

Northrop Frye, *The Secular Scripture*

The author is dead. So professed famously Roland Barthes and Michel Foucault, even as they continued to publicize their authorship on the covers of their books.[1] At one point this odd gospel gained much currency in academia, even spilling into the mass media tickled to report on the kooky theories from professors of that slippery formation known as postmodernism. Such intellectual posturing has, of course, nothing to do with real-life threats to real-life authors who, for one reason or another, incur the disfavour of those for whom sightseeing means seeing the world through the sights of a gun. After the tragic executions in Nigeria and the lifting of the *fatwa* that freed Rushdie to appear for photo-ops at high-profile book fairs, the number of known authors on the endangered list has indeed dwindled. The Jordanian Islamic Action Front has recently even denied that it had issued a *fatwa* on Khalid Duran for his *Children of Abraham* (2001) – this in response to accusations to that effect by the American Jewish Committee, the book's publisher. Evidently both the AJC and the JIA have learned their lesson about the value of book-selling publicity from the Rushdie affair. Indeed, an inspection of the nuts and bolts of the publishing industry reveals that real challenges to authorship come from the directions altogether overlooked by Barthes and Foucault, such as fiction factories, novelizations, direct mail-order publishing, or multimedia-packaging.

But what about the death of the book? Are there reasons to believe that this is another myth, albeit one that refuses to be laid to rest? "People Don't Read Any More," proclaim banner headlines in – of all places – the print media. Others draw attention to a recent Gallup Poll that appears to diagnose a new trend: aliteracy. "I didn't finish one book," demurs a typical undergraduate who aced her English course, "I skimmed every second page."[2] Such a willing suspension of belief in reading is said to affect even educated professionals, including American teachers who, in the same Gallup Poll, confess to the same aliteracy rate as their students: 50 percent.

The book is a thing of the past, we hear, slain by the twin assassins of TV and Hollywood flicks. Yet, as Patricia Holt reports in *Publishers Weekly*, a full one-third of all motion pictures made annually in the United States are based on previously published novels. Nor is the umbilical connection between books and films anything new. During the silent film era, Penguin's Reader's Library raked in massive profits from novelizations that appeared on bookstands even as the marquees hit the town. Von Harbou's famous *Metropolis*, *The Sea Beast* (with Douglas Fairbanks), *My Best Girl* (with Mary Pickford), or *Cobra* (Rudolf Valentino) were all made readily available to people who preferred the allure of the printed page to the moving pictures. And as for the death of the book, statistics tell a different story. The postwar era has experienced such a runaway boom in publishing (see below) that the book industry keeps dispatching red flares calling for some form of reduction in numbers.

These days the pundits add the Internet to the reasons why books are allegedly working under a death sentence, this despite the fact that two-thirds of the world does not even have a telephone.[3] Books are going the way of the dodo, chip in hi-tek gurus, clipping to their belts (next to the pager, iPod, and cellphone) the e-book. This hand-held computer uses plastic inserts the size of credit cards that can hold the contents of entire novels and even provide the illusion of page turning. Succumbing to this kind of futuristic hype, in which books were mere roadkill on the information autobahn, in the 1990s academic libraries drastically scaled down purchases of new volumes, as if expecting e-ducation to go digital by Y2K. Yet, although the hype and its devices have been around for some time now, the paper-bound, dog-eared book refuses to throw in the towel – and perhaps for a good reason. After all, quipped the director of Princeton University Press, "Who wants to go to bed with a floppy disk – or with a microfilm projector?"[4]

Let us examine, then, the facts behind the demise of the book. Despite all forecasts and most people's media-fed impressions, book publishing has flourished since the dawn of the TV era. UNESCO and other sources (Escarpit; Curwen) report that worldwide book production, as expressed in number of titles, has increased more than threefold between 1950 and 1980. The accepted estimate for 1950 is 230,000 titles, with the total climbing to 725,000 titles in 1980. This rate of increase is much higher than that of the world's population, which, during the same period, grew from 2.5 billion to 4.5 billion.

There are of course known methodological issues that surround such global tallies, beginning with the basic collection problem: how detailed and/or reliable are a country's output surveys? One could further wonder about collection lags (how often do governments run their surveys?), missing data (why do some nations not report findings in certain years?), discrepancies (why do national estimates sometimes depart from UNESCO tallies or show illogical spikes and troughs from year to year?), or even absence of reports from certain countries altogether. In spite of these and cognate problems, cross-checks reveal a high degree of consistency across various reporting agencies, and the picture is unrelenting. The total number of book copies printed, pegged at 2.5 billion in 1950, was 9 billion in 1980, more than 13 billion in 1996, and racing towards 15 billion as the twentieth century drew to a close. In other words, with one volume per person worldwide in 1950, thirty years later there were two – a 100 percent increase in little more than the lifespan of one generation – and around the turn of the millennium, closer to two and a half.[5] That same generation passed the baton to ours, which, after the year 2000, continues to produce books at the same supercharged rate.

Still, these annual figures do not amount to much until understood within a proper *cumulative* context. More than half of all the books ever published came out after the first hydrogen bomb; more than half of all wordsmiths who ever put pen to paper did so after the birth of TV. An inverted pyramid or a giant time cone, its apex in the past and its cavernous maw in our face, is how Dali might have painted the book world as we know it. Take all the books and add the output from the myriad literary journals, magazines, fugitive publishing, underground presses, and the like, and you can begin to realize the amount of words deposited year in, year out, on library bookshelves, already filled to the point of bursting. Despite the nostalgic idealization of the Renaissance as the time when one could allegedly keep up with the flow of print, those days (if they ever existed) are gone forever, never to come back.

The figures closer to home are even more unequivocal. It is hard to square the myth that people do not read anymore with the fact that book production, the quantity of bookstores, and total sales fail to display any signs of decline. Quite the contrary. The number of new titles released each year in the United States more than quadrupled between 1950 and 1991, with respective figures of roughly 11,000 and 49,000 (after peaking at 50,000 in 1985). In the same period the number of bookstores shot up from over 8,000 to more than 25,000, climbing to within a handshake of 30,000 as I write these words. These trends are, needless to say, not confined to the United States. The approximate number of new titles released in Great Britain, for example, in 1955 and 1995 was, respectively, 14,000 and 90,000.[6]

I suppose it is possible to question the correlation between book publishing and book readership, so to honour the skeptic, let us follow the link between book publishing and the intermediate stage: book purchasing. Here the numbers are even more eloquent. Driving a stake through the heart of the myth of a non-reading public, the total 1991 book sales were thirty-five times greater than in 1950, ballooning from under $0.5 billion to $16.1 billion. The mushroom cloud of money to be made in publishing books, in the age in which no one supposedly reads them, just keeps getting bigger and bigger. In 2000, net sales in the United States have crept close to a tidy $25,000,000,000 – expanding, according to the American Book Industry Study Group, by another 3 percent in 2001.[7]

Even though the twin Anglo-American markets are the giants of publishing, they make up just a fraction of the global trends moving in the same direction. The numbers again speak for themselves. Rounded up, the growth in the international book title output between 1990 and 1996 looked more or less like this: China up from 74K to 110K, Germany up from 61K to 71K, Spain up from 36K to 46K, and Italy up from 25K to 35K.[8] Even Canada found a front seat on this runaway train, climbing from 8K in 1990 to an estimated 20K in 1996.[9]

"HONEY, I BLEW UP THE BOOK"

The book publishing business – the one that has to do with big name authors and big money and sexy ladies and sexy literary gentlemen – has nothing to do with book publishing. It gets the attention of the press and the people who are dinner-party knowledgeable, but it gives a black eye to what real book publishing is about.

Don Fine (Arbor House)

If you ask Lemuel Gulliver, he will tell you that bigger is not necessarily better and that one ought to be careful about greeting these

colossal numbers with a triple *"Helas*!" There is no straight correlation between quantity and quality in the world of publishing – at
least none has ever been established – and even less in the world
of art. It used to be that books were written because their authors
had something to say; nowadays many write to find out *if* they have
anything to say. Moreover, averaging statistical data frequently
conceals an uneven distribution of readership. In 1951, for example,
10 percent of the adult population accounted for 70 percent of book
reading, and 10 percent of buyers were responsible for 80 percent
of sales.[10] Changes in demographics and gains in general education
notwithstanding, it is at least conceivable that the percentages may
be similarly skewed today.

The fact that there are many more outlets for buying novels cannot hide that the lion's share belongs to a handful of bestseller-and-
moccacino chains whose priorities are often at odds with those of
book lovers and book buyers. Worse, balance-sheet considerations
mean that most booksellers refuse to buy first novels altogether and
balk at storing titles that do not promise better-than-average sales.
A generation back, Howard Kaminsky, the president and publisher
of the vastly successful Warner Books, ruefully commented: "Six
years ago, we were publishing perhaps twenty books a month. Now
we publish fourteen, including reissues. And our sales are about
six times what they were six years ago. We publish more books by
publishing fewer books."[11]

Be that as it may, a sure sign of the publishing industry's vitality
is the keen interest that Wall Street has evinced in its operations.
With skyrocketing college enrolments and post-Sputnik investments in education, research, and libraries, the postwar decades
were boom years for publishing. The key players thrived by becoming public stock companies and funding a tsunami of expansion
(Random House, Houghton Mifflin), diversifying into other fields
(Macmillan, Harcourt), swallowing their smaller brethren (Harper
and Row buying out J.B. Lippincott; the Hearst syndicate adding
the hardcover Arbor House to their softcover Avon Books), or succumbing to the widely publicized "urge to merge" (Doubleday and
Dell, Viking and Penguin). Others ended up grafted onto multi-

media corporate giants. Matsushita Electric, for example, acquired not only the Music Corporation of America but, riding coattails, the Putnam-Berkeley Publishing Group. By the early 1980s Doubleday remained the *only* family-owned business, before it too was absorbed by Bertelsmann, the German communications conglomerate that became the template for the menacing dot-com empire fought by Bond in *Tomorrow Never Dies*.

The clearest index of how profitable book publishing has become may be the speed with which the movie industry got into the act. MCA, Filmway Pictures, Gulf and Western, and others – all now own reputable publishing houses. Gulf and Western, for instance, boasts Paramount, Simon and Schuster, as well as Pocket Books in its entertainment division, with Warner Communications having founded its own Warner Books. Oprah Winfrey, the queen of daytime TV and a media titan in her own right, has in the meantime branched out into her own book club and a literary magazine. In a 2003 ceremony she received accolades on top of a standing ovation from the Association of American Publishers for her contributions to publishing.

Besides establishing beyond reasonable doubt that book reading is not in decline, what else do recent statistics document? Two patterns must be singled out. One is the negligible percentage of titles traditionally accorded attention by literature curricula – time-tried classics, poetry, and new literary fiction – among this renaissance of reading. The estimates for book distribution through US general retailers are quite revealing. For the four most relevant categories of fiction, their respective shares of the 1999 market were: popular fiction (31.5 percent), bestsellers (12.1 percent), classics (0.9 percent), literary fiction and poetry (0.3 percent).[12] Of even greater significance, however, is the comparative index to contemporary book culture. To put it mildly, the situation is even more lopsided, with the classics, literary fiction, and poetry amounting to less than 3 percent of all four fiction categories under discussion. The picture is equally lopsided elsewhere in the world: an astounding 45 percent of all books and periodicals sold in Japan are the popular *manga* cartoons.

Two quick rejoinders. First, book distribution numbers can sometimes mislead due to the common practice of remaindering unsold copies, which can reach a jaw-dropping 40 percent of total run.[13] Second, a counterpoint: the above is at least partly offset by the presence of other fiction categories (i.e., juvenile), which, when taken into account, bring the picture back to where Harry Potter left it in the last paragraph. A cross-check with more recent data compiled for the American Booksellers Association by the market researchers from the NPD Group suggests that the above figures are, in fact, highly accurate. Popular fiction's share of consumer purchases of adult books not only remains constant but also closely matches the figures from distribution. In 1991, for example, pulp fiction (comprising Adult, Espionage/Thriller, Fantasy, General, Historical, Male Adventure, Mystery/Detective, Occult, Religious, Romance, Science Fiction, Suspense/Psychology, TV Movies, and Western) claimed no less than 54.9 percent of the buyer's market to the highbrow's 2.9 percent. Once again, the 1998 figures give the lion's share of 51.9 percent to popular literature, with 3.9 percent going to Art/Literature/Poetry (the latter comprising Art/Architecture, Literature-Classics/Contemporary, Performing Arts, Poetry/Plays, and Pop Arts).

It is true that, in terms of titles released annually, highbrow fiction commands a greater share of the market than distribution figures allow. But there yawns a gulf the size of Norman Mailer's ego between the public and the custodians of letters with regard to what they buy and read, and what they peg their cultural literacy on. The knee-jerk defence that the highbrow 3 percent constitutes the cream of the literary crop must contend with several rejoinders. Quite apart from the accuracy of such claims (to be examined in Chapter 2), such elitism seems misplaced when considering the literary system within its socio-cultural context. Moreover, a defence of this kind could compel only to the extent that popular novels received the type of critical analysis accorded to the classics, which they manifestly do not. When pulled out of obscurity, however, with their jackets dusted and their pedigrees suppressed, genre writers prove rewarding subjects for all manner of socio-aesthetic manoeuvres, as evidenced by a spate of MLA panels on Stephen King, Bram Stoker, and Raymond Chandler. Recent studies, such as Walton and Jones's *Detective Agency* or Paula Rabinowitz's *Black and White and Noir*, elevate an entire pulp genre to a form of historical sensibility that blurs the line between popular fiction and serious socio-political commentary.

Outside of allegations of inferiority and inability to pollinate culture with commendable ideas and attitudes, there are quantitative reasons for educational and curricular inattention to popular fiction. More books have seen the light of day since 1950 than in the whole literary tradition stretching as far back as *Gilgamesh*. "The point has long since passed," conclude the editors of *Five Hundred Years of Printing*, "when any library or bookseller can stock more than a fraction of the books in print, or when every book which merits reviews receives any" (243). Noting the "enormous number of manuscripts received by any editor," the authors of *Books: The Culture and Commerce of Publishing* maintain that, "Were editors to rely solely on formal means of manuscript submission ... publishers would soon go out of business" (73). Doubleday, for one, estimates that each year it receives an average of 10,000 manuscripts "over the transom" (the industry's term for unsolicited) alone, of which only a few may be signed on.[14]

In the infant years of the new millennium, the estimated number of new titles published worldwide in any given year approaches one million. More than 300 paperback titles are released *monthly* in the United States. The number of *Heftromans*, inexpensive sixty-four-page pulp fiction novelettes that flood the unified German market, exceeds 200 million a year. More than ever before in the history of Western civilization, the production and consumption of books has reached inflationary proportions. Neither the market nor the critical superstructure can sustain such "Honey-I-Blew-Up-the-Book" growth.

An instructive metonymy of this state of affairs may be the world of scholarly and scientific publishing. At the formation of the Association of American University Presses in 1932, only eight presses were reported at an informal meeting of directors. Fifty years later there were more than seventy, and in the first years of the new century, 125. The flood of publications in professional journals and conference proceedings is so urgent that most institutional libraries have imposed draconian limits on book acquisition. In the 1980s it gradually became necessary to publish indices to indices of publication titles in an attempt to cope with this deluge of information. One can only wonder how much time such meta-indices can buy, and how many years we are from publishing indices of indices of indices. Computer databases that facilitate search and access do not, after all, attack the information glut but merely alleviate its symptoms.

BURIED UNDER PYRAMIDS OF BOOKS

You don't expect me to know what to say about a play when I don't know who the author is, do you? ... If it's by a good author, it's a good play, naturally. That stands to reason.

George Bernard Shaw

With the volume of writing growing at a head-spinning rate, the literary culture loses its ability to function critically, buried under pyramids of books that no one will ever have time to read. Yet our critical strategies, inherited from the days when books were scarce enough to command individual attention and attract universal response, are not designed for this quantitatively (and qualitatively) novel environment. Out of what had started – and for centuries continued – as a genteel trickle, swelling into a middle-class river and finally into a modern deluge of print, highbrow critical filters still siphon off a minuscule fraction, though no longer trying to maintain the appearance of knowing the totality of literary output. This select group, its aesthetic status already bolstered by virtue of having been separated from a field so large, is then awarded the luxury of in-depth analysis.

The essence of this process is satirized by the folksy aphorism ("better read than dead") concerning two kinds of books: those that are bought and read, and those that are autopsied as part of institutional curricula. One can detect behind this polarity the capricious machinery of canon selection, which later ossifies into a picture of granite-like solidity. Few contemporaries could compete with Ring Lardner for popular and critical acclaim, with Hemingway among the many cognoscenti who lauded and applauded his popular style. Lardner's syndicated sales far exceeded Hemingway's, and his best fiction, such as the celebrated "You Know Me Al" series, earned him critical accolades around the country.

Yet today the posthumous author of *True at First Light* (1999) is a classic, while Lardner's stories languish in the vast cultural cemetery known as Popular Fiction. Lardner was, of course, a satirist and humorist working with the vernacular mastered during his years as an itinerant sportswriter, a fact that ought to earn him a place in the populist tradition of Dickens or Twain. Is it the lowbrow stigma of having had baseball as his first subject matter that cost him the laurels lavished on writers who, for example, had made their careers on bull fighting or marlin fishing? But then, why should Bernard Malamud attain the first rank in American letters, given that he inaugurated his career with a novel about baseball (*The Natural*)?

The adage that social history is written by the winners is no less true for literary history. Surrounded by the reassuring heft of Norton anthologies, one might almost believe their immanent nature. Yet reality is, as always, more complex and prosaic. Despite Hawthorne's warm praise, *Moby Dick* lay fallow until the Hollywood decades of the twentieth century, while critics and readers alike saw nothing extraordinary in this ponderous whaling tale. All this changed only in the wake of some high-profile and high-impact film versions of Ahab's quest. Suddenly Melville was a genius, and careers were to be made from the study of the intricacies of his now masterful prose and the subtleties of his now profound symbolism. For centuries Jack Donne was an appreciated but otherwise unremarked versifier of the metaphysical persuasion, until T.S. Eliot nailed him to the entrance of his own poetic church. Baudelaire – then Borges – hit this very nail on the head by observing that writers create their own predecessors even before Bloom hammered it home in *The Anxiety of Influence*. While earning his bread as a Faber and Faber editor,

Eliot adamantly rejected a little book about a bunch of quarrelsome pigs called *Animal Farm*. Zora Neale Hurston, now firmly in the canon, was until recently absent from any literary textbook (she died destitute, working in a nursing home).

In the end, it all comes down to one thing. An encounter with a literary work of art is not like stepping on a rake in a dark shed: a smack on the head and a sudden vision of light. Errors of judgment have been made and are almost certainly being made all over again. In one of the first studies of this problem, Russell Lynes scoured the historical record to document how often the commonplace of one generation becomes the refined vogue of the next, or the elite aesthetics of one time the vulgarity of another. What enters the canon is not so much a matter of intrinsic value, reports Lynes, as of sometimes very arbitrary decisions about what is highbrow and what is lowbrow.[15]

Questions about canon formation have been in the foreground for at least a generation, but they are worth airing again as their answers have far-reaching curricular consequences. Although we do not profess literature or literary studies in this manner, elevation to the canon often has less to do with the transcendent *je ne sais quoi* than with the historical and pragmatic self-interests of individuals and institutions. A prior verdict about the genealogy of a given novel – popular or "literary" – affects the verdict on its aesthetic attributes, given that highbrow prose is typically interpreted in a symptomatically a-generic fashion.

Today it is still iconoclastic and contrary to established practice to appraise works from the top of the literary Ararat in terms of popular genres. Could one justify reading *Crime and Punishment* as a murder mystery, manqué because suspenseless? Or *The Old Man and the Sea* through the schema of a fishing yarn? How about *Doctor Faustus* as a so-so satanic horror or *The Assistant* as a failed Harlequin romance? The answer, echoed by a growing number of studies, is a preliminary "Yes."[16] It appears that, at least in terms of the popular-canonical division, readers often find what they set out to find: repetitive formula in the former, genre-busting originality in the latter. Reverse the background assumptions and you'll be surprised how much the new bottle alters the wine.[17]

In contrast, little of such finessing takes place among works booted to the *Trivialliteratur* end of the spectrum. A categorical benefit of a doubt does not appear to extend to writers whose artistry may bear comparison with classics of world literature but who prefer to create within the framework of an instantly identifiable lowbrow genre. In this sense, at least, cinematic *auteur* studies have been more progressive, reconciling artistic individuality with generic structuring. Critical problems of this nature are exacerbated by the inadequacy of most approaches to genre, which bear, even today, the indelible stamp of structuralism (I give this problem due consideration in Chapter 3).

POPULAR EQUALS GENERIC EQUALS BAD

Our present museums and galleries to which works of fine art are removed and stored illustrate some of the causes that have operated to segregate art, instead of finding it attendant of temple, forum, and other forms of associated life.

John Dewey

Notwithstanding a growing number of integrated scholars, the inherited and tacitly embraced view of genre fiction can still be summarized by two equations. Popular equals bad because if it were any good it would not be popular in the first place; and popular equals generic equals bad because it appeals to so many by virtue of being simplistic, schematic, and repetitive – in other words, by exhibiting the distinctive traits of its lowbrow heritage. This is hardly an accident. Popular fiction of sufficient antiquity, such as Shakespeare or Dickens, is regularly embraced by the institutional taste-makers but not as pulp fiction. Aestheticized modes of interpretation truncate the popular roots, conceal them under layers of critical accretions, and transmogrify popular fiction into *objets d'art*. This is quite common in literary history, and understandably so, for without it there would be little literary history to speak of.[18] *The Decameron, Don Quixote, Romeo and Juliet, Robinson Crusoe, Tom Jones, Gulliver's Travels, The Rubaiyat, Don Juan, Emma, Huckleberry Finn*: the literary canon today is chock-full of works written for the public agora and not for the academe.

For all their theoretical diversity and analytic nuance, Western theories of aesthetics generally legitimate four types of artistic impulse. These are: mimetic (art as a reflection of life), functional (art in the service of society), emotional (art that affects members of society), and formalist (art that embodies beauty and skill in its form).[19] It must be acknowledged once and for all that, throughout its career, popular art in general, and popular literature in particular, has availed itself splendidly of these aesthetic duties. Consider, for example, the mimetic impulse. Popular fiction has always painted a vivid picture of its time, sending its Robinson Crusoes around the colonial New World, its Oliver Twists around industrial London, and its Steve Carellas around the rotten apple of New York. Recently it even competed with the press as a journalistic mirror of the death throes of the Soviet Empire.[20]

As for the functional criterion, the same novel that used to debase public morals with scandal and trashiness, if one were to believe its early detractors, has long since become the medium of choice for literary expression. On its way it has educated the public, stoked national pride and unity, and, despite denunciations to the contrary, helped keep morals intact. Russell B. Nye's *The Unembarrassed Muse* painstakingly documents how the nineteenth-century domestic novel used sex, sentiment, and religion to teach that "conventional sexual morality was best, that deviation from it was dangerous, that immorality was punished by terrifying results" (26). Naturally not all genre fiction is so squeaky clean. But sex and violence sell the highbrow as much as popular art. And for every murderous rapist-sadist Popeye given sanctuary in the Faulkner canon, there is a Popeye Doyle hunting dope fiends on the pages of *The French Connection*.

It is no different with emotional appeal or, in a more distinguished lexicon, catharsis. Have you ever seen footage of hordes of screaming and swooning teenagers at a Beatles' concert? Have you ever watched the Marx Brothers' Chevalier-imitation routine without going into convulsions? How about the repulsion and revulsion reported by readers of the brain-chomping scene in *Hannibal*? Or the heartthrobs for the countless Romeos and Juliets of popular romance, so unfailingly successful as to be condemned as tear-jerkers? Even though John Lennon berated the elites for merely rattling their jewellery in distinction to the masses' genuine applause, no one would seriously disown affective responses to classical concert goers or postmodern fiction readers. But without tipping the emotional scales in favour of either side, it is hard to deny that much of popular art is created and consumed precisely because of its emotional appeal.

Which brings us to the fourth kind of aesthetic legitimation, based on stylistic (formal) attributes of the work. This is the point where many of us almost involuntarily trot out the familiar conceits that generic fiction is seedy, its plots worn out, and its aesthetics designed for mass consumption. Yet the accusation that pulp fiction has no artistic merit could only be filed by those ignorant of the quirky horror novels of Thomas M. Disch, the urban procedurals of Ed McBain, the neo-noir efforts of Philip Kerr, the literate spy fiction of John Le Carré, the revisionist westerns of Larry McMurtry, the scientific fiction of Stanislaw Lem, the tragicomic fantasies of Karel Čapek, or the stylish erotica of Erica Jong. For that matter, one of the funniest, most politically engagé and most skilfully assembled comedies of the last generation was the madcap *Road to Omaha* from the writer touted as incapable of anything but "ludlums" – espionage thrillers of the most trite and repetitive sort.

As even this thumbnail sketch reveals, much like the lay bards of old, popular writers of today continue to satisfy the aesthetic needs and represent the values of their public. An endlessly dynamic and self-organizing cultural formation, popular fiction is part and parcel of the same Plato-Longinus-Kant aesthetic axis and the same philosophy of art that legitimates our classics. And little wonder about that. It is often read by the same individuals and created by the same artists; and it appeals to the same values, using similar techniques and narrative formulas (more on this in Chapter 2).

My point here is not that all genre fiction is good literature, because much of it manifestly is not. There are good reasons to believe that much of it goes in one eye and out the other, and that it is meant to do so. There are good reasons to believe that much of it is no more than a short-lived and forgettable experience for its readers. Granting all that, popular literature is by now a universal forum for the propagation and assimilation of ideas. It refers to and comments on all aspects of contemporary life, in the end informing, and in some cases even forming, the background of many people's values and beliefs. This includes intellectuals who, after hours, are avid consumers and in some cases producers of popular culture. For, as one of us concedes, "while we seem to be taking only inno-cent pleasure in our popular readings, we are always at the same time inserted into a cultural value system."[21]

THE SPIRIT OF DOOMSDAY APOCALYPSE

Today literature and the arts are exposed to a different danger: they are threatened not by a doctrine or a political party but by a faceless, soulless, and directionless economic process.

Octavio Paz

So much for aesthetic theory and popular fiction. But what about the market invasion of cheap paperback bestsellers and their com-mercial threat to the book culture in the decades following the Second World War?

Between the arrival of the first printing press in Massachusetts Bay in 1638 and the end of the eighteenth century, about 50,000 books, pamphlets, broadsheets, and newspapers were printed, most cheap paperbacks. In fact, the first clothbound book, Char-lotte Eaton's *Rome in the Nineteenth Century*, did not appear until 1827.[22] Nor is the bestseller a twentieth-century invention: Susanna Rowson's *Charlotte Temple*, published in 1793, was not only *the* best-selling novel of the century, but it continued to retail for another 100 years, becoming one of the best-selling titles of the nineteenth century as well. Combining sex and melodramatic characters, and alluding to well known national events in an effort to provide a topical and socially meaningful frame of reference, the novel mined a recipe that proves its selling power to this day. Nor is Rowson's example an isolated one; in fact, popular literature has rarely shied away from contemporary issues and social causes in need of dramatization. Equally vital was the social mobility and visibility that popular fiction provided to women writers, even as belles lettres remained the boys' club. As early as 1872, for instance, 75 percent of novels published in the United States were written by women, giving a voice and a creative outlet to a disfranchised and regularly neglected half of society.[23]

The first big wave of paperbound books arrived after 1830, triggered by the replacement of the Gutenberg screw press with the high-speed cylinder press, which, for the first time, allowed publishers to reach a mass market. These modern paperbacks were, for the most part, pirated popular British novels sold for a quarter in peacetime or shipped in bales to the front lines during the Civil War. One of the most sought-after commodities on this massive reprint market was the wonderboy of London Town's popular press, Charles Dickens.[24] It was not, however, until the paperback boom of the 1890s, sparked by the introduction of cheap case-binding machines, that the public's appetite for genre novels became a matter of national debate. Genre fiction was denounced from the pulpit and the political soapbox for depleting the moral fibre of the country – the same country that did not see fit to ratify women's rights until 1920.

Typical was the New York Society for the Suppression of Vice and the Society for the Prevention of Crime, which advertised the goals of doing away with crime and vice by, inter alia, suppressing all literature about crime and detection. In the spirit of doomsday apocalypse, these precursors of Leavis and Bloom campaigned in earnest to curb the production of popular novels by law. In order to abolish criminality by abolishing it from the printed page, they even got the Massachusetts legislature to prohibit selling minors books or magazines containing criminal news, police reports, accounts of criminal deeds, or stories of lust and crime. In a rap familiar from endless repetitions – not least from Senate subcommittee censorship hearings on rock lyrics – in 1918 the American Booksellers Association bound its members to "discourage the publication and sale of books of pronounced immoral character."[25] In this principled way the watchdogs of morality laboured to save the innocents from the sl/easy allure of fictional crime – both common and commonly overlooked in later Dickens.[26] Still, the victory could not have been complete, as seen from the need for the 1954 comic book burning spree and a "grassroots" appeal to Eisenhower for comic book prohibition, both proudly sponsored by the Chicago Citizens' Committee for Better Literature.

The 1920s saw another paperback revolution when E. Haldeman-Julius launched the cheapest of all mass-market lines, the Little Blue Books, sold for the first time with the aid of full-page newspaper ads. Priced at a nickel, with hundreds of numbered titles to order simply by circling, these books became an American institution. They also brought growing numbers of people into the circle of fiction readers in a feedback process of social change that saw the spread of public libraries, compulsory elementary education, and a decline in illiteracy. The paperbacks received another boost in 1939 when Robert F. de Graff created Pocket Books, alchemizing the quickly yellowing (owing to a high acid content) pulp paper into gold. Packing racy, modern content in catchy, multicoloured covers, mass-printed by rotary presses, and sold through newsstands and outlets run by print-media wholesalers, these twenty-five-cent book-wonders sold in the millions. Available during the Second World War through the Armed Services Editions, they offered countless soldiers reading material, laying the groundwork for the vast expansion of the postwar literary market.

If history makes one thing evident, it is that paperback publishing and commercial pressures have been around since the dawn of literary culture in America, disproving the contention that mass fiction kills literary culture. After all, if it were so, the latter would have been dead for a long time now.[27] Numerical explosion excepted, today's publishing trends and concerns are no different from yesterday's. It may be true that nineteenth-century publishers thought of themselves not as merchandisers but, rather, as business men of letters, intent on promoting good literature. It did not save them, however, from charges of commercialization and sellout, which, if anything, demonstrate once again that the cultural battle lines of today were drawn much earlier than is commonly supposed. In 1843 the well known *North American Review* bemoaned: "Literature begins to assume the aspect and undergo the mutations of trade. The author's profession is becoming as mechanical as that of the printer and the bookseller" (Douglas 82). In 1890 *Publishers Weekly* thundered at the creeping threats of commercialism. "This is an age of ambition ... If literature and art are to be treated as common merchandise ... it will make commonplace the manners of our people and their intelligence restricted to the counting-room" (Coser 17–18).

Such sentiments reached a crescendo during the clerical and political crusade of the 1890s, in the heyday of a popular fiction boom that swept the United States between 1890 and 1920. This is made apparent again on the pages of "The Commercialization of Literature," an outspoken and influential article featured in the November 1905 issue of the *Atlantic Monthly*. "The more authors seek publishers solely with reference to what they will pay in the day's market, the more publishers bid against one another as stock brokers do, and the more they market their wares as the soulless articles of ordinary commerce are marketed, the more books become soulless things" (578), remonstrated Henry Holt, then the dean of American publishers.

Before we examine these and related charges in Chapter 2, one thing is worth keeping in mind. While in absolute numbers popular literature may indeed produce more inferior writing than does its highbrow cousin, it is not at all certain that this is true in *relative* terms. There is simply no systematic data to give credence to the reflex supposition that popular literature contains a higher *proportion* of bad prose than does its counterpart. The question of percentages is not mere quibbling. Rather, it is the key to the mindset mass-produced in schools, universities, and public institutions. After all, in terms of publishing clout and cultural appeal we are dealing with a genre Goliath and a mainstream midget. With many skilled artists working in popular genres, it is at least arguable that a fraction of popular literature is art. But because of the disparity in size, a fraction of the popular market may rival or even exceed the totality of the canon. In absolute numbers, in other words, there may be more accomplished and meaningful writing produced at the popular rather than at the "literary" end of the spectrum.

Although unsettling, this conclusion flows from fairly common sense premises. One reason why it has not received the fanfare it deserves is that it has a potential to completely upturn the coverage model of literary education still practised in the majority of our institutions. It is true that statistics can be used to prove anything – including the truth. And statistics strongly support the blossoming of a Melville or a Malamud – indeed any number of them – in one of the many popular genre hothouses of our literary culture.

PEOPLE WILL CONTINUE TO READ BOOKS

A few years ago, I freely admitted to a reporter that when it comes to reading for pleasure, I don't curl up with a "great book" of literature.

Andrew Ross

Having explored some aspects of the history of popular fiction publishing, I would like to close with a brief look at the shape of things to come. Apart from quasi-futurological postmortems staged from time to time in the mass media, little editorial space is given to the book culture of tomorrow. As an example of recurrent trend-mongering, which, from a largely ahistorical perspective, foresees the end of various socio-economic processes, this is no academic ho-hum.[28] A few years before the twentieth century, the German Patent Office nearly got boarded up because of a mistaken conviction that there were no further inventions to be made. Similarly, in the era of CD-ROM, MP3, VHS, VCD, DVD, DVC, 3D, and HDTV, book reading may seem defunct or at least moribund. Assuming that people will continue to read, I focus my attention below on popular fiction in contrast to those academic studies that, speaking of novelistic trends, typically address themselves to their highbrow manifestations.[29]

As higher education and material affluence spread, we can expect that genre fiction will continue its radial expansion. Creating new forms of expression, it will tackle an ever-widening range of social, cultural, and technological issues, smashing readership records in the process. Gains in readership will be partly offset by general humanistic training losing ground to scientific and technical training. Literary symbolism and imagery will become indebted to technology, advertising, and other sources recognizable the world over. Rhetorical polarization of the popular and the canon apart, cultural eclecticism and aesthetic free trade will continue to swell the ranks of the commercial nobrow culture, completing the transformation implicit in Jerry Wald's 1958 slogan: "There's no such thing as highbrow and lowbrow any more."[30] In a sometimes overlooked aspect of panculturalism, the global percentage of from-English translation, which *Index Translationum* already puts at around 50 percent, will increase further as the language of GM and MGM solidifies as the world's new *lingua franca*.

Popular writers will borrow from belles lettres in order to better serve the public. "Serious" fiction will openly embrace popular narrative techniques, genres, and subjects in an effort to broaden its readership base. Both groups' efforts to target the dominant class of readers will continue to erase the stigma affixed to popular literature, its producers, consumers, and critics. Increased cultural prestige will secure it more appreciation and interest from academics and from talented artists. In their hands we will see the rise of new genres and their hybrids targeting specific classes of readers, a process that will fragment the reading public into even more specialized interest groups. This will furnish us with minibestsellers: books that sell out within the confines of a particular region, cultural environment, or interest group but pass unnoticed elsewhere.

Although the media trumpet the death of book culture, the facts paint the opposite picture. Every index, from total sales, the annual number of new titles, to the index of diversity (different titles per million of population) shows a steady rise. As these figures continue to grow, the fate of individual books will become almost completely tied to advertising and promotional "booming." Selection will become artificial, oftentimes determined not by readers but (in advance) by marketers. Still, as long as the press panders to sensationalism, human interest angles, and celebrity gossip, while Hollywood gorges on special effects, super-colour, speed-editing, and nascent 3D technology, the novel will remain safe from these image and throughput-oriented rivals.

All the same, in order to facilitate access, to lower costs, and to heighten interactive appeal, literature will increase its use of other media. The general trend in leisure consumption is saturation: longer movies with surround sound, artificial sensory environments like Disneyland or Virtual Reality, Imax theatres, High Definition interactive TV, laser disk or DVD editing. The coming generation of e-z writers will harness the Internet technologies to this end. As a result we will see downloading of books from the Web (to eliminate printing costs), personal printing (desktop publishing), posting of books in progress with allowances for readers' input (maybe in the manner of Stephen King's forays into Web publishing), multiple versions (remixes) and updates (e.g., Tom Clancy, *Op-Center 5.1*) of already published novels.

Ditto for interactive fiction, where readers can affect the tenor or even outcome of a book, and authorless novels posted on the Net and freely modified by anyone with access. Multi-authored books may be started by one person and developed by others, à la *La maledizione del faraone* (1995), a short mystery authored by four Italian writers. Begun by Eco and abandoned a quarter of the way through, this novel was completed in succession by each of the co-authors (Pontiggia, Riotta, and Tabucchi) without collaboration or consultation with the others. Their sympathetic parody of the Indiana Jones subgenre embodies a set of complex theoretical assumptions about the "open work" and is a marvellous exponent of the

38

possibilities inherent in the merger between the popular and the intellectual.

Other multimedia developments will include treatments, where the original author retains the rights to the core concept (e.g., plot line, conflict structure, character) but submits it as a narrative skeleton for others to develop into possibly quite diverse novels, somewhat in the manner of the narrative multimedia incarnations of James Bond. A related development will be a rapid burgeoning of audio books and interactive computer games (à la Thomas Disch's *Amnesia*, a pioneer in the mid-1980s). In the long run, the emergence of multimedia octopi, with tentacles in film, TV, cable, video, computer games, magazines, newspapers, book publishing, MP3s, and other niches of the entertainment and leisure industry, is one of the trend-setters for the future, leaving no one outside its sphere of influence. All of us, whether MTV or PBS partisans, have grown up among Hollywood blockbusters, Sunday comics, Disney schmaltz, and laughtrack-doctored sitcoms.

The entertainment and artertainment deluge will reach inflationary proportions as more material becomes available in hard copy and electronically. National literary boundaries will erode under the pressure from progressive worldwide anglicization, increased freedom of movement (personal emigration), electronic publishing, and better machine translations. A genuinely interdisciplinary orientation of the humanities will direct much professional interest into popular, ethnic, sociological, and scientific studies never imagined by Pater-type purists. All this means that literary studies will reintegrate itself with the social sciences, re-enter the social arena dominated by the popular media, and renew efforts to establish its relevance to the reading public at large.

The popular arts of the modern Western world are, in fact, articulated with an elaborate and effective system of aesthetic propositions; and, moreover, these are closely related to the aesthetic principles that have been discussed relative to Western fine arts for the last two and a half millennia.

Richard L. Anderson, "Popular Art and Aesthetic Theory"

Preliminaries aside, it is time to test the faith of the cardinal critiques of genre literature. My goal is to reconstitute more than a century of debate about its aesthetic, axiological, and functional attributes and, wherever necessary, to reclaim them from precipitous or ill-founded conclusions. For this task I synthesize a long range of arguments propounded from the early days of popular culture criticism, some collected in the two classic compilations by Rosenberg and White: *Mass Culture* (1957) and *Mass Culture Revisited* (1971). I also marshal evidence from a growing array of literary studies, which, while typically confined to individual genres or historical eras, help clarify some of the global issues at stake.[1] Finally, I take note of the socio-aesthetic analyses from fields as diverse as sociology, philosophy, and popular music, eminent among them Herbert J. Gans's anatomy of American taste cultures, *Popular Culture and*

High Culture (1974), and Richard Shusterman's *Pragmatist Aesthetics* (1992).[2] It may be somewhat redundant to point out that I take the debates summarized herein to be settled in popular fiction's favour. If I try to provide a comprehensive aesthetic survey of the debates about it, it is in the hope of elucidating something about the nature of popular and nobrow art.

Although the issues are indisputably complex, on closer inspection the derelictions ascribed to popular literature turn out to be for the most part inaccurate. As I demonstrate, at times they apply with equal force to the canon, giving additional ammunition to those who accuse curricular taste-makers of double standards. While examining each charge in detail, taking issues and not their proponents to be of consequence, I largely refrain from elaborating separate strains of arguments or nuances of individual censures. The tenets from Chapter 1 concerning the rising tide of print apply with equal tenacity to mass culture and popular fiction criticism, accruing over decades of heated polemics. It would be impossible to engage directly even a fraction of existing critical commentary without vindicating Daniel Dennett's aphorism that a scholar is a library's way of making another library. Fortunately, even though the controversies in question are thoroughly interdisciplinary – literary scholars, cultural critics, philosophers, anthropologists, historians, psychologists, sociologists, and even politicians have staked out their positions – the capital arguments turn out to be limited in number, even if glossed in innumerable variations.[3]

The most persistent critiques of popular fiction can be separated into four related groups.

1   The negative character of popular literature creation: unlike high literature, popular literature is mass produced by profit-oriented hacks whose sole aim is to gratify the base tastes of a paying audience.

2   Its negative effects on literary culture: popular literature borrows from "serious" fiction, thus debasing it, and lures away potential contributors, thus depleting the latter's pool of talent.

3   Its negative effects on readership: the consumption of popular fiction produces at best spurious gratification, and at worst it can be emotionally and cognitively harmful.

4   Its negative effects on society at large: popular fiction lowers the cultural level of the reading public and encourages political, social, and cultural dictatorship by creating a passive and apathetic audience rendered highly responsive to the techniques of mass demagoguery and propaganda.

The first argument can be separated into three causally related charges. The first is commercialism: popular literature is not a branch of art but a profit-oriented industry. The second is uniformity: seeking profit, this industry is said to create a homogenous product that caters to the lowest common denominator. The third is alienation: the above transactions turn creators of popular literature into assembly line profiteers who surrender the expression of their individual skills, emotions, and values to make it in the marketplace.

As a first-pass response, it must be acknowledged that popular literature naturally operates on the premise of maximizing audiences and/or turning a profit. But so does much of highbrow fiction. This is especially true nowadays, when government subsidies have become scarce and wealthy patrons few. It is true that one cannot yet buy books by Roth or Bellow printed on rolls of toilet paper, as is the case with some homegrown products (e.g., Morrow's *Book of Lists* or Doubleday's *People's Almanac* – for a nominal price of three dollars per roll). Oh, Dawn, a New York company, promotes its publication list in this way in the hope that people, after using the toilet paper in the standard fashion, will remove to the bookstore and get the paperback for a more leisurely and uninterrupted read.

Yet similar processes are at work in the case of canonical writers whose names function precisely as trademarks deployed to promote sales. Who would think of purchasing a bad first draft of a self-aggrandizing safari memoir (*True at First Light*) if it were not fronted by the name of Hemingway? The fact is that many did buy it for exactly that reason. Bottom-line pressures may in fact be more acute for prestige fiction, if only because its limited market makes the struggle to make a living that much harder. As a result, ambitious writers often choose to work with popular genres or techniques – as Art Spiegelman did in his Book Critic's Circle Award and Pulitzer-winning comics *Maus* and *Maus II* – to broaden their appeal in a bestseller.[4] In general, the myth of Pure Art, which lies behind the anti-commercial bias of this critique, fails to adequately explain why so many writers of Odets's or Faulkner's stature should be drawn to the greenback pastures of Hollywood.[5]

As for uniformity, although academic readers pride themselves on their highly individuated tastes, just because as a group they form such a small and select audience, the literature that appeals to them is in fact homogenous and uniform to a remarkable degree. This is no surprise, as imitation and formulaic solutions are no less common in "literary" than in popular fiction. A good example is Mailer's *The Naked and the Dead*, a successful and much anthologized war novel that also happens to be highly derivative of other successful war novels. In plot and structure, for instance, it closely imitates Remarque's *All Quiet on the Western Front* and Barbusse's *Under Fire*, two trend-setting First World War bestsellers. The book's focus on a platoon of soldiers of mixed backgrounds in order to trace individual reactions to combat is a stereotype of epic proportions. In this respect *The Naked and the Dead* is no less formulaic than all those John Wayne war flicks, with a Martinez, a Minetta, a Goldstein, and a "Polack" Czienwicz in every unit. The same goes for the narrative technique, where Mailer's flashback vignettes openly mimic Dos Passos's *U.S.A.* The latter's "Camera Eye," for example, is resurrected as "Time Machine," and the only marginally more innovative "Chorus" draws heavily on Dos Passos's experiments with montage.

There are, of course, countless case histories of this kind, of which Homer and Joyce, or Marlowe and Mann, may be the best known. Stream of consciousness, a bona fide highbrow technique pioneered by Eduard Dujardin in the 1880s, was imitated by everyone who would be anyone in modernism, to the point of ossifying into a separate subcategory: the stream of consciousness novel. Interpretations of Updike in terms of *The Scarlet Letter*, which he revisits with a persistence that verges on obsession, have become something of a cottage industry in literary scholarship. Trends of this kind are plain even to a sociologist like Gans, who observes that many "'serious' novels have made the theme of the artist as a young man, borrowed originally from Joyce and D.H. Lawrence, into a formula, featuring a stereotypical young man striving to develop his identity as an artist."[6]

An intellectual who reaches for a minimalist story knows in advance what to expect from its pared down style or plotless design, in a manner comparable to popular genre categories. Hard as it may be to accept, William Stuckey's research reveals that even such a loose assembly of the artistically prestigious as the Pulitzer Prize-winners betrays a significant number of thematic, narrative, and character-related schematics.[7] On the other hand, Frank Luther Mott's preliminary findings from "Is There a Best Seller Formula?" suggest that there is no sure-fire trick to produce a popular winner. Or, which amounts to the same thing, if there is one, "it is lost in the variety of forms, qualities, appeals, characteristics" (292). So much for highbrow uniqueness and its triumph of invention over convention.

MAKE A BUNDLE BY WRITING A POTBOILER

I'm not trying to be taken seriously by the East Coast literary establishment. But I'm taken *very* seriously by the bankers.

Judith Krantz

As for homogeneity on the popular front, in many ways the sheer size of its cultural environment determines some of its structural and even aesthetic qualities, such as originality and diversity. Given its numerical magnitude, popular fiction invades and explores every literary niche as part of a self-organizing process known as adaptive radiation. Competing to stand out from the crowd while cashing in on conventions familiar to readers, popular literature routinely takes liberties with genre formulas. Doing so, it ends up diversifying to a much greater extent than does highbrow fiction (sociologists of empirical bent are hereby challenged to submit this conjecture to verification). Because the competition is so numerous and so fierce, there is a great deal of pressure to transform the formula, be it theme, plot twist, or narrative technique, in order to surprise and score a winner at the sales counter. This is no different from canonical genres such as the sonnet, which, from Petrarch to Sting, had also undergone massive metric, thematic, and rhyming transformations while remaining identifiable as a sonnet.

The perception that popular fiction is blandly homogenous, or that it erases distinctions between one work and another, is in many cases demonstrably false. Connoisseurs of popular genre books find dramatic differences between them and between the styles of writers who write them, much as academic readers differentiate the predictable (anti)conventions of the (anti)novels of Alain Robbe-Grillet and Jean Genet, or the minimalism of Marilyn Robinson or Anne Beattie. Recognizing this awkward fact, Abraham Kaplan has come up with a clever countermove designed to deflect attention from the highbrow penchant for formula. He proposed no less than that repetitions within popular arts are indicative of stereotyping, whereas repetitions in the canon – for instance, "the marked resemblances among Elizabethan tragedies or among Italian operas" – are only stylizations.[8] The failing is thus not in the repetition per se but in the deficiency of the first occurrence. No argument is fashioned, of course, to prove that first occurrences of popular genres are necessarily deficient, because none could be. Instead, to rescue the proposal from self-destruction, another criterion is prodded into place: the fault of a popular fiction stereotype is that it "so little resembles anything outside it" (354).

Once more no argument is advanced in defence of this fiat, and not a single example is hustled up to shore up this conclusion. And counterexamples abound. Since I have already noted several literary ones, let me turn to cinema. A flurry of media attention has lately accompanied the closing of local bookstores, gobbled up by chains of prefabricated outlets for merchandizing print-units. The issue should be of immediate concern to all book lovers, highbrow and lowbrow alike, and one would expect it to be featured in works of fiction. Although I recall no art films lamenting this trend, it was swiftly fictionalized in *You've Got Mail*, a romance-comedy with two of Hollywood's bankable stars, Tom Hanks and Meg Ryan. The central issues of the film, the disintegration of a book-selling tradition and the novel means and pitfalls of finding romance over the Internet, did resemble the "outside" of this cinematic fiction because they were taken from it. My exhibit B is *The Full Monty*, a buddy comedy from across the Atlantic. This indy picture not only laid bare a few labour class naughty bits, it also brought home the emotions of fathers struggling to live up to their duties towards their children, of husbands struggling to live up to their sexual duties towards their wives, and of laid-off family providers struggling to live up to their self-image. So is it really fair to say that the film is merely a genre stereotype that fails to resemble life as we know it?

When critics like Adorno augustly accuse genre creations of "inducing relaxation" because they are "patterned and pre-digested," they invariably fail to condemn the Petrarchan sonnet, as patterned a form of literature as any.[9] It is only from the vantage point of highbrow aesthetics that all popular writing looks ripe for pre-fab relaxation. How much relaxation is induced by Ira Levin's *Rosemary's Baby*, which climaxes with the defeat of the heroine and the triumph of Satan? How about the unthinkable – the death of the protagonist in Desmond Bagley's *The Enemy* or Len Deighton's *MAMista*? How pre-digested is *The Investigation*, in which Lem lays out an old-fashioned detective tale only to shatter its conventions and to deny even the possibility of a resolution? How many formulas has Lynda LaPlante been chained to in *Prime Suspect*, when she rewrote the book on the police procedural? As a matter of fact, research shows that even highly conventionalized subgenres like the conspiracy thriller are anything but rigidly schematic, with some of its popular fantasies plumb contradicted by the formula.[10]

This is not to dispute the existence of fiction factories such as Lyle Engel's Book Creations Inc., whose eighty-plus authors manufacture up to 3,000 titles a year by filling out story outlines provided by the Engel enterprise. Nor is the above to be construed as an en masse validation of aesthetic aspirations that often just do not come into play for makers of pulp fiction. But the fact is that genre literature is not automatically synonymous with generic hack-work. Just like the avant-garde, popular fiction mutates, radiates, and diversifies constantly, in the course of the last century alone giving us such new types of writing as science fiction, the hardboiled novel, the police procedural, the techno-thriller, the comic book, and the graphic novel, to name a few, together with their countless thematic and structural subtypes.

As far as the charge of alienation is concerned, available data indicate exactly the opposite of what critics from Dwight Macdonald on have insisted is the case. The proverbial image of a highbrow litterateur who does not care to communicate with her readers but creates only for herself, and a genre hack who suppresses his own values and caters only to the appetites of the audience, is simply false.[11] From the innumerable examples that belie this picture, one can begin with the late Robert Ludlum, who, with just under one-quarter *billion* copies sold, single-handedly defined the popular in contemporary fiction. In the Irangate era (1989) introduction to the new edition of *Trevayne*, itself written in the aftermath of the Watergate scandal, Ludlum summed up his feelings about the Nixon and Reagan presidencies in these words. "For me, one of the truly great achievements of man is open, representative democracy ... But wait. Someone is always trying to louse it up. That's why I wrote *Trevayne* nearly two decades ago. It was the time of Watergate, and my pencil flew across the pages in outrage. Younger – not youthful – intemperance made my head explode with such words and phrases as Mendacity! Abuse of Power! Corruption! Police State!" (v). Hardly the words of a browbeaten hack who relinquishes what is dear to his heart in order to pander to Mencken's booboisie.

The example of Irving Wallace has the added piquancy of being a lesson in political correctness in reverse. Following his 1965 publication of *The Man*, Wallace was attacked by James Baldwin for having the chutzpah to write about blacks in times of acute racial tension and strife. Baldwin's remarks left little doubt that the best-seller added insult to injury by daring to hypothesize a black man in the White House. Wallace's answer? Someone *ought* to write about the possibility of a black American president and drive the political message home, and a popular writer like Wallace, who could reach millions of readers (and voters), was best suited to this task. Politically engagé? Socially conscious? Artistically ambitious? Maybe. But surely not bereft of self-expression for the sake of pandering to the ignorant masses.

Critics like to ignore the fact that many authors of popular novels are highly educated and skilled artists. In the days before *The Postman Always Rings Twice*, *Double Indemnity*, and *Serenade*, James M. Cain was the recipient of a graduate degree in literature, a college professor, an editor of *The New Yorker*, and the author of *Our Government*, a serious if satirical collection of political essays. Raymond Chandler was a proficient speaker of German, French, and Spanish; a dabbler in Greek, Armenian, and Hungarian; a whiz in mathematics; and an expert in Greek and Roman history, culture, and literature. Later in his life he even reflected on this intellectual and academic background in a letter to his publisher, Hamish Hamilton. "It would seem that a classical education might be rather a poor basis for writing novels in a hard-boiled vernacular. I happen to think otherwise. A classical education saves you from being fooled by pretentiousness, which most current fiction is too full of."[12]

Popular and financial success may precisely allow writers to swim against the current, liberating them from prevalent tastes and fashions. Between Richard Condon, assured of sales no matter how much he expressed rather than suppressed his views on politics as organized crime, and a postcolonial poet aiming to make a splash on the academic circuit, it may well be the popular writer who enjoys more creative space in which to manoeuvre. It was exactly in this spirit that Mark Twain launched his famous broadside at Henry James, insisting that he wrote for the millions while James wrote solely for the upper-class few. Many, if not most, creators of popular literature are educated and skilled artists who simply prefer to work within established formulas. As a Yale Classics professor, Erich Segal was an expert on time-honoured patterns of sentiment and melodrama before he trotted them out in his 1970 smash hit, *Love Story*.

Nor is it true that intellectuals do not defer to their audience's tastes. After the critical success and financial fiasco of *The Sound and the Fury* (1929), the newly married Faulkner openly vowed to make a bundle by writing a potboiler. It would be *Sanctuary*, a novel of sex and crime set in the same Southern milieu he had explored on past occasions. In the introduction to the book's 1932 Modern Library edition, the author took a rare step for a "serious" writer by stating flatly he was out to make money. "I had been writing books for about five years, which got published and not bought," he complained. "I began to think of books in terms of possible money. I decided I might just as well make some of it myself ... [I] invented the most horrific tale I could imagine and wrote it in about three weeks" (v). When, on 26 March 1931, the *Memphis Evening Appeal* review excoriated Sanctuary as a "devastating, inhuman monstrosity of a book that leaves one with the impression of having been vomited bodily from the sensual cruelty of its pages," it was precisely to the extent that it galvanized the public with its trashy content.

There is no doubt about Faulkner's success in creating a horrific and lurid tale. Upon reviewing the original script, the shocked publisher is on record as having protested: "Good God, I can't publish this. We'd both be in jail." *Sanctuary* indeed contains enough sensational material to vie with Hearst's yellow journalism of the era. It goes well beyond blood simple violence – car wreck, forceful confinement, sadism, impotence, corncob rape, wanton murder, brothels, lynching, perjury, and hanging – to smash sacrosanct psychological taboos. In Faulkner's hands Temple, a teenage rape victim, blooms into a predatory nymphomaniac who calls her assailant Daddy. In a salacious ménage-à-trois she revels in sex with a lover he finds for her, while "Daddy" Popeye himself whimpers and slobbers at the foot of the bed. Was Faulkner creating only for himself in a sovereign disregard for his audience?

DECRYING THE GLASS AS HALF-EMPTY

Another unsettling element in modern art is that common symptom of immaturity, the dread of doing what has been done before.

Edith Wharton

The second set of charges against popular literature, which singles out its alleged effects on high literary culture, falls into two types. The first is that popular fiction borrows from highbrow fiction, thereby debasing it. The second is that, by offering powerful economic incentives, genre literature diverts talent away from more intellectual pursuits and thus lowers the latter's overall quality.

To begin, one could ask what is wrong with popular writers borrowing from intellectuals? It seems that such crossovers ought to be lauded rather than deplored inasmuch as they introduce aspects of high culture to readers who would otherwise remain outside it. Instead of decrying the glass as half empty, one might rejoice in its being half-full, given that such cross-pollination spreads the select techniques and content of high literature among its popular counterpart, ennobling and enriching the latter rather than debasing the former. In the past, however, it has frequently proven too big a pill to swallow for those who would keep the public a safe distance from the classics. Emily Brönte's canonical romance, *Wuthering Heights*, sold over 300,000 copies by dint of being marketed as a Pocket Book. Several years later, in the comic book format, it sold millions. Yet, instead of words of approbation for a cross-cultural breakthrough, it was greeted with flag-waving denunciations of cultural debasement, proving once again that, as far as popular culture goes, you're damned if you do and damned if you don't.[13]

Karl Marx hectored that highbrow culture arises from the desire of the elite to distance itself from the middle class. As the latter gradually learns to absorb the highbrow forms, this spurs the elite to move on to more esoteric pursuits. This cyclical model implies that it is natural for the avant-garde to alternate between periods of intense experimentation and stagnation, during which the general culture plays catch-up to the new techniques. If true, this means that there isn't – and never could be – any threat to high culture despite occasional alarms about its appropriation by the masses. Indeed, on this view popular literature again performs an invaluable cultural service as a Socratic gadfly that keeps high culture creatively alert. Wherein, one might ask, does the middle ground lie? Perhaps in the words of Delmore Schwartz, who, in the midst of the early 1950s comic book wars, offered this advice in "Masterpieces as Cartoons": "Each adult and literate human being who feels that literature is one of the necessary conditions of civilized existence can set the example of reading *both* the original classics and the cartoon version" (471).

Perceptions of literary debasement are further compromised by their selective bias. Borrowing and imitation have always been two-way streets, with many committed intellectuals crossing the tracks for no other reason than to create popular art.[14] Čapek and Lem, both Nobel Prize nominees and aesthetic sophisticates, built their careers on genres, themes, and techniques of the lowbrow variety (see Chapters 4 and 6). As a matter of fact, genre writers frequently delve into the same inventory of technical and formal techniques as do the avant-garde, and they do so independently of the imitative impulse. It is for no other reason that, tracing the epistemological imperative in *Postmodernist Fiction*, Brian McHale gives a nod of approval to such bestselling populists as Doctorow, Vonnegut, Heller, and Woody Allen. Their intertextual, ironic, and epistemological urbanity, often combined with radical narrative self-reflexiveness and linguistic panache, is perhaps the best counterargument to the proponents of popular culture debasement.

Professing the canon we revel in its profuse allusion and intertextuality, forgetting to remind our undergraduates that even kitsch, the whipping boy of popular culture, has often been used to fertilize the higher plains. Conclusive evidence has accrued over the years that many avant-gardists used elements of kitsch in their literature and art to scandalize their audiences and to elevate themselves out of obscurity.[15] Scholars by no means integrated concede that an "important, though rarely suspected, advantage of kitsch is that it lends itself naturally to irony – and irony is, among other things, an obvious privilege of sophistication."[16] Gilbert Highet, himself not above condemning popular culture as a vulgar showoff, admits that kitsch is not always facile and graceless, often displaying a complex outlay of creative effort.

In the end, even if popular literature borrows more from highbrow fiction than the other way around – by no means a slam dunk hypothesis – it may be because its audience is larger and requires more literary production. Moreover, this particular critique is trapped by its own logic. Mutual lending and borrowing have been going on for so long that, if the charge of debasement were indeed true, then highbrow fiction would not exist today: it would be by now thoroughly debased. Either the charge of debasement is wrong or serious fiction written by serious writers and dissected by serious critics is now nothing but debased popular literature anyway. *Quod erat demonstrandum.*

The fact that popular literature lures away talented writers is correct to the extent that we overlook the fact that popular writers also try their hand at more ambitious projects, lured by their cultural prestige. A classic example may be Thomas M. Disch, a virtuoso of New Wave science fiction and the horror story. In parallel with his genre pursuits, he also published volumes of poetry, directed Broadway plays, adapted operas, and established himself as a sought-after theatre critic. Characteristically, in the middle of his busy sci-fi career he took time off to co-write *Neighboring Lives*, an ambitious, literary, and poorly selling Victorian *roman fleuve* about the life and times of Thomas Carlyle.

While on Victorian fiction, one of the most drastic measures to curry literary prestige must have been that devised by Conan Doyle. It is no secret that Sir Arthur was distinctly contemptuous of the detective and adventure stories (such as *The Lost World*, the prototype of *Jurassic Park*) that brought him renown. Parallel to the exploits of his ace consulting detective, Conan Doyle thus plied a "serious" literary vein in the historical mode (e.g., *White Company*), hoping it would bring him acclaim from the highbrows. The allure of pound sterling was clearly not foremost in his mind when he killed Holmes in "The Final Problem" at the apex of the latter's popularity. However, Dr. Moriarty's triumph was short-lived. Holmes's demise provoked an outcry across Britain during which fans wore mourning bands in public, with the result that, in the end, the detective had to be brought back to life in "The Empty House." Willing to forgo his most lucrative creation for the sake of literary posterity, Sir Arthur would be discomfited to learn that today no one cares a tinker's cuss for his historical dramas, while Holmes is a classic of world literature, revered in the works of such contemporary greats as Borges and Eco.

This is not to say that all genre practitioners just itch to desert the popular Muse or that those who do invariably pull it off. John McDonald, author of a commercially and critically successful crime series featuring a private eye, Travis McGee, has also tried to write outside the formula that brought him so much success. Although sympathetic to these efforts, in "Up from Elitism" Ray B. Browne contrasts the McGee novels with MacDonald's books outside the genre, rating the latter as less than successful. Still, the example confirms that at least some popular writers entertain literary ambitions and bet their money on them, even though such ambitions do not automatically compel them to try to become the next avant-garde. More important, it is not at all clear that even if popular fiction was legislated out of existence, highbrows would rush in to fill the void. Not all creators can write for popular audiences, as the repeated failure of distinguished novelists in Hollywood, such as Huxley or Fitzgerald, has borne out. The pattern was already clear to Henry James. In "The Next Time" his hero, Ray Limbert, sets out to write a potboiler after a series of distinguished but non-selling *opera*, only to produce another unpopular art novel.[17]

Besides, writers who post an occasional bestseller need not automatically be inclined to turn their noses up at ambitious fiction afterwards. A musical version – first on Broadway, then a Gene Kelly-directed film – of Thornton Wilder's early play, *The Merchants of*

Yonkers, brought the author the proverbial jackpot in royalties as the 1964 smash hit *Hello Dolly*. Instead of trying to replicate his box-office coup, however, Wilder embarked on another of his epic literary endeavours, the farewell *Eighth Day*. Similarly, after the success of *The Thanatos Syndrome*, which in less than two weeks bolted into the top ten on US bestseller lists, Walker Percy devoted himself to crafting a series of essays on semiotics, posthumously collected as *Signposts in a Strange Land* (1991).

Popular success may in fact provide artists with the means to pursue more esoteric projects that might never have been written if they had had to seek regular employment in order to put food on the table. Biographers agree that, if not for the financial bonanza from *Animal Farm*, Orwell would probably not have had the resources to complete *1984*.[18] The financial precariousness of the literary métier is a byword, and it is no secret that most authors, from Shakespeare down, had other resources to pull them through. Some of the top names in the canon have been customs officers, deans of cathedrals, doctors, government clerks, editors, or insurance executives. Some have been writers of popular literature. In the end, for authors and publishers alike, prestige and popular projects have always worked side by side in the literature business. André Deutsch kept both V.S. Naipaul and Peter Benchley (of *Jaws* fame) in his publishing stable, while Jonathan Cape printed not only Kingsley Amis but also Ian ("my name is Bond, James Bond") Fleming.

THERE ARE FEW MME BOVARYS IN REAL LIFE

There is no such thing as a moral or an immoral book. Books are well written, or badly written.

Oscar Wilde

Charge three, popular literature's negative effect on society, assumes a number of incarnations. First, popular literature is said to be emotionally debilitating because it provides only spurious gratifications and brutalizes readers with gratuitous sex and violence. This is the qualitative version of this critique. The quantitative version abandons the charge of wantonness and argues simply that mass fiction is inundated by sex and violence – in implicit contrast, presumably, to the canon. Popular literature is also said to be intellectually debilitating because of its emphasis on escapist content, which inhibits its readers' ability to cope with reality. Finally, popular literature has been accused of being culturally debilitating because it prevents readers from partaking of more serious and difficult types of writing. All three of these charges are predicated on the assumption that the behaviour postulated by the critics actually exists, that the content of popular fiction actually contains models of such behaviour, and that there is a causal link between the two. All are contradicted by available data.[19]

Of particular interest is Achim Barsch's "Young People Reading Popular/Commercial Fiction," an extensive 1997 study of the status and reception of the typically German popular fiction phenomenon, the 64-page pulp fiction booklet (*Heftroman*). Its findings squarely contradict the vices traditionally attributed to lovers of popular literature. Not only is there no typical reader of genre fiction – readership is distributed more or less evenly across the income, social, and educational spectrum – but pulp fiction buffs are quite simply avid readers. In addition to Heftromans, they frequently consume vast amounts of belles lettres and non-fiction. They make complex and differentiating judgments about the contents of what they read and about the distance between fiction and their personal lives, and they are emphatically not pathological escapists. Although diversion from everyday stresses and sorrows is an important reason for turning to popular fiction, numerous multilayered and sophisticated motivations were found to come into play in readers' contacts with the booklets. A relatively high incidence of rereading was another of the study's findings, linking the reading patterns of popular literature enthusiasts even more closely to those of highbrow consumers (more on this in Chapter 3).

Barsch's findings are confirmed across the entire spectrum of popular literature patrons. They extend even to readers of romances, traditionally pitied as a low-grade social group hooked on low-grade formula. The harlequins may be trashy, patriarchal, and clone-prone, but their readers often engage in critical and oppositional interpretive transactions. Studies conducted by Janice Radway, especially for *Reading the Romance*, show that many women construe their reading as an act of self-assertion as well as a declaration of temporary independence from their marital and parental roles.[20] Empirical findings consistently record the presence of discriminating and critical attitudes among popular culture audiences, a distinction that academic consumers of high art typically arrogate only to themselves. You don't have to be a boob, research shows time and again, to enjoy the boob tube.[21]

Some established voices go even further. In the eyes of Borges and Northrop Frye, for instance, the intuitive wisdom of storytellers of romances and other popular genres determines and defines the literary tradition. Unadulterated by academic "isms," popular genres combine into a cultural symphony made up of variations on the old and the fertile creations of the new. In fact, if one is to believe Frye's tenets in *The Secular Scripture*, it is the mythic imagination of the popular forms that guides the elites out of their cycles of artistic exhaustion. In general, there is little evidence that the vast majority of North Americans who regularly partake of genre fiction are atomized escapists incapable of getting a grip on reality. If anything, what scant data exist – particularly from community and leisure studies – indicate that most people from the lower-middle and middle-middle class (i.e., the group most "at risk") are not isolated brutes living out escapist and violent fantasies but, rather, active members of family, peer, and social groups.[22]

This is not to deny that some popular novels betray the characteristics of which they are accused. My only point is that content attribution, the standard critical practice of inferring effects and attitudes, is a singularly unreliable and demonstrably fallible method. The very same method would find a lot amiss with most of what the canon professes as art. Few, however, pillory Updike for titillating academic sensibilities with spurious annals of anal sex in *Roger's Version* or fault Malamud for making his protagonist copulate with a beast in *God's Grace*. Gore, incest, violence, and sociopathy have been staples of world literature since before *Oedipus Rex*. Thackeray used to openly bewail the conventional pieties of the Victorian age, which prevented him from jazzing up his prose. And the amount of lascivious, offensive, and politically incorrect material culled from the bard's canon for Michael MacRone's *Naughty Shakespeare* (1997) proves that he was indeed the baddest of them all.

In general, popular fiction, which mainly addresses itself to its widest consumer, the middle class, is frequently more conservative and puritanical than is the avant-garde simply because it strives to cater to the middle-class social and sexual ethos. When *Classics Illustrated*, the 1940s and 1950s comic book giant, brought out such canonical must-reads as *A Midsummer Night's Dream*, *Crime and Punishment*, and *Gulliver's Travels*, it actually felt compelled to clean up some of their content for the sake of a popular (often juvenile) reader. Swift's ending, for example, would lose some of its perceived misanthropy; the bard's bawdiness would be bowdlerized; and Dostoevsky's Sonia, a prostitute, would vanish altogether. Such liberties ignited accusations of tampering with the classics, which provided some ammunition to those who saw popular fiction bashing as a game of "heads I win, tails you lose."

People choose literary content to fit their individual and social preferences rather than vice versa. Most readers of popular fiction have a crassly pragmatic attitude towards what they read. They do not generally buy whatever lies on the bestsellers rack but, instead, select books that satisfy their needs and values. As a rule they are also not particularly attuned to the verbal and symbolic content of what they read, which makes them, if anything, less susceptible to the "trash" they consume. Indeed, if my own experience is typical in this respect, readers who use popular fiction for pleasure and diversion would never dream of patterning their lives after the books they read with such passion. There are few Mme Bovarys in real life, and for the people who enjoy popular literature as a breather from everyday life, a fast-paced dose of action or faraway fantasy serves them better than does plodding realism.

It has been argued that, insofar as popular literature often expresses and reflects their aesthetic and social values, popular fiction readers form a taste culture. As such, their decision as to what type of books to buy and read is at least in part a matter of choice rather than cultural and ideological brainwashing. Those willing to pay for genre novels presumably find value and satisfaction in them, and it would be difficult to deny that, for them, popular literature performs an appreciable cultural role. Similar tenets have begun to emerge recently from philosophers scrutinizing popular culture. In the analytic vein, for example, Nöel Carroll has advanced several arguments to the effect that genre fiction evokes the same processes of intellectual involvement as does high literature, albeit using different themes and methods.[23] These findings appear once again to debunk the debunkers of popular fiction by revealing an appreciable degree of discrimination in its consumers. Jerry Springer aside, recipients of popular culture are not all passive receptacles, as the flop of some hyped-up Tinseltown money-guzzlers (e.g., Costner's raspberry-showered *Postman* or Travolta's *Battlefield Earth*) evidence.

The supply and demand of the literary marketplace form a feedback loop. There are good reasons to believe that popular fiction, instead of luring gullible readers away from serious art, responds to the demands of the reading public (or at least to what genre writers and their publishers perceive these demands to be). If I am correct – that is, if turning to popular literature is at least in part a matter of choice rather than a Pavlovian response – then the charge that Joseph Wambaugh is the only obstacle between an average reader and *Crime and Punishment* is simply untrue. Besides, some elements of the literary avant-garde reach mass readership via the mediation of popular fiction, giving the latter a constructive role to play in a broadly conceived cultural education.

POLITICAL, SOCIAL, AND CULTURAL DICTATORSHIP

The comics may be said to offer the same kind of mental catharsis to its readers that Aristotle claimed was an attribute of the drama.

Loretta Bender, MD

The fourth and last set of reasons for keeping popular literature away from curricula in the numbers it deserves takes two forms. On the one hand, it is alleged that the mass presence and appeal of popular literature lowers the general cultural level of the reading public. Its other ill-effect on society is said to be paving the way for political, social, and cultural dictatorship by creating a passive and apathetic audience that can easily fall victim to propaganda and totalitarianism.

On reflection, the facts seem to be at odds with both of these perceptions, despite centuries-old endorsements of the "our-standards-are-in-decline" scenario. One of the oldest – and, in this context, funniest – of such plaints is practically indistinguishable from today's Letters to the Editor. "Our youth now love luxury. They have bad manners, contempt for authority. They show disrespect for elders and love chatter in place of exercise. They contradict their parents ... and tyrannize their teachers," crabbed Socrates 2,500 years ago.[24] Our art must have the resilience of a Bailey circus strongman, it seems, to have withstood millennia of the slide down the cultural chute. And, if so, then all fears about its incipient corruption can be put to rest. Or maybe it's just the opposite: our high art and culture have indeed succumbed long ago, with Irving, Poe, and Dos Passos a proof of how degraded and degrading it has become over the ages.

As Gans reports in *Popular Culture and High Culture*, the fact of the matter is that, during the last century, the dominant cultural level in the United States has not only failed to decline but has actually risen from that of lower-middle class to middle-middle class. So much for the lowering of cultural standards due to popular arts, which, I need hardly remind you, flourished during the period in question. Those who persist in believing that things have indeed gotten worse can compare what we have today with what the English public consumed in the nineteenth century. From penny periodicals to penny dreadfuls, from *Vice and Its Victim; or, Phoebe, the Peasant's Daughter* to Marinism and half-baked plots, some popular fictions of the last century were dreadful enough to become cult classics on a par with sci-fi flicks from the 1950s.[25]

Since all preceding arguments are an *en masse* refutation of the fourth charge, one may wonder whether the apocalyptic arguments have any basis in fact. The answer is "Yes," although only if we overlook the tendentiousness evident in most comparisons of past and present cultural productions. Conservatives who maintain that popular literature leads to a decline in standards tend to contrast the highest achievements of the past with the mediocre of the present. This is widespread enough for Ingrid Shafer to spoof it in an ironic litmus test of literary value in the popular arts. With numerous examples to support her case, she reconstructs the critical argument as follows. If a novel is popular, then it cannot be any good since only difficult and revolutionary literature is good, and the buying public would not buy what is revolutionary and difficult. If it's contemporary, then it cannot be good because, by definition, it is not a true and proven classic. The exception is a contemporary classic – namely, a work ahead of its times and readers – in which case see above. Sums up Shafer: "Talk about going around in vicious circles!"[26]

Similarly, the argument that literary culture would immediately improve if pulp fiction did not stand in its way does not convince. If anything, the postwar experience of the iron-curtained parts of Europe persuades to the contrary. For decades the communist regimes sought to replace capitalist pop culture with one of a decidedly more propedeutic and soc-realistic flavour. The results, as we know, were less than spectacular, and, in the end, the governments caved in against the grassroots demand for domestic equivalents of Western genres. One example from my youth is Maciej Słomczynski, card-carrying intellectual and canonical translator of Shakespeare, who applied his talents to the detective novel under the pen name of Joe Alex. Urbane and ironic, he playfully piled genre cliché upon cliché in a chart-topping series of whodunits, ingenious enough to nonplus the discriminating connoisseur.

Undoubtedly it is feasible to manipulate popular literature consumers. Like any cultural product, pulp fiction is not immune to being saddled with latent ideological content liable to pacify the public by concealing the top-heavy nature of the world's power relations. In less technical terms, we are talking here about the tried and true program of preempting dissent and discontent by providing cultural opium to the masses. To their lasting credit, mass culture critics like Bernard Rosenberg have unerringly zeroed in on "the ways that mass communications can and do anesthetize us"

(7). True to his word, on the next page of "Mass Culture Revisited I," Rosenberg does a compelling and concise job of recapping how mass media occasionally sway, or even mould, public opinion.[27]

The words may have changed over the years, the post-Foucauldian version sounding perhaps more sophisticated than Dwight Macdonald's straightforward attack on popular culture as an instrument of political domination. But, far from changing, the problem remains as acute as ever. If only for this reason alone, we need intellectually vigilant readers and critics on both sides of the fence. Nor does the fact that popular fiction has been spared the brunt of attacks directed at other popular media (mainly, it seems, television) mean that the charges, even if not to the same extent, are not transferable. However, contrary to the conservative opinion that has sounded the alarm bell for centuries now, the evidence marshalled in this chapter shows conclusively that there are few reasons to believe that popular fiction has a lasting harmful effect on highbrow literature, on its consumers, or on society as a whole. In this I am reassured to find support in Richard Anderson, who also concludes that, while much of popular art "overtly or implicitly expresses and validates the values of the status quo," it provides "no effective way to establish the exact extent to which particular popular art forms serve established propaganda."[28]

A ROSEBUD OF CRYSTALLINE PURITY

The crisis of culture in liberal-democratic society is due, in the first place, to the fact that the fundamental social processes, which previously favoured the development of the culturally creative élites, now have the opposite effect, i.e. have become obstacles to the forming of élites because wider sections of the population take an active part in cultural activities.

Karl Mannheim

Raymond Chandler – oiler, business exec, purveyor of hardboiled crime, and stylist supreme – is emerging posthumously as one of the more original and entertaining authors of the twentieth century.

Celebrated as the creator of Philip Marlowe, PI, he is also the author of penetrating essays on modern fiction and the vagaries of its reception. Many of these classic studies record the dismay of an ambitious artist at the critical disdain directed towards genre fiction. Chandler's opinion – echoed in recent years, notably by Eco – is that neither uncritical plaudits nor apocalyptic censures are adequate to the scale and complexity of the popular fiction phenomenon. Between "the one-syllable humors of the comic strip and the anemic subtleties of the litterateurs," maintains Chandler, "there is a wide stretch of country."[29] In *Apocalypse Postponed* Eco stands the entire debate on its head by declaring that the alarmist and consolatory voices raised against mass fiction are actually "the most sophisticated product on offer for mass consumption" (18).

Mapping Chandler's country may be, however, less straightforward than the metaphor suggests. In the real world one can easily settle where the interstate ends and a country lane begins. Not so in the world of modern fiction, where the interweaving influences, borrowings, imitations, and appropriations often obscure the extent of one's artistic territory. Globalization may be the buzzword in business and cultural studies, but in literature it has always been a part of the landscape.

Today divisions between nations, literatures, taste cultures, and individuals are not only hard to define but also even detect. Space-age multi-channel communications, mass marketing strategies, and a culture of imitation of genuine trend-setters make this process even more difficult.[30] Browser technology allows creators to surf for ideas and to refine searches without end, greying the border between what's original and what's recycled. Hypertext webmasters yoke texts and writers in configurations the latter could have never foreseen and might never have authorized. Questions about the authorship of these new supertexts are really questions about cultural divisions and aesthetic categories gone nobrow.

Interpenetration between popular art and high art has always taken place, with or without the consent of the curators of the particular version of the canon. Little wonder that those interested in distinguishing the highbrow from the lowbrow often find themselves stymied when tracking the origins of styles, schools, or influences. The experience is not unlike watching the line between sand and water on Arnold's Dover beach. With the tide high, then low, and with individual waves thrashing about, who is to say where one ends and the other begins?

Not all popular literature is, of course, worthy of praise and scrupulous analysis. But among its wares, almost a priori consigned to the cultural basement, there are works equal (less several hundred critical articles and academic theses) to the canon. According to the basic axiom of "eliterary" education, popular fiction has little social or aesthetic merit and, therefore, little claim to a place in literary history. Yet despite these by now standard voices, what you get is not what you see. An abundance of independent studies documents even the Victorian sensation novels as anything but passive instantiations of a vacuous genre formula.[31] Quite the contrary: premier popular writers such as Charles Reade, Mary Braddon, or Wilkie Collins purposely subverted the very melodramatic conventions they deployed with such skill. Frequently drawing on newspaper reports of criminal trials and the proceedings of the Divorce Court, they not only tackled pregnant social issues but also openly disputed conventional ideas about status, morality, and even romance itself.

Eliterary education accepts the literature of entertainment from the past but *not* as the literature of entertainment. Where once there were low comedies closing the day for the drama-weary Hellenes, we now honour stage classics of antiquity. Where once there were adventure melodramas for the merchant class, we now see prose masterpieces of the pre-Romantic age. Popular forms are frequently shunned by the elites until novel forms replace them, at which point the entertainment of the past starts to claw its way up into the domain of respectable art. The case could be made for much of today's establishment, including the theatre, opera, or classical music, and even for poetry in Plato's day. Moreover, the pattern continues to unfold right before our eyes. The Library of America, committed to preserving American classics from Poe to Faulkner, has recently incorporated Dashiell Hammett into its prestigious canon, a writer known in his day for action-packed private-eye classics in which the only thing faster than a bullet was one-line wit.

In the end, institutional dogma apart, popular literature created for the mass enjoyment of mass readership may be as true a medium of literary artistry and aesthetic continuity as the canon, circulating and recycling plots, narratives, and characters that have proven their enduring worth. If, to paraphrase Auden from "In Memory of W.B. Yeats," the words of dead men are modified in the guts of the living, then, instead of deploring, we should welcome genre fiction's very trademarks. Its predilection for well tried formulas and its penchant for recycling may, at the end of the day, be a good way to preserve the great motifs of literature for new generations of readers. And the generations to come may yet see in our potboilers a product of high art.

Having examined some of the most persistent criticisms and misconceptions of popular literature, not surprisingly I must conclude that almost all of them are groundless. Statistical surveys, aesthetic analyses, and empirical research prove time and again what, for the longest time, only institutional myopia prevented us from teaching to our students. Aesthetic standards spring up in all communities, from the nomad cultures and pre-Columbian Americans down to the rhyming poetry of modern rap and the mosaic of popular prose genres that supply writers with preset patterns within which they can develop their individuality.[32]

Aesthetic and cultural theories change over time, and even our Western views on art have had numerous incarnations in their journey from the pre-Socratic and early Hebraic thinkers down to Scott McCloud's *Understanding Comics*.[33] Institutional aesthetics is less a Rosebud of crystalline purity and more like a moving picture of the life of Charles Foster Kane: a time-indexed jigsaw of opinions, cross-influences, and accretions. However, there is no reason to be afraid of acknowledging the time-specific value of our classics. It ought not to detract from the power of Da Vinci's Gioconda to recognize the fragility of the claims to aesthetic immanence made on its behalf. Many prefer to believe in the transcendence of our classics, even though the boom-and-bust cycle of the Mona Lisa's aesthetic stock over centuries of shifting aesthetic paradigms is a matter of historical record.[34]

This double standard extends to a whole range of aesthetic critiques. Genre novels have been sniped at for growing long and overdrawn, presumably in contradistinction to the economy of highbrow fiction. While there are some writers who fit the bill – Tom Clancy's self-indulgent and jingoistic Jack Ryan opus leaps to mind – fat and flat describes equally well David Foster Wallace and his 1,000-plus pages of *Infinite Jest* from the postmodern canon. It may be that, with prices of paperbacks climbing, genre authors aim to provide maximum bang for our buck, pushing the average number of pages up. But if you like your prose lean and mean, then pulp fiction is still your best bet. Kept in check by the demands of the marketplace, it tends to deliver a compact product in a to-the-point style designed to keep the pace brisk and the reader awake. Look no further than the oeuvres of William Marshall (mystery), Louis L'Amour (western), or Desmond Bagley (espionage), legendary for their brevity and pith.

Rather than constituting a cultural menace, popular fiction performs an appreciable socio-aesthetic role. Moreover, more often than we like to tell our students, it not only aspires to, but succeeds at, being art on a par with what goes into the regularly revised editions from Norton. From the arguments in this chapter it should be evident that, as institutional taste-makers, we have little to gain by continuing to ignore popular fiction, except a further degree of isolation and irrelevance to society at large.

Popular literature demands serious and sympathetic analysis, free of prejudice on the one hand and anti-canonical backlash on the other. While much of genre fiction can stand next to works hailed as lasting triumphs of world literature, much more of it deserves to be treated as the only thing it tries to be: gripping and informative but ultimately ephemeral entertainment with no aspirations to bowl over the establishment. Some of it is demonstrable schlock, which makes the task of discrimination among its various offerings and the education of readers who persist in reading it all the more worthwhile. But to separate a good thriller from a bad one, or a good crime story from a bad classic, we need to approach literature – in whatever form it manifests itself – with a pure mind and interpretive apparatus of sufficient refinement.

3   Genres and Paradoxes

Bond is sent to a given place to avert a "science-fiction" plan by a mon-strous individual of uncertain origin and definitely not English ... In facing this monstrous being, Bond meets a woman who is dominated by him and frees her from her past, establishing with her an erotic relationship interrupted by capture by the Villain and by torture. But Bond defeats the villain, who dies horribly, and rests from his great efforts in the arms of the woman, though he is destined to lose her.

Umberto Eco, "Narrative Structures in Fleming"

Nöel Carroll's article, "The Paradox of Junk Fiction" (1994), raises a number of important points about interpreting mass fiction, setting the stage for the pragmatic turn in interpreting genres. Carroll's ingenious inquiry is designed to illuminate the seemingly odd behaviour people exhibit when reading popular literature. His minor premise is that popular (or, in his idiom, junk) fictions, often repetitive and formulaic, tend to belong to well entrenched genres typified by "an extremely limited repertoire of story-types" (226). The major premise is that popular novels repeat these generic stories ad infinitum, with only minor variations, so that the reader who has read in the genre "knows in rough outline how the story is likely to go" (ibid.).

Before advancing any further, let us consider questions raised by these twin assumptions. First of all, how limited is the repertoire of popular genres? As we saw in Chapter 2, studies of literary forms and their reception repeatedly return the verdict that genre variations, regularly dismissed as minor, are in fact profound and extensive. It would be hard, in fact, to find a wholly typical genre narrative inasmuch as most rely on a complex mix of conventions and often substantial departures from them. Stretched over hundreds and thousands of stories, such variations end up being remarkable in both number and character. This is what makes a genre system rich and unpredictable, even though any single novel may depart from it only to a certain degree.

Hammett's *The Glass Key*, O'Hara's *Appointment in Samara*, Hemingway's *To Have and Have Not*, Cain's *Double Indemnity*, Chandler's *Playback*, Himes's *Cotton Comes to Harlem*, Kerr's *A German Requiem*, or Mosley's *Devil in a Blue Dress* are all hard-boiled fiction. Yet they are as distinct from one another as are the biographies of the men who wrote them. On the other hand, a story-type comparison of Flaubert, Dreiser, Zola, and Hardy would have to conclude that these classics of naturalism do indeed operate within a limited and repetitive repertoire. Stories of low-class origins, socio-genetic determinism, and the struggles to escape its dictates, crowned with inevitable failures, are repetitive and formulaic, especially next to the variety of highly individuated styles and storylines in the hardboiled masters.

The theme of star-crossed lovers has been exploited in all kinds of serious fiction, yet the peripeties of the lovers' encounter, romance, and inevitable downfall are, in effect, as predictable and formulaic as is every "new" Bond adventure. Once we filter the background through an appropriately selected structural lens, the differences between *Romeo and Juliet*, *Wuthering Heights*, and *The Great Gatsby* begin to disappear. At this point the reader who has followed Shakespeare's plot knows in rough outline how the story is going to develop in Brönte and Fitzgerald, surface variations notwithstanding. A skeptic might argue that this argument misses the point because serious literature cannot be reduced to its story-type. If so, then this simply proves that it is no different from a legion of popular novels, of which the hardboiled classics are only one example.

Carroll unveils the paradox of genre fiction in the following way. If, "in some very general sense," readers already know the story in question, "why are they still interested in investing time" (226) in reading it? The misty phrase, "in some very general sense," is worth pausing over as it goes a long way towards providing us with an answer. The appeal to some very general sense in which a proposition is true signals, I venture, a futzing of the issue, without which the paradox would lose its apparent intractability. The next remark does nothing to dispel this impression. Making essentially the same point, it reiterates that "consumers of junk fiction are generally reading fictions whose *stories – or story-types –* they already know" (227; emphasis mine). This statement obscures the potentially enormous difference between individual stories and story-types. It is simply incorrect to conflate the two, as though knowledge of the generic plot-line were sufficient to enable us to know all there is to know about a particular story.

Even if we granted Carroll the limited number of story-types in a genre – by no means a proven proposition – the knowledge of a story-type still does not entail knowledge of the story in question. My hardboiled and star-crossed lovers counter-examples reveal why this is so. The differences between stories of the same story-type can be, after all, as profound as those between *Romeo and Juliet* and *The Great Gatsby* – or as those between *Double Indemnity* and *A German Requiem*. In fact, the difference could be as profound as those found among all four novels combined in that the latter two also happen to be tragic love stories. This makes the equation between stories and story-types even more arguable for, if a genre can accommodate the diversity of Shakespeare, Fitzgerald, Cain, and Kerr, then hardly anyone could be faulted for steadfastly returning to a pattern that is, in fact, not much of a pattern at all. That is why I suggested earlier that the putative paradox is perhaps no paradox at all as there is nothing odd or irrational about readers persisting to read in a particular genre. Given the potentially vast differences between individual instantiations of a paradigm, I may remain glued to the page even though my grasp of the story-pattern may tell me that it's not likely that the hero and heroine will emerge unscathed by their affair.

Kathy Seldon (played by Debbie Reynolds) is not truthful when she tells Don Lockwood (Gene Kelly) in *Singin' in the Rain* that once you've seen one of his movies, you've seen them all. By that same logic, the daily paper, which always dishes out the same limited repertoire of wars, crimes, economic downturns, political cover-ups, and celebrity gossip, would not be worth reading. Newspaper story-types, as experience instructs, hardly change at all and are limited in number to begin with. Yet I imagine most of us see nothing irrational about a daily half-hour with the local *Courier*, *Gazette*, or *Times*. In the end, it is not necessarily the case that a rough anticipation of the story-type kills the story. Even though we guess at Kathy's deception, we still relish the moment when she admits to Don that she had seen no less than eight or nine of his productions.

The question, "How can we be interested in consuming stories we already know?" is misleading. We do *not* know the stories we consume even if we can at times reliably guess at their story-type. Reading popular fictions is not a mindless and submissive process. On the contrary, it requires the constant exercise of one's interpretive powers. Carroll concurs: "even though you already know the story type inside and out ... each different novel provides you with an opportunity to exercise your interpretive powers on a different set of details and misunderstandings, and, most importantly, on different *kinds* of misunderstandings" (234).

Approaching reading as a transaction between the author and the reader, mediated through the novel's simultaneous play *with* and *within* the convention of a genre, analytic philosophers find a great deal of value in popular literature. The pleasure from and active involvement in this literature derives from its ability to stimulate and exercise our powers of observation, inference, and interpretation. We read on to learn more about the story, to see our predictions thwarted or confirmed, or to devise answers to gaps, puzzles, or questions posed by the plot and the characters. In other words, we interpret popular stories cognitively, much as we do prestige fiction.

This goes against the apples-with-oranges view of literature, wherein the putative difference in lowbrow and highbrow standards is said to render them incommensurable. One of the most venerable legacies of cultural elitism is, after all, that popular literature induces interpretive passivity and general mental flatlining. To hold that it may in fact be intellectually and interpretively as engaging as are the classics may strike skeptics like Leo Lowenthal as ill-informed. Yet, as I showed elsewhere, *all* fictions demand nuanced – even if for the most part unconscious – cognitive processing even on such a fundamental level as storyline integration.[1] There are no narratives so transparent or trite as to require zero intellectual contribution on the reader's part. Even such a basic process as recognizing a poem as a poem presupposes "conventions of reading which the author may work against, which he can transform, but which are the conditions of possibility of discourse."[2]

The same kind of processing need not, however, imply the same degree of processing. Surely *Don Quixote* calls for a greater amount of concentration and mental involvement than a western, say, *The Lonesome Dove*? The objection is clever, and the underlying question simple: can we replace a quantitative distinction with a qualitative one? I don't think so. Reading Cervantes for enjoyment, letting himself be carried by the picaresque mock-adventures of this entertaining romance, the reader certainly does not employ his intellectual faculties in optimal fashion. On the other hand, when one ponders McMurtry's epic as a critic and scholar, it engages the reader cognitively and rewards every instance of intellectual processing. The reverse, of course, also obtains: when one reads the latter epic for fun, and the former for cognitive payoff, both perform admirably again. The skeptical argument is clever because, if correct, it would associate complexity exclusively with the classics and simplicity exclusively with formula fiction. But literature itself provides a vast number of examples of why this will not work. Just plug canonical Aesop and a platinum-selling science fiction such as *A Canticle for Leibowitz* into this equation.

Apart from providing an opportunity for cognitive work, which can be as basic as trying to guess whodunit or as complex as Pellegrino's ortoevolutionary inquiries, genre novels are equally capable of provoking emotional or moral responses. Our continued interest in junk fictions, therefore, derives from the same source as does our interest in the canon: exercising our faculties for processing narratives, making emotive discriminations, and forming moral judgments. Carroll goes even further, arguing that knowledge of genres "may make our active engagement with junk fictions more zestful in the way that playing games with well-defined rules enables us to hone our abilities more keenly" (237). Viewing interpretation as a literary game has a long tradition that has not, however, fully tapped the modelling potential offered by game theory. Later on I outline a few game theory insights into the problem of genres and literary interpretation.

A related though separate phenomenon is that of literary recidivism. In its simplest form it poses a similar question: How can we consume with relish and abandon *the very same* stories we have already read once – or even many times – before? For there is no doubt we do just that: just as there are frequent rereaders of Shakespeare, so there are frequent rereaders of genre stories.[3] The proper answer to this question is sure to require a full-scale study of its own. I would wager, however, that it will be informed by the truism that, although stories don't change, we do. Theories of cleansing and catharsis may be true to varying degrees (in the same sense that lovemaking with the same partner need not become less rewarding through repetition). Besides, rereading a novel need not (in fact, it almost never will) generate the exact same set of experiences. Critics keen to harness the basic tenets of information theory sometimes forget that a work of literature is not *just* an information carrier.[4] This is why foreknowledge of the plot line does not prohibit a rewarding reread. Linguistic flavour, character development, and moral nuance are only some narrative facets that can sustain many happy returns to an already familiar novel.

But even informational redundancy is not a foregone issue. Returning to a favourite book may be experientially like using a microscope for enhanced resolution. Your eye may be drawn to the finer detail (e.g., of mood, utterance, description) that may have escaped during the first contact, which is often dominated by a natural rush to find out what happens next. Finally, the answer may lie in the shortcomings of our cognitive faculties. We have imperfect memories. We forget. I have by now reread Ed McBain, Martin Cruz Smith, and Brian Azzarello/Eduardo Risso countless times, yet each time, after a longer interval, I experience a sense of discovery (if only of forgotten elements), anticipation (if only of familiar passages), and aesthetic satisfaction (if only of integrating the unfolding of a complex design).

THE PARADOX DISSOLVES INTO THIN AIR

As an artist, of course, I hate genres. They cramp my style and pigeonhole my burgeoning creativity.

Sean Stewart

Thomas J. Roberts has recently offered an account of reading genre literature that also bears on the paradox of junk fiction. In his view, the experience of a popular novel is typically mediated through the experience of an entire genre system. "Genre reading is system reading. That is, as we are reading these stories, we are exploring the system that created them" (151), argues the author in *An Aesthetics of Junk Fiction* (1990). Naturally, system reading is not the sole reason we turn to popular literature, as the preceding sections sought to establish. All the same, Roberts makes a thorough case for recognizing the effect of genres on our reading of popular novels – or, as I would argue, on all literature, period. It is only against the background assimilated from previous contacts with a given *class* of writing that we can track the attributes of the particular story we are reading. Variations within genre conventions or the absence thereof, along with the level of artistic skill involved, are only some intertextual features appreciated solely in the context of comparative and contrasting reading within a system.

Roberts's thesis has provoked a range of responses too great to analyze here. One of them, however, has an interesting upshot for the paradox of junk fiction. Not surprisingly, it has been advanced by Nöel Carroll, who concedes that most readers – including journalistic as well as academic critics – do read comparatively within any given genre. Nevertheless he insists, with some justification, that we commonly read novels for the sake of the individual story rather than for the genre of which it is a part.

How does this illuminate the paradox? First, if the reader spends an evening with a book for the sake of that story, and not that story vis-à-vis its genre, then the paradox dissolves into thin air. Recall that the paradox involved describing a situation in which a reader persists in reading fictions that, in a sense, she already knows. But you can't recognize that you already know a story unless you bring other stories just like it into the picture. This, however, means taking a comparative look across literary genres. So if you read for the sake of the individual story alone – cordoning off other narratives as well as their categories – then the paradox does not even come into play. Reading popular fiction thus represents no irrationality on the reader's part.

Interestingly, if you read the story as filtered through the background of other stories, the paradox still fails to obtain. In this case the interpretive task and the intellectual fun derived from playing the present narrative off others like (or unlike) it is a perfectly sensible reason for spending time with a genre novel. On Roberts's account, let us recall, readers' interest is grounded precisely in comparing and contrasting literary attributes across a variety of novels in a genre. And such variety may be a source of rewarding contact, even with stories that, in some very general sense, one already knows. That seems to have been the case in ancient Athens. Achaean spectators attended several tragedies in a row in order to compare plays by different authors in the same genre, using the same plot line (e.g., the story of Orestes). Much of the humour in the comedies derived, on the other hand, from the Greek viewers' recognition of standard elements of tragedy being made incongruous and laughable in their crossover context.

So much for the paradox of junk fiction. We have seen previously that reading popular literature can be a source of intellectual, moral, emotive, and aesthetic satisfaction on a continuum with the canon. Now we have additional reason to believe that there is nothing irrational about doing so. Reasons why people read books differ and, as Uri Margolin reminds us, are not always guided by refined aesthetic considerations. Our behaviour may be dominated by a simple "desire to maintain an integrated course of action with the same players, suspense, a thematic point, overall aesthetic design, or even the very tellability and sheer novelty and surprise expressed by the question 'S/he did'?"[5]

Although in the minds of many readers the term "genre" still applies only to popular literature, my arguments above ought not to be taken as applicable only to popular fiction. Reading inside a genre is at the same time always reading outside a genre. Spotting clichés or appreciating novelty inside a given literary form inevitably means drawing on the comparative experience of novels outside it. This point may still be underappreciated even among the more perceptive writers on the subject. Janice Radway, for example, proposed early on that popular texts are "primarily *formulaic* in that they rarely function outside a reader's competence."[6] If what I suggest above is correct, then singling out formula texts is a smokescreen since there are no readings that take place outside a reader's competence. To appreciate the absence, presence, or just transformation of a formula, you must already have absorbed that formula, making the reading of genre literature and mainstream fiction once more a comparable experience.

For this reason I would like now to turn the spotlight on genres and consider their role in the more general context of our interactions with literature, whether during a late night subway ride, a lounge fest on a Club Med beach, or a prep session for a grad seminar. Asking how genres figure for the author and the reader during the tacit transaction into which they enter – one by dint of writing the story, the other by dint of reading it – will help us model the interpretive mechanisms that come into play when readers sit down with a book. Genres are an integral component of our interactions (be they entertainment- or dissertation-driven) with literature. For all this, it is hard to shake off the feeling that the ruling profile of genre studies, which made it into a classificatory assembly line, has borne little tangible fruit. Moreover, all proposed genre "grammars" are too painfully simplistic in their one- or two-dimensional mappings to capture the dynamics of literature as we know it. In fact, the very proliferation of axes in these systems shows them to be essentially arbitrary, casting further doubt on their exactness.[7]

In *Kinds of Literature* Alastair Fowler furnishes a suggestive sample of the axial tower of Babel. Here goes: "authorial-interpersonal (as in Hernadi's scheme); private-communal (Hernadi); the 'height' of the world imitated (Frye and Scholes); rhetorical height; economiastic-vituperative (Averroes); comedy-tragedy (Langer); thematic-nonthematic; psychological polarities, such as subjective-objective or introvert-extrovert (as in Frye's scheme), or 'specific continuous forms'; rhetorical and stylistic spectra, such as opacity-transparency or metaphorical and metonymical (as in David Lodge's scheme)" (247). The list is by no means exhaustive, and countless other binary oppositions could be brought into the picture. This is inevitable, considering that all these systems rely on circular reasoning to jump-start their structural base. The difficulties are compounded by the fact that literary categories are based on anything but uniform criteria. Distinctions follow such sundry factors as theme (*Bildungsroman*, war epic); length (triple-decker, short short story); versification (haiku, villanelle); reading public (penny dreadful, dime novel); iterated edition (serial novel, sonnet cycle); genological priority (anti-utopia, revisionist western); and so on.

This is not to say that the descriptive approach is wholly without virtue. It provides for a measure of ordering of structural characteristics shared by different stories as well as for a broad charting of literary creativity. In the long run it may even help to jump-start a paradigm shift, in the sense of Lévi-Strauss's dictum that "Darwin would not have been possible if he had not been preceded by Linnaeus."[8] But by and large we must move beyond producing shopping lists of structural resemblances simply because such literary taxonomy often ends up resembling literary taxidermy. Who needs genre tabulators to tell them what kind of novel they're enjoying? The matter is open to empirical test. Are there really that many Dan Quayles out there who need to be prompted that Atwood's *Handmaid's Tale* is to be read with the dystopia, Larry Bond's *Red Phoenix* with the techno-thriller, and Pérez-Reverte's *Club Dumas* with the detective mystery in mind?

On the other hand, the matter of *how* we arrive at these judgments is of immense interest and importance. Genres are, of course, an influential subset of literary conventions in general, conventions that function as invitations to certain ways of reading. Research into the mechanisms that let us identify and follow these conventions traditionally splits in two ways. The first option involves reception theory in the empirical mode, which relies on mostly psychometric studies of the reading process.[9] The second option involves looking into the behaviour of writers and readers with a view to modelling the interdependent nature of their quid pro quo. Here, broadly speaking, genre "moves" made by the author are at least partly inflected by the anticipated "moves" to be made by the reader. More formally, genres and conventions in general are treated as interpretive strategies used cooperatively and reflexively (in the Gricean sense) by the author and the reader.

The view of literary conventions as elements of cooperative strategies of communication has as yet few exponents in literary studies. Some researchers have indeed proposed that genre studies ought to move in the direction of interpreting the "operations of reading." Others stress that the relation of literary works to the genres they embody is "not one of passive membership but active modulation ... [which] communicates." Peter J. Rabinowitz's preliminary argument for why "genres can be viewed as strategies that readers use to process texts" is also serviceable as a guidepost for what you'll find below.[10]

All the same, much like the entire school of reader response, such observations have yet to mobilize others for, by and large, literary conventions and genres in particular continue to be approached as acontextual entities. As such they are assumed to be accessible via a structural shortcut of one kind or another and thus to be independent of the interpretive "collapse" of a given novel into a given genre. But the methodological foundations of this contextless view are quite precarious and have already been shaken by the pragmatic effects of genre syncretism and speciation. Though we like to forget it, literary conventions are as prone to mutations as Gregor Samsa, metamorphosing in response to the complex literary transactions into which writers and readers enter with each new work.[11]

A SERIES OF GHASTLY BODY THEFTS

A logical theory may be tested by its capacity for dealing with puzzles, and it is a wholesome plan, in thinking about logic, to stock the mind with as many puzzles as possible, since they serve much the same purpose as is served by experiments in physical sciences.

Bertrand Russell

The analytic framework I have in mind departs from the view of genres as labels for mostly context-free building blocks (themes, motifs, character types, etc.) associated with this or that group of books. This disclaimer would be superfluous if it were not for the persistent belief that genres are somehow empirically definable and immutable. Old habits die hard, it seems, and the habits in question are seasoned indeed. As far back as the Renaissance scholars were wont to believe in the Platonic permanence of literary forms and conventions. They conceived of genres as systems that are always the same, that make no concessions to times or audiences, that impose upon the poet a strict obedience to unalterable rules. This model bears the same relation to any real-life literary form as does a stone lion in front of a Natural Science museum to its fighting, feeding, fleeing, and reproducing pal in the Serengeti.

It is easy to see how this premise could lead to a skewed perception of literary forms and, through it, to a skewed perception that the task of genre studies is mainly classificatory. It was often thought, for example, that the production and refinement of genre definitions is – or even ought to be – the top priority for the critic. All you need is to analyze a group of stories, identify their recurrent elements, and systematize the latter in cluster form. It's like a genrecipe from a literary cookbook: a droid, a dragracer, and a Druish Princess baked on a transgalactic desert for two hours gets you a sci-fi Big Mac *à la* Lucasfilm. Other inferences have also been made, one of the more tenacious being that obstacles before genre critics were, by and large, quantitative, limited to determining the number of building blocks necessary and sufficient to tag a book as a member of a given class.

It is not hard to point out what is wrong with this approach, and indeed, its refutations are many, coming both from literary studies and philosophical aesthetics.[12] An influential example of the latter is Kendall Walton's "Categories of Art" (1970). The author begins by distinguishing three kinds of features that can be isolated over different categories of art: standard, variable, and contra-standard. In literary works these correspond to set elements primarily associated with genre patterns. In detective fiction, for example, the perpetration of the crime is a standard element, the vagaries of plot are the variables, and the lack of solution is a contra-standard element. If you ever played Clue, you would know that no one bats an eye when Colonel Mustard bites it: it's all standard fare in a mystery. Whether he bites a bullet or a poisoned éclaire, however, is not known in advance and is thus one of the variable elements in this equation. Finally, as the game demands a solution and a culprit, it is contrary to the players' expectations and game standards if the butler gets away with murder.

Walton's thesis is that aesthetic qualities of art are determined not just by purely textual (or, more generally, structural) features but also by these features *as seen through the work's category.* To illustrate this point, he introduces a possible world scenario involving an alien society with a singular genre of artistic expression. These are *guernicas*, works of art much like Picasso's cubist painting, only in various bas-relief dimensions. Walton considers the art features of the three-dimensional guernicas and compares them to the aesthetic appeal of the flat, two-dimensional work by the Spanish artist. He concludes that, side by side with the artworks of the alien society, some attributes of Picasso's work will come to depend on the particulars of the guernica category. Sums up the philosopher: Picasso's painting "seems violent, dynamic, disturbing to us. But I imagine it would strike them [the alien society] as cold, stark, lifeless ... in any case *not* violent, dynamic, and vital" (347).

Walton's fantastic scenario may make some readers uneasy, particularly regarding its transfer to our everyday experience with flat guernicas. I thus reassemble the argument using an actual literary case. Stanislaw Lem's early novel, *The Investigation* (1959), relies on a nuanced and complex interplay between two genre categories: classic detective fiction and the ghost story. A page-turner bound to haunt even the hardened buffs of mystery, it follows Lieutenant Gregory of Scotland Yard as he strives to explain a wave of trouble in local morgues. Corpses in various stages of decomposition begin to disappear in hair-raising circumstances that, despite all odds, seem to point towards "resurrection."

The crux of Lem's genre experiment lies in reaching to the detective novel for a framework within which to develop his ghost-story theme. It's a truism that the detective story is one of the most structured genres around. The perpetration of the crime always triggers an investigation that leads to the discovery of causes (means and motives) and, through them, to the apprehension of the criminal. By smashing the conventions Lem spotlights their deterministic structure and, by extension, the deterministic principles that govern our thinking. The world in which a series of ghastly body thefts is touched off not by a psychopathic bodysnatcher but by a statistical fluctuation is a world very different from the one to which we are habituated. Our culture, symbolized in the story by the criminal law, is simply not equipped to deal sensibly with events that are subject to laws of a more fundamental nature – Nature's laws.

The solitary seeker of truth, the investigative routine, the red herrings, the eccentric scientists, the air of bafflement and menace, the humanless "crime" – all return in the companion book, *The Chain of Chance* (see Chapter 6). But where the later novel climaxes in a resolution, the investigation from 1959 is crowned with fiasco and a flurry of muddled hypotheses. The truth is not out there, mocks the author, rewriting the canons of detective fiction with a little help from the ghost story. Lieutenant Gregory – and, via him, the reader – is forever banished to ignorance even as a corps of Lazaruses freed from *rigor mortis* dance in front of his eyes. Where the supernatural lies by definition outside the rationality of forensics, the scene of the crime demands the application of techniques certified as tried and true. Has a crime really occurred? The detective must believe it must have, even as another ghost staggers out of the morgue.

The point here is that the appreciation of Lem's novel is not independent of the appreciation of the genres within which it is set. Relying on text alone, one might judge this crime yarn a failed undertaking, written without skill or attention to plot development. A writer who sets up a mystery only to leave it unsolved commits a crime against convention, opening himself to the charge of incompetence. But the extratextual knowledge of crime fiction *and* the ghost story plays the rules of one genre off the rules of the other, altering the grasp not only of the story's aesthetic properties but also of such structural elements as the plot. For while the standard features of the detective story demand a resolution of the mystery, the ghost story, in contrast, is built on the premise of the unexplained and inexplicable. The inconclusive ending, which thwarts the detective story's "must have" resolution, is thus a masterful move rather than a consequence of lack of skill. A statistical, and thus rational, account of the corpses' resurrection is another factor contra-standard to the out-of-this-worldness of the ghost tale. In order to appreciate it, however, the reader must go beyond Lem's text and consider the genre conventions relevant to the narrative. In terms of *both* detective and ghost story, *The Investigation* is bold, cunning, and original – features that are not at all obvious if we limit ourselves only to what's on the page.

Once we accept this pragmatic change in perspective, other conceptual dominos begin to fall as well. The logical concept of class, for instance, no longer does to describe the relations among stories set within a genre.[13] It seems we need to loosen the logical strictures and to forsake the notion of a necessary structural intersection between all members of a particular category. Genres don't function like empirical classes but, rather, as invitations to a literary game of a cooperative kind, played out in a book-specific context. A better way to look at genres is thus in terms of the convergence of reciprocal expectations. Coordination, not classification, you might say, is the name of the game.

GENRES AS INTERPRETIVE LANDMARKS

Sometimes what appears to be another example of a known game turns out, on more careful study, to be an entirely new one, and a game which appears to be new often turns out to be a variation of a known one.

Eric Berne, MD

So far I have offered some loose insights into the nature of genres as interpretive landmarks used by authors and readers. I now briefly place these intuitions within a rigorous context of communicative exchange and game theory. Of key interest to us is the type of intention involved in a communicative act, first outlined by Paul Grice in "Meaning" (1957) and developed in subsequent papers.[14] The bedrock of Grice's analysis is the concept of reflexive intention. In the simplest terms, a reflexive intention is one that is intended to be recognized as having been intended to be recognized.

Genre interpretation is readily expressed as a variant on the Gricean communicative model. Put somewhat tediously, the reader infers from the presence of standard elements of a genre that the author intended her to recognize them as standard elements of that genre. From this the reader can infer that the author intended her to recognize that the standard elements had been used intentionally, and that she was meant to recognize this. This is how Lem harnesses the common ingredients of the detective story. Clues like Scotland Yard, Inspector Gregory, forensic techniques, crime scenes, and so on, send a strong signal that they are there for a reason. The reason is to enable the reader to realize that these clues are there precisely so that her interpretation can take into account these and other features of the detective story.

The analysis of the reading process can profit from being recast in terms of game theory. The spectrum of games in which we engage in our lives stretches from total cooperation at one extreme to total conflict at the other, with the majority falling between the two. It is no different with reading literature, although typically the reading process is not a zero-sum game, where the preferred outcome for one side entails a corresponding loss on the other.[15] Quite the contrary: in many cases the range of interpretation favoured by the author will coincide with the optimum reading strategy for the reader. Formally speaking, literary genres, or, more generally, literary conventions, correspond to at least weakly dominant strategies in iterated cooperative two-person non-zero-sum games.[16] In what follows I highlight some of the research potential of this approach.

Let's start with the basics. In game theory terms "game" does not connote playful behaviour. Any situation open to normative analysis, from birthday cake division to superpower negotiations, is a game. The literary process is paradigmatically a two-person game. In the variant minimum (typical), a single reader engages a single author in a game of Reading-Your-Book. Variant minimum is therefore open to modelling and empirical testing as a direct interaction of two individuals involved in a particular instance of the reading game (e.g., you reading my book). In the variant maximum, the author – who could be several individuals, like in the Tel Quel or Oulipo writing groups – is engaged in a game against the entire literary system.[17] One can, of course, model the second player as any assembly of readers in between: as big as a nation or as small as an undergraduate seminar. The second model, while also open to direct manipulation and testing (for instance through class-room questionnaires), could profit from statistical analysis across a variety of contexts (e.g., sales, library loans, scholarly citations or acknowledgments, selective response polling).

Both game theory and empirical research instruct us that the more cooperative the game, the more significant the ability to communicate. Thomas Schelling's influential *The Strategy of Conflict* makes an especially useful contribution to the understanding of cooperative behaviour. The author goes to great lengths to show how salient game points are used reflexively to coordinate players' moves. All literary conventions – from the general (such as genre) to specific rhetorical or symbolic devices – also work in this manner. Like palimpsest post-it notes, they signal the flexible rules of the literary game in progress.

In contrast to semantically depleted games such as chess or poker, whose rules can generate all possible configurations of play, reading is a free-form game where some, perhaps even many, rules can be made up as the game progresses. There is thus plenty of room for vagueness, ambiguity, or even radical misinterpretation. This is as it should be. Literary games are en-vironment-rich, and it is to be expected that, in contrast to matrix analyses, their sensitivity to framing will be reflected in interpretive openness to both the nature and nuance of the game.[18] The nature of any cooperative game may change profoundly with a change in contextual details since often these details lead to the stabilization of a non-antagonistic outcome. A theoretic framework could help us model how coordination varies in each case by analyzing its effect on varying degrees of cooperation between the author and the reader.

After all, the rules of any interpretive game are not carved in stone. As stabilized as they may become during the course of the story, they are always subject to adjustment or even revocation. Cautions Schelling: "the propositions of a *normative* theory [of partly or fully cooperative games] could never be derived by purely analytical means from a priori considerations" (163). Where communication is short of perfect, where there is uncertainty about players' value systems or choices, or when an outcome is reached by a sequence of moves, an essential component of cooperative games must necessarily be pragmatic and context-sensitive. Not even the most comprehensive payoff function could capture the contextual message of a writer who gambles on sharing a certain point of view with unknown readers. As a species of cooperative game, literary interpretation will thus once again heavily depend on the players' shared sense of pattern, regularity, convention, or even cliché.

Another avenue for literary research is the study of the effects of different narrative embodiments, all based on the same game with the same basic genre skeleton. Earlier on we ran into one such star-crossed-lovers skeleton in Shakespeare, Brönte, Fitzgerald, and Cain. We could examine the role of various framing scenarios responsible for generating colossal aesthetic differences between books based on the same game. Although the range of conflicts underlying literary fictions may be limited, the effect of narrative variables could be empirically examined in a controlled setting. In this way we could approach the questions of genre strictures from another angle, rendering justice to the narrative richness and complexity of popular literature while acknowledging the fundamental nature of the structures upon which *all* literature relies.

Before closing the book on genres and literary divisions, there is time to address one more set of questions bearing on the relation between highbrow and popular literatures. Up to this point I have gotten away with using terms like "highbrow" and "popular," even while building a case against perceiving them as distinct categories. But, I can almost hear you say, since they shade into each other, how can publishers and advertisers distinguish Joyce's *Finnegans Wake* from Wambaugh's *Finnegan's Week*? The same goes for booksellers. Any local retailer can furnish proof that distinctions continue to be made, with fiction separated into Literature and Bestsellers before the buying public has a chance to get involved in the process. Decisions about highbrow-lowbrow status must perforce be made on the basis of some criteria, and the nature of such criteria is well worth a glance.

If there are no intrinsic (essentialist) features to separate popular from highbrow fiction, then there must be pragmatic rules that take up the slack. Error-prone as they may be vis-à-vis unknown books and unknown writers, especially those that defy easy classification, several factors typically come into play.

1   The name and reputation of the publisher, or (if applicable) the series of which the book is a part. Since the point is unremarkable, we need only note that most of today's publishing stables nurture authors from across the spectrum under their wings (see Chapter 2).

2   The name and reputation of the author. Bernard Malamud, secure alongside Roth and Bellow as one of the Big Three in twentieth-century Jewish American authors, bears the credentials of a bona fide litterateur. This canonical badge identifies him, makes him attractive to intellectuals and academics, and reserves his seat on the textbook-business train (see Chapter 1).

3   The size of the initial run. The first printing of Malamud's *Dubin's Lives* (1979) was a solid 76,000 and sold very well. The first edition of his next offering, *God's Grace* (1982), was only 30,000 and the sales were disappointing. Reflecting the pre-publication perception of the novel's inability to hack it on the academic market, this low printing became a self-fulfilling prophecy of the publisher's lack of faith in its intellectual prestige and highbrow credentials.

4   The literary DOW-Jones ranking of the book's genre. Dealing with biography and the literary-academic milieu, *Dubin's Lives* fell squarely within the conventional pieties for a highbrow novel. *God's Grace*, a fantasy with talking animals, belly laughs, coherent anthropology, sensational sex, and a magical premise failed to inspire confidence regarding its appeal to the "literary" market. It didn't matter that it was allegorical and intertextual enough to demand a lifetime of critical exegesis: fantasy isn't prestigious enough. Malamud himself entertained no illusions about lowbrow genres and highbrow intellectuals, soberly

observing that "there are some critics nowadays who feel a man can write nothing of importance unless he is dealing with some aspect of society using the method we call realism."[19]

5 Interest from outlets for distribution, frequently reflected by the book's appearance. Major bookselling outlets like Costco Wholesalers typically don't carry novels that underwrite grant proposals and dissertations – novels most likely to appear in drab and sombre hard covers. On the other hand, academic libraries rarely carry the complete works of a Len Deighton or an Elmore Leonard, especially if they are printed in glossy, day-glo paperbacks with stencilled lettering and "Pick Me!" graphics.

6 Prior history with regard to the expectations of professional readers. These are critics, scholars, and reviewers who may be interested in plugging the book in highbrow and academic media. If you are an outstanding mainstream figure like Eco, then you can play around with serious and even serial crime with no fear of being reviewed solely in *Clues* and *Armchair Detective*. If you are an outstanding genre entertainer like Hugh Laurie, then you'll get an omnibus review on page D13. If you are neither, then you will get your desserts according to practices 1 to 5 above.

HYBRID, CROSSOVER, AND NOBROW

In most major departments of literature in the Western world popular writings are automatically considered inferior to real and serious literature ... In addition, journals dealing with literature tend to be controlled by editors from the most respected and academically conservative departments.

Ingrid Shafer

While empirical, statistical, and analytical evidence redeems vast areas of popular literature from the standard attributions of vice, curricular indifference continues as the order of the day. Professors and other institutional taste-makers go about their business as usual, investing inordinate amounts of energy in the visible minority of literary production. Meanwhile the publishing cornucopia refuses to rectify itself, so that every day the ratio of fiction circulating in society to the fiction noted by academics and art critics gets more and more lopsided.

With the realization that genre prose may be producing literature qualitatively on par with the canon and in numbers too vast to absorb within the current system, one can see an extreme type of response, reminiscent of Nelson's feint at Trafalgar. Turning a blind eye liberates aesthetic conservatives from the genres and genre fiction that stands behind them – all by dint of denying that they are out there at all. The history of literary studies has, of course, witnessed prior attempts to exorcize the ghost of literary categories by philosophers such as Croce. More recently, Maurice Blanchot was willing to proclaim that a "book no longer belongs to a genre" and that "literary forms, that genres, no longer have any genuine significance."[20] Literature – for the French critic synonymous with highbrow fiction – was said to have erased the genre intermediary between individual works and that ultimate category, literature in toto.

That such sweeping fiats have actually rallied some professionals around them owes more to the neglect of genre literature and genre theory than it does to their argumentative coherence. One reason why Blanchot's anti-generic (or ageneric) stance fails to get off the ground is his reliance on the very categories he seeks to depose. Todorov's classic illustration that there has never been a literature without genres may be another.[21] But the issue of genre identity cuts much deeper. It raises its Hydra head whenever we grant individual status to any novel without recourse to the immense majority of fiction from which it is assumed to stand out in a significant way. The very act of inclusion in the canon presumes consigning a host of other books to obscurity.

Decisions of this kind ought to be made with a better understanding of popular literature and popular genres. Unable to read everything, critics often depend on publishers to guide their professional attention towards or away from entire categories of writing. The shortcomings of this practice are bad enough in confrontation with unknown authors, but they are even more spectacular in the face of novels, genres, or hybrids that display significant novelty. When in 1991 Art Spiegelman's graphic novel, *Maus II*, hit the *New York Times* bestseller list as fiction, the classification was determined more by its genre than by its wrenching Holocaust drama. It was not to last, however. Following a letter from the author in which he cogently defended his non-fictional intentions, this singular comic book was hastily moved to the non-fiction section.[22] *Maus II*, a Holocaust comic book and a category buster, proves once and for all that separating genre and serious literature is like trying to decide which is greater: six of a kind or half a dozen.

Writers react to genres, even if only to react against them, and a decision not to develop a story within (or without) a popular convention implicitly recognizes that convention and its influence. A proper understanding of literary forms is thus vital in the study of *all* narratives, not just those with roots in the foothills of the canonical Mount Olympus. Yet, although smoke still lingers after the recent wars of the canons, it is hard to shake off the feeling that the hostilities have been waged by confederations of remarkably similar persuasion vis-à-vis genre literature. The dispute, it seems, has been an internal affair, a civil war between the equivalent of a dead-white-male-conservative South and a gender-class-sex-ethnicity-race-mindful North. Divided as they are, they stand united in their suspicion of genre fiction, with critical patrols busy left and right lest migrants from the literary barrios sneak in.

Exceptions confirm the rule. Following multi-million-dollar advances and staggering publishing figures, Stephen King began to attract attention on campuses, so that these days one can occasionally encounter his name on undergraduate syllabi. Ironically, the few popular writers who become subjects of study by tapping into academics' preference for pouring new wine into old bottles (horror as neo-gothic), may have an adverse affect on the rest. Boosting certain writers or formulas – for example, turning vampires into sex symbols and Ann Rice into the flavour of the moment – means overlooking hundreds of others who are no less deserving of socio-aesthetic analysis. Those who create in less identifiable genres or styles, or even more interestingly, in their nobrow hybrids, fail to register on the critical radar for lack of the media hype surrounding bestsellers. *Newsweek* may praise Disch, a quirky no-brow virtuoso of almost any genre he plied, as "the most formidably gifted unfamous American writer." But, as he himself is the first to admit, "Publishers don't quite know what to do with me."[23]

So what about artertainers like Karel Čapek, Raymond Chandler, and Stanislaw Lem, who write ambitious fiction in the idiom of popular culture? What about nobrow literature that strays away from both academic and bestseller formulas in search of success? Refusal to follow the herd is surely a sign of literary aspiration, aesthetic sophistication, and whatnot. But nobrow fiction – too intellectual for the *Dynasty* set, too popular for the Sunday Art Supplement critic – seldom commands the advertising push to pluck it out of commercial and academic obscurity. Neither lite entertainment nor heavy-duty art, when nobrow fiction fails to go platinum it falls between the cracks and vanishes from both public and scholastic radar. In the end, such absence of evidence of popular-genre art becomes the evidence of absence.

The institutional decisions we make, the consequences of these canon-making decisions, and the grounds for making them are all public knowledge.[24] Yet, despite evidence to the contrary, the profession of professing the canon has been built around the fiction that there are intrinsic merits to determining the differences between serious prose and formula entertainment. Condensed intellectual content, reflection on the role of art, metaphysics, and self-reflexivity – almost by default these telltale signs of high artistry are associated with the 3 percent of literature that is in circulation.

Never mind the classics that are remarkably like the early Beatles: simple, direct, without even a hint of avant-garde pyrotechnics. Look no further than *The Old Man and the Sea*. Never mind self-reflexive and art-sensitive popular hits like Osvaldo Soriano's *Triste, solitario y final*, whose condensed intellectual content perfectly complements their popular entertainment appeal. *The French Lieu-*

tenant's Woman, Sophie's Choice, and *The English Patient* are all fine prose, yet all three got "legs" in bookstores only in the wake of big budget film adaptations. The question is: if popular reprints and a retroactive academic thumbs-up as a consequence of Hollywood remixes do not detract from artistic stock, then why divorce entertainment appeal in the popular form from art by default? This is hardly a revisionist claim. Nabokov's revelation in *Evgenii Oniegin* that Pushkin drew heavily on popular French romances was not intended to (nor did it) detract from the accomplishment of the Russian artist.

Hence the idea behind taking a fresh look at the art of Čapek, Chandler, and Lem in Part 2 of this book. As the critical reception of *War with the Newts, Playback,* and *The Chain of Chance* makes clear, our judgments easily flounder in the face of nobrow writers and books that simultaneously target both ends – as well as the middle – of readership and reviewership. Recasting Larry Tesler's apt quip that Artificial Intelligence is whatever has not yet been engineered by the cognitive sciences, genre fiction is whatever has not yet been assimilated by the taste-makers' canon. Targeting both ends of the cultural hierarchy, Čapek, Chandler, and Lem split the difference between the basement and penthouse, standing united in their disregard for formulaic solutions, whether highbrow or lowbrow, in books that give new meaning to hybrid, crossover, and nobrow.

Does *War with the Newts,* at its apex the byword of intellectuals in Europe and America, merit eking out its days as an obscure science fantasy? Does *Playback* deserve the dubious distinction of being maligned equally by fans and foes of Chandler's noir? Does *The Chain of Chance* deserve honourable citation only as a narrative afterthought to *The Investigation?* For answers to these questions we must turn the page on theory and move on to fiction.

Nobrow: Varieties of Artertainment

4 Karel Čapek and the Politics of Memory

I read Karel Čapek for the first time when I was a college student a long time ago in the Thirties. There was no writer like him – no one who so blithely assumed that the common realities were not as fixed and irrevocable as one imagined. Without adopting any extraordinary tone of voice he projected whole new creatures and environments onto an oddly familiar non-existent landscape.

Arthur Miller, Foreword to *Toward the Radical Center*

Of the many enigmatic things about Karel Čapek's career, not the least enigmatic is Karel Čapek himself. He was never so pleased as when taken for a gardener by deliverymen who were duped by the sight of a man in old clothes toiling among flower beds. Although he enjoyed socializing, he disliked crowds, even those mobbing him on his frequent travels abroad. He stopped writing for the theatre at the zenith of his worldwide fame as a playwright and did not return to it until shortly before his death. Deploring the efficacy of his fiction, he poured his creative energies into journalism, only to be nominated for the Nobel Prize in Literature in the year of the Newt. Urbane, cosmopolitan, with a doctorate in aesthetics, he cultivated the vernacular of the common man. An intellectual sophisticate, he was a connoisseur of genre chills, kills, and thrills.

His fondness for popular forms was not restricted to fiction. Where James Agee celebrated the grassroots of America in *Let Us Now Praise Famous Men*, Čapek celebrated the grassroots of culture in a miscellany of essays, some collected in English as *In Praise of Newspapers*. Enlivened by his trademark humour and kris-sharp wit, this slender volume is a primer on the popular culture of the day. Daily press, tabloids, popular humour, anecdotes, slang, fairy tales, folk traditions, detective fiction, proletarian art, and even pornography – all get their fifteen pages of fame. It is difficult to appreciate this kind of openness today, when discourse on sado-masochism, graffiti, and gangsta rap has crossed over the tracks to Main Street. But mass culture and popular art still implied barbarians storming the gates in the days when F.R. Leavis was professing elitism in *Mass Civilisation and Minority Culture* (1930). And yet where Leavis is imperious, Čapek is only curious; and where Leavis condemns, Čapek commends. His remark that the average man prefers a thriller to the collected works of Marx would be but a plaint about the sign of the times in Leavis's mouth. For Čapek it's a preamble to a cheerful admission that, in this respect, he *is* the average man.

In Praise of Newspapers shows a remarkable degree of sympathy, at times almost reverence, for popular art. Even pornography, for which the writer has no love lost, ranks discussion as a branch of literature, albeit one guilty of a cardinal sin: sexual deceit. At other times his attention to the Jazz Age entertainment industry would lead him to write on motion pictures, studio stars (he idolized the Fairbanks smile in "The Fairbanks Smile"), and on the Dream Factory itself. As a movie critic Čapek again gave mass culture two thumbs up. Its virtues, he points out, are being popular, true to life, and democratic. "I want to confess that I expect art to be some kind of entertainment," he wrote in the miscellany. Its longest essay, devoted in its entirety to Sherlock Holmes and Holmesiana, ends with another confession: "it does me good to find pleasant things in the realms of bad reputation."[1]

Besides leading him to Baker Street when visiting London, Čapek's lifelong affair with detective fiction led him to explore it in many stories, of which *Tales from Two Pockets* may be the best and best known. In pursuit of the metaphysics of crime and punishment, he was drawn to the cerebral English tradition rather than to the American hardboiled tradition (like Chandler, he was something of an Anglophile). Much like in the earlier *Wayside Crosses*, Čapek fleshes out his policemen, criminals, victims, and occasional bystanders with the sparsest of means, often with a single stroke of a quill. His backdrop is the prison, the police house, or the city beat. His plot thickener is murder, theft, adultery, or even an event that defies forensic lore though mysterious enough to kindle an investigation. But even as he exploits the detective genre, his crime tales are sometimes hard to recognize as kith and kin of Gaston Leroux or Agatha Christie.

What makes them less than commonplace is, much like in the Maigret *noirs*, the commonplace feel about them. The characters are common owing not to their station in life but, rather, to the timeless drama of conscience and expiation. The day of reckoning turns the greatest sinner into an Everyman, his soul reduced to a size that fits all, and that is why Čapek, like Simenon, never condemns. *Comprendre, pas juger*, is the MO of the French writer; understand, not judge, is the motto of the Czech. Evident in every tale in the *Pockets* book, it is nowhere more eloquent than in the court scene from "The Last Judgment." When a multiple killer comes before Him, expecting to be condemned to hell, God steps aside, leaving punishment in the hands of human judges. Compassion flows from understanding, reveals the Almighty to the accused. "If judges knew everything, absolutely everything, they could not judge, either; they would understand everything, and their hearts would ache. How could I possibly judge you? Judges know only about your crimes; but I know everything about you" (159).

The almost palpable weight of human tragedy conveyed through Čapek's "Judge not, lest ye be judged," shows how much can be said in the idiom of popular mystery. Murder and crime sell because they speak to everyone in a language that cuts to the soul like a knife cuts to the heart. Detective fiction appeals both to the tutored and Sunday reader not despite being schematic but *because* of it.

Princes and goatherds alike can appreciate the drama of wrongdo-ing, the math of the pursuit, and the poetry of justice. Writing is for the entertainment of all, argued Čapek, much like "the very earli-est literature [that] spoke to the greatest number, to princes among men as much as to those tending the goats."[2] In this sense his entire career may have led to *War with the Newts* and its nobrow fusion of high modernism and popular entertainment. An oxymoron? Only if you believe that between genre thrills and intellectual Himalayas *tertium non datur.*

THE TOYS ARE US

The SF device of substituting robots for human workers allowed Čapek to express, in the telegraphy of allegory, the moral truth that the industrial system treated human laborers as though they were machines, sowing thereby the seeds of an inevitable and just rebellion.

Thomas M. Disch

After the publication of *War with the Newts*, with Hitler winning the political and military game of chicken against the rest of Europe, it became clear that Čapek's warnings had fallen on deaf ears. In a eulogy cast as a fictional letter, Thomas Mann's daughter, Erika, consoled the author in his distress. "Your story of those sly, clever creatures which were first trained by man for all sorts of uses, and which finally, turning into a mob without soul or morals but with dangerous technical skill, plunge the world into ruin, this story is so contemporary and exciting, so comical and entertaining, that it wins friends everywhere."[3]

A modernist landmark in a high-octane adventure, the book was stylistically eclectic and eccentric enough to shame a Broadway revue, perplexing critics to no end. Peopled with sapient and human-like lizards, it looked like a kind of fantasy, albeit with science to balance the fiction. However, since the author used the newts to dissect contemporary civilization, it ended up being reviewed as a manqué kind of utopia. Properly speaking, most modern utopias are actually *u-chronias*, given their temporal rather than spatial estrangement. But not *War with the Newts*. Wild and fantastic as it is, there is nothing futuristic or other-worldly about it.

In the Epilogue to the first book edition – the story was originally serialized in a prominent Prague journal, *Lidové Noviny* – Čapek chided those who would dilute its impact. "There is no utopia here, only the present. There is no speculation about the future, but a mirroring of that which exists and the surroundings in which we live ... I cannot help it; literature which is not concerned with reality and with what is actually going on in the world, which does not react as strongly as word and idea possibly can – such literature is not my concern."[4] This view of high art as popular entertainment in the cause of social change animated everything he wrote until his death in 1938, on the eve of the bloodiest war in history.

By 1921 his philosophical and whimsical plays, *R.U.R.* and *The Insect Play*, were a raging critical and popular success. Rapidly translated into dozens of languages and staged all over the developed world, they were on their way to becoming some the most performed works of the century. Čapek was a household name from North America to Japan, while the word "robot" – attributed to Karel, although coined by his brother and occasional co-author, Josef – made literary and scientific history. Yet after 1927 and the publication of another play, *Adam the Creator*, almost overnight Karel stopped writing for the theatre. Convinced that he had to reach his readers in a more direct way, he forwent the source of his critical and popular acclaim, throwing all his creative energies into journalism instead. It is hardly a coincidence that *War with the Newts* is a *roman feuilleton* that, mimicking and mocking a myriad of tabloid conventions, reports on the state of the world tailspinning into a world war with an emergent superpower – the Newts.

The publication of this genre-bender caused a worldwide stir, running the gamut from calls for laurels to calls for lynching. In the United States it was extolled in top-echelon national magazines, including *Time*, the *New Republic*, and the *Saturday Review of Literature*, with Harry Levin opening his piece in the *Nation* with a perceptive: "It is hard to see, after this book, how the Nobel Prize

Committee can go on ignoring Karel Čapek."[5] Regrettably, the Swedish Academy proved loath to antagonize Hitler, lampooned in the figure of a war-bent dictator of the Newts and, failing to muster the nerve to honour the short-listed Czech, gave the prize to Eugene O'Neill instead. Urged by the Swedes to quickly submit another book that would "not attack anyone or anything," the author is said to have replied with deadly sarcasm: "Thank you for your good will but I have already written my doctoral dissertation."[6]

Taken on its own merit, without the shadow of world war menacing Europe and its literary gate-keepers, Čapek's allegory is an all-round winner – as long as you don't attempt to pigeonhole it in conventional categories. *War with the Newts* is the literary equivalent of a variety show that, in 200-odd pages, succeeds in lambasting the excesses of arms trade, science, religion, the League of Nations, modernism, intellectualism, anthropocentrism, historical objectivity, labour (mis)management, nationalism, capitalism, expansionism, fascism, bolshevism, communism, colonialism, imperialism, militarism, racism, the media circus, the sensation-seeking press, the fashion industry, and, not least, Hollywood's nouveaux riches and their studious extravaganzas. Čapek's satire has the lightness and the sting of Ali at his peak, while his Ferrari-machined plot skims from one narrative stunt to another, making readers convulse with laughter while cringing in self-recognition.

War with the Newts is like *Gulliver's Travels*: simple enough to delight a dilettante, deep enough to drown a philosopher, playful and ironic enough to reward even the most discriminating and cultivated reader. Call it nobrow, call it artertainment, or, in the words of F. Buriánek, call it a masterpiece whose "witty parodies can be enjoyed especially by a cultivated and literature-sensitive reader."[7]

The rollercoaster plot opens with the discovery of a sapient lizard species who, in the hands of an old sea-dog, Captain van Toch, soon become efficient pearl divers. The operation expands, the Newts are shipped around the world, and in no time the captain is having an audience with G.H. Bondy, captain of world industry. Their breakthrough powwow creates the Salamander Syndicate, paving the way for the industrial, mass-scale use of this intelligent and by now articulate species. As their exploitation intensifies according to the iron logic of twentieth-century slash-and-burn capitalism, the Newts become essential grease for the machinery of global trade and progress. Hunted, killed, enslaved, exhibited in circuses, bred in captivity, tortured, abused, preyed upon, and trained for war, they reenact Čapek's condensed version of an everyday in the life of our civilization. In the process, with prognostic audacity that proved all too accurate, *War with the Newts* gives us a terrifying foretaste – or for us, descendants of the Second World War, a sickening after-taste – of Nazism. Like Hitler's meticulously administered geno-cide, which processed human bones for fertilizer and human skin for lampshade leather, the executives of Bondy's Salamander Syndi-cate plan an industrial processing of the Newts. During the board meeting that would have been a jewel of comedy had its modest proposals not been so ghastly, the German member of the executive even ponders the value of these human-like creatures as a source of meat or skin.

Even though the mightiest work of art is powerless in a head-on confrontation with a machine gun, it can whip its readers into action, especially with a satire so lethal as that in *War with the Newts*. Dreading another world war, Čapek is desperate to stave it off through his comic and ironic masterpiece. When the world lies in ruins, he warns, there will be no one to blame because everyone will be to blame. On the last pages, Mr. Povondra's son spells out this ABC of guilt. "Everyone did it. The different countries did it, finance did it. They all wanted to make the most out of those Newts. They all wanted to make money out of them. We used to sell them arms, and what not. We are all responsible for it" (337–8).[8]

Indeed we are. We armed Saddam Hussein when he was warring against Iran. With Reagan's help we then defied Congress to sell arms to Iran, and we used that tainted money to supply weapons to the Contras, who were waging war against a democratically elected government in Nicaragua. We paid and armed Noriega when it suited our myopic foreign policy. We armed the Taliban and trained bin Laden in the days when it was expedient to call them freedom-fighters. We saturated the world with weapons and munitions in the name of balancing the budget, and now we wage undeclared wars on destitute Muslim countries in a vain effort to wash our hands of responsibility.

In his uncompromising (if good-natured) way, Čapek derides such self-serving thinking. History is on his side, teaching how seven decades ago such realpolitik beguiled everyone into appeasing the Nazi crusade for a greater Third Reich. Fittingly enough, at the end of the book Chief Salamander turns out to be a man, Andreas Schultze. Like Hitler, he is an ex-First World War NCO who whips the Newts into conquistadorial frenzy while being showered by world powers with arms, munitions, and credit. But there are human Quislings happy to front him during parleys with the defeated nations of Earth. These lawyers-for-sale talk the talk of real-life British and French PMs who would buy Hitler off with the sovereignty of the Rhineland, Austria, and Czechoslovakia. Povondra Senior is the spitting image of Chamberlain or Daladier when he mouths his pious mantra: "the Newts can't get to us, that stands to reason" (334). His faith is as unshakeable as is the faith in prewar defence lines, or the pre-9/11 illusion that those who live by the sword don't perish by it. In the end, just like Čapek had forewarned, neither the obsolete belief in neutrality nor the Maginot line would prove of any consequence to the Wehrmacht Panzers. The West and its promise of democracy were not dead. They just smelled funny.

With men acting like Newts, the reverse is even more evident. Sexual and emotional makeup apart, the sapient salamanders are like us from head to each of their five toes. Smart, adaptable, and impatient to ascend the ladder of industrial civilization, the all-too-human Newts become a blank page upon which every political, cultural, and religious formation projects its prejudices and hostilities. Their peaceful nature gets a doctrinal work-over from Dr Hans Thüring who hails the Baltic newts' Aryan traits, claiming they are lighter in colour (i.e., blonder), walk more erect, and exhibit cranial superiority to other members of their species. Flexing their military and industrial muscle under Chief Salamander, the newts rapidly morph into Hitler's Germany with their territorial demands echoing the Third Reich's hysterical calls for *Lebensraum*.

War with the Newts is a blistering allegory on the rise of Nazism and on Europe's ill-bred policy of appeasement. But it would be an error to chain Čapek's masterpiece to any single critique or theme. His madcap satire is quite simply an anatomy of our civilization, of which Adolf Hitler as Salamander Supreme is only one cancerous symptom. German national socialism, American expansionism, Soviet communism, and Newt militarism are simply different faces of an age-old lust for power. In a clue for the alert reader, the Newts' power grab, dressed up as a war for Independence, falls on 3 and 13 July, in a mocking bow to the American and French Revolutions, celebrated on 4 and 14 July, respectively.[9] In the world where neutrality means selling weapons to both sides, the tapa boys of Captain van Toch are power toys that humans greedily play with, heedless of their destructive potential. Only Čapek leaves no doubt that you are what you play with. The toys are us, or, as he wrote at the end of his 1934 novel, *Ordinary Life*, "Each of us is we."

THE GREEK WORD FOR MAN: ANDROS

I am convinced that a community of human beings is a far more useful thing than a community of ants and that if the human being is condemned and restricted to perform the same functions over and over again, he will not even be a good ant, not to mention a good human being.

Norbert Wiener

Today, alongside H.G. Wells, Karel Čapek is remembered mainly as an early practitioner of science fiction. The perils of modern warfare, the accountability of scientists for providing smart weapons to dumb politicians, the technology of might is right, the illusions of totalitarianism, the disillusions of industrial utopia ... In the technological minefield of post-Y2K none of his tygers have lost their fearful symmetry.

Science and technology are, indeed, guideposts in Čapek's search for a definition of an individual and his role in a democratic society. But thanks to his stylistic bravado and an almost Spartan economy of expression, the justice that Conrad needed the entire *Heart of Darkness* to bring to the visible world, Čapek dispenses in a page or two. He gives Europe full credit for bearing the white man's burden and bringing the torch of progress to dark lands, if necessary by torching cultures resistant to the progress of civilization. Captain van Toch is no Mistah Kurtz. Genuinely fond of his pearl-diving salamanders, he even rewards them with knives and harpoons. Bondy is also a decent chap, deeply sincere about his earnings, mindful of his fellow men who sit on the board of the Salamander Syndicate, and attentive to the Newts' needs when it optimizes their market value.

Irreverent and ironic in the manner of Shakespeare's fool, Čapek dons the funny hat and laughs at the world with the frozen face of Buster Keaton. In the American South the arrival of the dark-skinned Newts is a handy excuse to burn and lynch more blacks. In a science lab professors vivisect the newts in the name of science while their victims cry out in human tongues to God for help. The author's irony and sense of the grotesque pack more punch than any earnest sermon. After all, it makes little difference if the persecuted are black people or black newts because the latter's humanity is more than symbolic. As a prominent paleontologist contends, the salamanders may be living fossils of the early *Homo*. It's not for nothing that their genus name – *Andrias Scheuchzeri* – is the Greek word for Man: *Andros*.

Like Lem in recent decades, Čapek critiques scientism and technology worship not out of any neo-Luddite prejudice but, rather, out of a moral experience of the relation between people and machines. He elaborated this vision in a 1929 article, "The Rule of Machines," in words that remain true in the third millennium. "There is no conflict between man and machine. Our machines are genial, but our social and human efforts are more or less bungling ... The relationship of machine to people depends largely on the relationship of people to one another."[10] True enough, questions about science, society, and the individual rarely appear independent of one another in his writings, be it fiction or journalism. His mixed reaction to London Town in the days before *War with the Newts* is a characteristic example. He admired the industrial and commercial oomph of the capital at its imperial height but despised its mass and slum uniformity. If people are as legion as ants, he remarked, human life cannot be worth very much. Soon enough the Nazis would prove him dead right.

Part pulp fiction, part modernist extravaganza, *War with the Newts* draws its bestseller mileage from many popular traditions. A pinch of fantasy à la E.T. Hoffman, a dash of beast fable, a soupçon of dystopia, a spoonful of Hollywood melodrama, and you have Čapek's recipe for a nobrow cliffhanger. It all begins with a Paramount-perfect adventure mystery and Captain Van Toch, who unceremoniously buttonholes you, the reader, in a comic rant that will run non-stop until your ears are full and your head is close to bursting and your throat is dry and you just have to sit down with him to a vat of beer to wet your whistle before you can find out what happens next. Spun in a seawolf patois against the backdrop of native-filled tropical islands, Čapek's tale of pearls and sunken treasure cashes in on the literary tradition familiar to all who burned the midnight oil with Stevenson, Kipling, or Jack London. No less familiar is his stock of colourful stereotypes, of which Van Toch, the first of the many subordinate players in the drama of the newts, is a prime specimen. Even as he pays homage to the genre, the Czech writer piles up clichés so adroitly that, representing his stock, the captain becomes its gentle caricature. A wily South Sea skipper, his figure (portly), manner (casual), habits (boozing), temperament (choleric), language (cursing), and trademark (volubility) are at once true to the image and distorted out of all proportion.

Not surprisingly, psychological nuance and depth are predominantly in abeyance among the hustle, bustle, and muscle of the adventure story and the historical sweep of dystopia. Negligent of full-blown characterization, the latter's conventions typically sacrifice character individuation for the sake of broad societal trends that individuals, such as they are in Zamyatin's commune of numbers or

Huxley's Alphaville, either resist or exemplify. This may explain why, despite a lifelong devotion to the individual, Čapek is content to cast his humans and human-like newts as character types. While the South Sea captain, the business tycoon, and Mr Povondra excel in their cameos, it is the two group protagonists/antagonists that are the principle actors in the gross choreography of the plot. A non-heroic and hero-less adventure story, Čapek's nobrow experiment may be the most daring departure from any popular formula.

A casualty of high aesthetics, until recently science fiction was not deemed fit for literary history books. A talented creator speculating about science had to slough off the stigma of a literary lightweight before receiving an imprimatur from the establishment. But is the reverse true as well? Does Čapek's close encounter with the Nobel Prize in 1936 mean that his book is not science fiction? As the Czech author's ascent as sci-fi's prewar precursor parallels his exit from the world stage, some of his themes, which have come to be identified with the genre, are worth another look.

1   Contact with alien intelligence, although on this occasion of terrestrial origin. Čapek's sentient and articulate Newts are more than a mere vehicle for his dystopian adventure. In his customary fashion, he carefully develops them as biological and ecological species. The author's scientific expertise is abundant as he multiples evolutionary, morphological, and anthropological appendixes that flesh out the new race. Nor is this type of projection ("Didn't Linnaeus already classify all species?") an arid artifice of fiction. Only a few years before the novel's publication, the world was abuzz with Douglas Burden's find of a giant lizard species on the island of Sumatra (i.e., the region picked in the novel as the cradle of the human-like salamanders). The Komodo dragon, okapi, mountain gorilla, and other big mammals (the most recent, the saola, identified as late as 1992) are only the tip of the iceberg of amphibian, marine, and insect species still awaiting discovery today.

2   Ecology and the perils of monkeying with nature. Decades before the birth of eco-movements (Greenpeace did not come into being until 1971), Čapek delineates the global, not to say holistic, effects of ill-bred environmental programs. He tracks with particular care the disastrous effects of the get-rich-quick policy of introducing Newts to habitats unprepared for their fertility and rate of expansion. Just like in real life, where non-endemic species often trigger a near-collapse of the local flora (e.g., when the lowly rabbit nearly overran the Australian ecosystem) disregard for long-term effects of environmental policies can bring about results mapped with deadly, if hilarious, accuracy in *War with the Newts*. Raising the subject of global "econsciousness" is one of the novel's prescient feats.

3   Intelligence and thinking in other beings. Research with primates, other mammals, birds, and even invertebrates indicates that cognitive processing is certainly not a human monopoly. Similarly, ever since Alan Turing's epochal article, "Can Machines Think" (1950), much debate and controversy has centred around the possibility of a thinking computer. Drawing attention to the problem, Čapek has few illusions. Faced with a bevy of behavioural evidence – language, science, engineering – that Newts are a thinking species, his learned professors would rather claim mimicry than allow that these creatures may be at least as sapient as Ronald Reagan or Lynda Lovelace.

4   Construction of a good and just society, whether through a blueprint for a utopia or a critique of its negative tendencies. References by Bondy and his cronies to the making of a new Atlantis, with freedom and justice for all, are a rank parody of this theme. The Syndicate's road to the future is paved with the blood, sweat, and toil of the enslaved Newts, bred in circumstances that cannot but evoke the genetic management of Huxley's Gammas, Deltas, and Epsilons. In the end, Bondy's Newtopia is nothing but

a totalitarian regime marching to the hymn of progress derided by the Little Tramp in *Modern Times.*

5 Futurological prognoses. Much is usually made of science fiction's extrapolations and visions and, unlike a Delphic oracle, Čapek is remarkably exact in his picture of what in 1936 was only a shadow of a world war. For us, book-keepers of Auschwitz and Buchenwald, it cannot but trigger the memory of occupation and concentration-camp slaughter. Territorial gluttony, government-run weapons trade, cynical violations of neutrality, ethnic cleansing, outright exterminations, mass transport of civilians in boxed railcars, special fenced-in camps ... What in 1936 was a feat of modernist imagination is a lesson in modern history for the new millennium.

6 The legacy of H.G. Wells. The literary conversation with Wells stretches from Čapek's early stories down to *War with the Newts.*[11] The war of the worlds between humans and submarine newts, coupled with the catastrophic results of their breeding in captivity à la *The Island of Dr Moreau,* has an unmistakably Wellsian ring about it. With the Englishman openly cited in the novel as an authority on utopias/dystopias, with the menace of heat rays bewailed in a hysterical English headline, with familiar scenes of invasion-spawned anarchy, *The War of the Worlds* is never far from the attentive reader's mind. The congruence between the two works was obvious enough even for a 1937 anonymous *Time* reviewer who disparaged Čapek's book as a lacklustre "Wellsian fantasy" (82).

7 The entire history of speculative fiction concerning society and its increasingly technological means of governance. The utopian axis, from Plato's Atlantis to Wells's *Modern Utopia,* and the anti-utopias of Zamyatin and Huxley, are the obvious paradigms for the problem of the (in)human use of human beings. Jules Verne's *20,000 Leagues under the Sea,* a science adventure in which a renegade human wields submarine technology against people, is another.

V. Černy believes that a more immediate model for the narrative vehicle – a new/old species of intelligent and talking animals – may be Pierre Mac Orlan's "La Bête conquérante" (1920). In this little known story a farmer, trying to slaughter a pig, lesions its brain in a way that allows it to acquire speech. In no time talking animals are everywhere, and while humans lose themselves in indolence, the beasts, pressed into the yoke of slavery and industrial labour, rebel and take over the world. Another template is the animal fable, from the didactic strain of Aesop to the irony of Anatole France's *Penguin Island* and *The Revolt of the Angels*. Finally, anyone familiar with London's *Iron Heel* and Von Harbou's *Metropolis* will find them behind the scenes of mayhem of the workers' revolt.

FRITZ LANG AND CHARLIE CHAPLIN COMBINED

In what way is the farce of minor Elizabethans better than the burlesque of today? The comedy even in Shakespeare is often a tickling of the ears of the groundlings that may have come off in 1600, but is tedious in the extreme today.

D.W. Brogan

In 1917 Čapek got his first job as a journalist, and while it is fair to say that his newspaper prose is invariably artistic, it is also true that much of his fiction is journalistic. The compliment could hardly be higher as, according to his first English-language biographer, "the sum total of his journalistic writing ... embodies the spiritual testament of one of the most humane, civilized, and flexible minds of our century."[12] And one reason why *War with the Newts* dishes out its nobrow melange in the colloquial idiom of daily news is that the news writer's *feuilletons* and ambitious literature are really the recto and verso of the same page in the book of life. "Literature is the expression of old things in eternally new forms," held Čapek, "while the newspapers are eternally expressing new realities in a stabilized and unchanging form."[13]

This is not to say that fiction is merely a less exact and exacting form of journalism. In the title essay from *In Praise of Newspapers* the Czech writer chastens the press for its love of gossip, melodrama, and "If-It-Bleeds-It-Leads" sensationalism. Immersed in his day, a typical journalist is like Sidney's historian. Too busy with individual facts to seek out larger, more permanent regularities of human existence, he cedes that role to writers of fiction. "My opinion is that literature should aspire to be something on the whole better than a document of its time," maintained the author. If anything, it should be *"in its time* a document of certain permanent human values, to be a document of human beauty, dignity and so on."[14]

War with the Newts exploits and spoofs the techniques of popular journalism to inquire about the meaning of individual life in a century of mass industry, mass culture, and mass death. Čapek's eye for the most risible aspects of modern civilization is as unerring as is the lens of a seasoned paparazzo. But, ever mindful of the common reader, he divests himself of the solemnity of Dostoevsky's Grand Inquisitor. Borrowing left and right from assorted facets of unanimism, futurism, and cubism in order to capture the perspectival nature of moral precepts, he repackages them into popular motifs from fables, fantasies, and utopias. It is entirely characteristic of Čapek, critics agree, that while his "essays and articles have high literary polish, his fiction and plays talk to the reader with the direct simplicity of a popular columnist."[15]

Informal and informative, *War with the Newts* is executed with the same satanic precision as the brothers Čapek admired in motion pictures. When Malamud joked that he was a rewriter of drafts rather than a writer of books, he might have been describing the Czech writer, who would polish his lines until their highbrow aesthetics disappeared behind the entertaining façade. This habit of reworking his material may, indeed, explain his return in 1936 to themes and characters from earlier days. Fertile and groundbreaking as *War with the Newts* is it did not spring from nowhere, either in literary or in intellectual terms. In 1922 Čapek even remarked:

"it seems to me I am always writing the same thing, that only the coat is a bit different."[16] That same year he serialized *Factory of the Absolute*, a novel that presages the later masterpiece in episodic structure, fantastic premise, and even in the figure of a robber baron writ large – G.H. Bondy.[17] Although artistically it was only a scaffold needed to ascend to *War with the Newts*, it delivered the same acrobatic mix of philosophy wrapped in comedy inside a fantasy.

Deliberately blending the popular with the avant-garde, *War with the Newts* is something else entirely. Stylistically flashier than a peacock's tail, this mosaic of styles and points of view mixes in every mode and trope that modernism and pop culture have to offer. Back in 1914, during his doctoral studies, Čapek contended that the soul of twentieth-century art was the projection of multiple spatial perspectives in a single picture. His commitment to "[the] grasping of objects from several sides and from several distances; the division and juxtaposition of an opinion," was the narrative analogue of what Braque and Picasso attempted in the pictorial arts by means of collage, distortion, and hyperbolic detail.[18] But, like in a cubist tableau, things in *War with the Newts* are not what they seem to be.

Scoring his narrative symphony in a key at once major and minor, Čapek's tongue-in-cheek narrator more than once turns it into a pastiche of its kind. Never at rest, meandering from the personal to the global and from the incidental to the historical, poking into the dusty corners of the world only to fan out into a bevy of media reports, he is the devil's apprentice of a story editor, cutting and splicing reels of feature and documentary material. Within a handful of pages he covers the gamut from the grandiloquence of the executive boardroom to waterfront slang, finishing with a parody of Joycean stream-of-thought from a teenage movie mogul wannabe. In these and countless other incarnations into which he slips with the ease and frequency of a campaign-trail politician, Čapek's voice displays the assurance and dexterity of Fritz Lang and Charlie Chaplin combined.

Structurally, *War with the Newts* is a triptych whose middle part, "Along the Steps of Civilization," is one of the cleverest and craziest seventy pages ever to appear in print. Ditching standard narration, Čapek fashions a quasi-journalistic scrapbook out of an assorted mass of newspaper cut-outs. Documenting the ascent of *Salamander Sapiens*, this maestro of spoof designs a palette of viewpoints and styles mirrored in the cornucopia of fonts, typographical conventions, footnotes, headlines, multilingual quotes, and even letter and margin sizes that must have given the typesetter a thousand migraines. Replete with mock-studious attribution of sources and credentials, this literary high-wire act even boasts a self-reflexive reference to the very *War with the Newts*. Making high modernism magical and fun, this nobrow "ent*artainer*" delights in reproducing

BUSINESS CARDS , posters, and FREAK SHOW BANNERS;

facsimiles of handwriting; **bold** or *italicized* gossip-column headers; journal-style notes; interview-type Q&A; scientific expedition reports; CAPITALIZED FRONT PAGE HEADLINES; typewriter fonts; old-time gothic print; minutes of a business conference; a mock-anthropological appendix à la Margaret Mead; a reproduction of a newt skeleton; excerpts from an essay in Spenglerian philosophy; and even STOP a handful STOP of telegrams.[19]

A humanist must perforce be a humorist, upheld the author, if for no other reason than that laughter is essentially democratic. With a flair for linguistic parody redolent of Groucho Marx, Čapek's wit is like Bond's vodka-martini: sly, wry, and entirely dry. "Do Newts have soul?" fuss the mass media in "Along the Steps of Civilization." Toscanini says no, because they have no music. Tony (sic) Weissmüller, Olympic swimming champion and Hollywood Tarzan, has nothing to say about soul, but he comments favourably on their swimming technique. G.B. Shaw says they have no soul but insists that in this they are in accord with humans. And the one and only Mae West? "They have no sex-appeal. And therefore they have no soul" (201).

It is, of course, hard to write about humour without ruining it completely, and for that reason the last word must go to Čapek himself. In 1928, in *The Gardener's Year*, he crafted the following prayer. "O Lord, grant that in some way it may rain every day, say from about midnight until three o'clock in the morning, but, You see, it must be gentle and warm so that it can soak in; grant that at the same time it shall not rain on campion, alyssum, helianthemum, lavender and the others which You, in Your infinite wisdom, know are drought-loving plants – I will write their names on a bit of paper if You like – and grant that the sun may shine the whole day long, but not everywhere (not, for example, on spiraea, or on gentian, plantain lily and rhododendron), and not too much; that there may be plenty of dew and little wind, enough worms, no plant-lice and snails, no mildew, and that once a week thick liquid manure may fall down from heaven. Amen."

THE VEIL OF SILENCE

Something that everybody wants to have read and nobody wants to read. [A classic.]

Mark Twain

With the Nobel Prize politicized beyond redemption, many of its recipients are controversial, to say the least. Pearl Buck, for example, was honoured in 1938, the year of Čapek's death, while Greene and Borges went to their graves empty-handed (no prizes are awarded posthumously). Still, when *War with the Newts* was brought to the attention of the Swedish Academy, it was only the last link in a chain of international triumphs that included previous nominations for the coveted prize.

And yet, after two decades of fame and acclaim, rave reviews and theatre attendance records, literary and critical tributes from literati of Wells, Chesterton, Shaw, and Galsworthy's stature, the Czech writer receded from the canons of world, and even European, literature. Writing for the *Nation* in 1990, John Clute accurately spoke of the "long death" that had befallen Čapek, who, following the Second World War, "was to remain virtually unpublished in his own country for half a century" (638). A year later Bohuslava Bradbrook felt compelled to begin her review with a fervent hope for the Czech author's return from oblivion. Cecil Parrott completed the picture in 1995, observing that, despite a publishing mini-revival in the early 1990s, Čapek continued to be "less well known abroad" (231).

It is difficult to account for this state of affairs. While Mann, Musil, Moravia, Kafka, Lorca, and a dozen others were rapidly attaining the status of perennial twentieth-century classics, Čapek had to wait until 1962 for his first English-language biography, which was also his first critical biography period.[20] He commands the highest praise from writers as diverse as Arthur Miller, John Updike, Kurt Vonnegut, Milan Kundera, and Stanislaw Lem, some of whom list him as a major influence. Yet the author whose plays and novels took Europe, North America, and the Orient by storm on more than one occasion ends up forgotten, as if an iron curtain insulated him from postwar sensibilities.

The veil of silence extends even into the writer's homeland. In 1990, in an effort to revive interest in his writings, Catbird Press put out a comprehensive Čapek reader entitled *Towards the Radical Center*. Taking stock of the writer's current fortunes in the critical introduction, Peter Kussi did not mince words: Čapek vanished even from twentieth-century Czech literature. Contemporary accounts spotlight two writers who have weathered well the turbulent postwar decades: Jaroslav Hašek, the one-book wonder (*The Good Soldier Schweik*), and Franz Kafka, who wrote almost entirely in German. "But a generation or two ago," Kussi reminds us, "the Czech author with the most solid reputation abroad, especially in the English-speaking world, was Karel Čapek" (11).

It is symptomatic that the very editors who would promote Čapek's art feel compelled to begin the account of his career by acknowledging his fadeout from cultural memory. It is, if anything, even more symptomatic that these same editors fall prey to the kind of amnesia that their volume is designed to overcome. For, incredibly enough, *War with the Newts* is spared but a single sentence – and a brief one at that – in the entire critical introduction to this tribute reader. Is Čapek's masterpiece, released into a depression-wasted Europe choking in the hands of fascist and nationalistic dictatorships on its way to a holocaust, merely a hollow echo from the distant past?[21] Is this why postwar history has been mindless of its ultra-modern author, who, apart from being a non-stop entertainer, is also one of the most polyphonic writers of our era? Elizabeth Maslen disagrees: his "wit remains witty – if only because the world of today is still paralyzed by dilemmas facing Čapek's world" (91). But if not that, then what is the reason?

Čapek's variety and nobrow eclecticism may be the first clues. Unlike Hašek and Kafka, who display to us one and the same side, he slips through aesthetic nets like a moray eel. There is no better example of this embarrassment of riches than *War with the Newts*. Science fiction and modernist bricolage rolled into one, it works as popular entertainment and prestige literature at the same time. As a work of art, it sets out to transcend the either/or highbrow/lowbrow categories, proving that *tertium datur* where popular culture and literary ambition come to play. An artists' artist and a storyteller for the common reader, Čapek straddles literariness and mass appeal in disregard for cultural labels. Nor are his versatility and aptitude in making art out of artefacts of mass culture an accident. He once declared that he intended to write one hundred novels covering all literary genres. In a 1925 article, "Karel Čapek about Himself," he reiterated this nobrow philosophy by claiming to learn from everything he could get his hands on and to write under the influence of everything he ever read.

Modernism may have fragmented literature into a myriad of schools and movements, each one with its own agitprop manifesto, but far from pledging allegiance to any one of them, Čapek resolves to be a nobrow democrat with a rallying cry of *e pluribus unum*. As his correspondence, prefaces, and numerous commentaries make clear, he simply is the missing link between popular and highbrow art. History may simplify the past in order to streamline it, but Čapek and his brand of artertainment refuse to succumb to aesthetic labels, as though they are aware that the latter come with an expiry date.

Will the Czech writer regain his rightful place in literary history books? Will his gift for blending popular art and highbrow entertainment revive interest in *War with the Newts*? Admitting "I am interested in everything there is," the writer may have inadvertently betrayed himself as a populist to the priests of the highbrow canon.[22] But not all hold it against him. "Čapek is full of self-contradicting ideas coexisting at the same time," marvelled Arthur Miller. "Čapek was fascinated by ordinary life, just as he was drawn to everything strange and exotic" (13), echoed Kussi. Doležel complimented the diversity conveyed by his "free play of unbounded verbal imagination." And Gannett summed up: "Čapek did an infinite variety of things."[23]

THE PRINCIPLES THAT GUIDED HIS WRITING

Čapek, a great and liberal man, died on Christmas Day in 1938, a mere atom in the general darkness engulfing Europe.

Brian Aldiss with David Wingrove

A look at the principles that guided his writing may help account for Čapek's lapse from postwar collective memory.

1   The postwar years were Cold War years, and artists who couldn't be enlisted in the them-or-us tug of war were of suspect virtue. Which side was Čapek on? Vexatingly enough, neither. A pacifist, humanist, and a free thinker, he was an opponent of progress or victory at all costs who didn't hide his contempt for militarist propaganda. "A war machine. A vast machine, a huge one. The swiftest, most effective crusher of lives" (160) – is what he called it in *The Insect Play*. If the enemies of our enemies were our Cold War friends, then Čapek had the rare honour of appearing unsound to both the Allied Scylla and the Warsaw Pact

Charybdis.[24] To victorious Americans, swept by rampant consumerism, his calls for social reform, redistribution of wealth, and pacifist independence sounded too red, especially coming from a state buried deep in Stalin's embrace. For the Soviets he was no less reactionary, if only because he could not be conscripted in the propaganda war against the West. He was, after all, the author of "Why I Am Not a Communist" (1924) who declined Moscow's invitation to the 1938 May Day parade. Even more to the point, he was a critic of the revolution, holding that people are just as selfish, greedy, and cruel after reforms as before them. As if on cue, Communist censors struck from the Czech edition the passage that exhorts the Newts to unite, in a hysterical spoof of the Party manifesto (it was reinstated only after Stalin's death).

2   In a time of extremes defined by dogmatic political stances, flag-waving propaganda wars, and Nixon- and McCarthy-stoked witch hunts, Čapek's neutrality and moderation must have looked like pinko reformism if not full-blown socialism. Didn't his Newts declare expansionist war on the world on the anniversary of the American Revolution? With writers and artists testifying before the Senate left and even right, few after the war had much use for an East European satirist who, equally critical of either system, swore loyalty only to his irrepressible wit, profound understanding of history, and defiant humanism.

3   In the century that unvaryingly confused bigger with better, the Czech writer cautioned all would-be architects of global progress: "Empires do not endure due to the wisdom of state dignitaries, but as a result of the needs of many millions of people who work at crafts of all kinds in order that they might live ... It is these private details that make up what we call the greatness of nations."[25] With the world and its problems getting more complex, with automation, weapons of mass destruction, genocides, geopolitics, and hemispheres of influence the order of the day, a

champion of the small and individual must have seemed an anachronism.

4   For all the ferocity with which he tore into the complacencies of our time, Čapek was never preachy or grandiloquent. Like Ghost Dog, the black samurai from Jim Jarmush's eponymous film, he often paid respect to little things, sparing Big Notions but a fleeting glance. Puckish and irreverent, he could be as side-splitting as Woody Allen in the mock-Dostoevskyan *Love and Death*, and as poignant as Woody Allen in the Dostoevskyan *Crimes and Misdemeanours*. Resorting to laughter, fantasy, and the grotesque, instead of throwing his philosophical weight around, may have cost him critical laurels. It is a dismal fact that geniuses of comedy hardly ever command the highest acclaim precisely because their art seems to lack the lustre of voluminous and self-important grand opera. And yet Čapek's greatness can be measured by the aphorism from his first collection, *The Garden of Krakonoš*: "Humour is the salt of the earth, and whoever is well salted will long retain his freshness."[26]

5   Čapek's doctoral thesis, "The Objective Method in Esthetics with a View to Creative Art," was a passionate defence of the objective and representational role of literature. Even then the young author distanced himself from the cult of art for art's sake and highbrow aesthetics as esoteric symbol-weaving. Literature was about drama – drama of (and for) the masses – not intellectual navel-gazing. For the emergent postmodern sensibility, awash in epistemological and narrative angst, his Horatian genre-coated pill of enlightenment would sound out of tune and out of time.

6   Čapek's art fell prey to the emerging opposition between highbrow and lowbrow. How could you take seriously a wordsmith who looked for inspiration "in pulp literature, not in the realm of exclusive creations"?[27] In his lifetime he was venerated as a modernist par excellence: intellectual, philosophical, political, and avant garde. But he was

always a little too comical, too enamoured of lowbrow genres, and just too readable to suit custodians of intellectual mystique. A relentless experimentalist, he was also a storyteller in the popular tradition, who found Joyce and his antics vulgar. Few reviewers fail to remark on how entertaining *War with the Newts* is, implicitly diminishing it in the eyes of those who, with Clement Greenberg, equate art with readers' prolonged resistance to it. How could a novel published serially in a daily paper, written in the idiom of popular press and Tinseltown B-movies, be art? Not that Čapek cared, convinced that the division between popular and highbrow was just another invention of the latter, who refused to acknowledge in the classics of today the comic artertainers of yesterday. Or, as he put it: "Folk humour will always enter into literature and will abide there by right of perpetuity; but in this case it will bear the name of Aristophanes, Rabelais or Cervantes."[28]

Another problem is the annexation of Čapek by the science fiction community. It may seem odd that well-meaning genre enthusiasts could have a hand in his disappearance from the annals of world literature. Science fiction attracts, after all, vast and eclectic audiences as well as a great deal of attention from the media – especially today, when its signature themes have achieved transcultural visibility and recognition. However, scoring big with Hollywood producers, the genre signed a pact with the devil. With the exception of wayward visionaries like Kubrick or Gilliam, what is released for general consumption is more often than not a sci-fi wiener dipped in fake-blood ketchup.[29] From *Jurassic Park* to *Deep Blue Sea*, from *Alien* to *Syngenor*, from *Starship Troopers* to *Leviathan*, bad science and bad fiction recombine in a subgenre of slasher horror where, instead of Freddie, Jason, or Chucky, the alien monster or velociraptor does the wetwork.

Keen to upgrade its image, science fiction apologists have displayed a propensity to aggrandize its domain, sticking the label on writers who have precious little to do with space opera or monster hide-and-seek. Many artists have been reluctant to play the role of the genre's redeemers. Ray Bradbury spent his career fighting to emerge from the literary event horizon known as sci-fi. "I write ancient mythology – Greek, Roman, Egyptian," he remonstrated in a 2001 interview. "I fought with them for years to take the [science fiction] label off."[30] With tributes to Čapek as a genre precursor decimating his stock as a serious artist, this *Anschluss* is all the more ironic in that, where Campbell and Gernsback-era 'zine writers were for the most part prophets of scientism, Čapek is suspicious of the inner vacuum and social irresponsibility permeating science. *War with the Newts* iterates time and again that the measure of civilization lies not in technology but, rather, in people's relation to technology. This humanistic and cautionary attitude is at odds with the technophile banalities from sci-fi's so-called golden era.[31]

With philosophy in lieu of cyberotica, science in lieu of fairy tales, and political satire in lieu of feudalactic empires, Čapek is an intellectual nova for an average Han Solo fan. This may partly explain why no studio has ever capitalized on *War with the Newts*'s blockbuster potential. Although tailor-made for the big screen, there was only one attempt at adaptation. In 1958 Kenneth Sylvia reworked it into a play, entitled *Day of the Newt*, in effect trivializing it into another *Day of the Triffids*, after a 1951 space-invasion hamburger by John Wyndham.[32]

It may also explain why Čapek is so unpopular even within the sci-fi world, to the point where the rank-and-file know him only as the inventor of the word "robot," if that. After all, although he mined some of its themes and conventions, he was not interested in the genre per se. The means rather than the goal, science fiction provided him with a set of narrative tools that enabled him to better express his distress with an inter-bellum Europe on a collision course with destiny. Few paid heed when he stressed, in "The Meaning of R.U.R.," that he was always more interested in people than in robots. A nobrow entartainer, he was, in Elizabeth Maslen's words, "a past master at moving from the ultra-literary to the colloquial" (83). And yet, as his career demonstrates, although something for everyone may be a winning strategy in politics, this is not always true in the politics of literature.

5   Raymond Chandler's Aesthetics of Irony

Murder laced with lust, mayhem spiced with nymphomania: this is the formula for the chief surviving form of the murder mystery in America, though, indeed, that form has not surrendered its native birthright of anti-feminism. It insists, however, on undressing its bitches, surveying them with a surly and concupiscent eye before punching, shooting, or consigning them to the gas chamber. Not only in the cruder and more successful books of Mickey Spillane, but in the more pretentious ones by Raymond Chandler, the detective story has reverted to the kind of populist semi-pornography that once made George Lippard's *The Monks of Monk Hall* a black-market bestseller.

Leslie Fiedler, *Love and Death in the American Novel*

From the early days of crime fiction's meteoric rise in popularity, critics tried to correct some of its formulaic tendencies.[1] One of the most unforgettable was Monsignor Ronald A. Knox, British clergy-man, editor and detective story writer who, in the Preface to the *Best Detective Stories of 1928–29*, laid out the ten commandments for crime mystery's Golden Age. Among other treats, his decalogue dispensed such structural gospel as, "Not more than one secret room or passage is allowable," and "No Chinaman must figure in the story."[2]

Still, not all of the early stabs at the poetics of the genre were so silly, and one of the more consequential was Čapek's own "Holmesiana, or about Detective Stories."[3] Taking stock of the detective literature he knew so intimately, the Czech writer understood that at its narrative centre lay not the crime, but the detective. Nor did he hesitate to prescribe what kind of sleuth stood behind a good crime story. A detective has nothing to do with himself, he proposed. A detective takes no notice of his feelings for he takes notice of facts and deeds. He does not ask questions about his own salvation, and he is the most perfect realist in the universe. As soon as he falls in love he loses his intellectual integrity.

If art denies expectations, invalidates rules, and generally transmutes water into wine, then Raymond Chandler is an artist. This is because Philip Marlowe, arguably the most famous literary creation of the last century, is the living antithesis of Čapek's recipe for a successful detective. Take, for example, the last injunction. At the end of *Playback* Marlowe is not only in love but fixing to get betrothed, and in *Poodle Springs* he even plays husband to a millionaire's daughter, in his spare time sleuthing a case involving pornography and murder, and doing a whole lot of soul-searching about his identity.[4] Playing with Čapek's rules by applying them in reverse, Chandler shows time and again that the genre is simply too creative, its poetics too flexible, and its characters too complex to conform to any critic's scriptures.

In his lifetime Chandler's unflagging attention to style, mood, and speech earned him acclaim from Hemingway, Priestley, Eliot, Burgess, Waugh, Steinbeck, Maugham, Perelman, and Auden, among others. The *Atlantic Monthly* printed his articles alongside Lippman's, Sartre's, and Einstein's. A writer of power, vision, and endurance, he was in, Auden's words, quite simply a contemporary American novelist who wrote "serious studies of a criminal milieu, the Great Wrong Place." As such, continued Auden, "his powerful and extremely depressing books should be read and judged, not as escapist literature, but as works of art."[5] No less august an opinion-maker than the London *Times* agreed. In what was literally the last word on the matter, its 1959 obituary honoured Chandler as an artist who, "working the vein of crime fiction, mined the gold of literature."[6] In 1995 the Library of America finally threw its weight behind the hardboiled master, editing two volumes of his writings and thereby inducting him into the national Hall of Literary Fame.

In this context it is an open question what drove Leslie Fiedler into maligning Chandler in *Love and Death in the American Novel* (see epigraph at beginning of chapter). As everyone knows, these affronts could be cooked up only by someone with limited experience of Philip Marlowe, a detective principled enough to make Job look like a sellout. The PI may be hardboiled, he may bedevil pretty blondes, but he does not go around punching, shooting, or consigning them to the gas chamber. As much a hard-nosed realist as an incurable (in *Playback* even sentimental) romantic, Marlowe not only takes note of his feelings but frequently of those of others. As for pornography, his infrequent episodes of love-making are understated in lyrical terms befitting a knight of romance. Look no further than *Poodle Springs* to find intimacy elliptical enough to suit an astronomer. No more than "a long sigh, and two people as close as two people can get" (8); the mood is no different from *Playback*, where the bedroom darkness yields only "that muted cry, and then again the slow quiet peace" (799).[7]

Fiedler's assault seems a case of an academic projecting his dislike of genre formulas onto one of its most celebrated practitioners – and missing his target by a country mile. While Chandler's prose is undeniably of the hardboiled school, it has shot and punched its way out of the *Black Mask* ghetto. Even in 1933, when most hacks hacked a million words a year to get ahead, his first story, "Blackmailers Don't Shoot," was a crop of five months of painstaking revisions, so much so that before the advent of word-processors it was finessed to flush right, as if typeset for publication.

A quarter century later *Playback* is another odd duck, which, instead of an instant detective classic, delivers a tongue-in-cheek retrospective of the entire hardboiled tradition. Laying open a world of billboard culture and criminals too well heeled to bring within hearing distance of a courtroom gavel, Chandler bids a parodic, if fond, farewell to the hardboiled school in a still unappreciated intertextual gambit. This entartaining novel has eluded readers and reviewers in search of a conventional Marlowe caper, where the wise guys are all ten-minute eggs and the detectives run at the mouth with bullet-quick wit. Many cannot forgive the ambitious writer for changing the rules of the game or, what amounts to the same thing, playing a different game altogether.

A BOMBSHELL REDHEAD ON THE RUN

Tales of imagination, then, that deal in murders, and in other species of iniquity, lead to the actual commission of similar sins.

Fanny Mayne

Eleanor King, alias Betty Mayfield, is a bombshell redhead on the run. No sooner does the court rule her husband's death of a broken neck an accident than, exonerated but fearful of her father-in-law, Henry Cumberland, she flees.[8] Determined to buy peace of mind with wads of Cumberland's cash, she gets off the train in Esmeralda trailed by Larry Mitchell, blackmailer and lounge lizard, and Chandler's by now middle-aged private eye. Marlowe tails Betty on behest of Umney, a big lawyer with a big cheque book and an even bigger attitude. Once on the case, in no time he finds himself on the wrong side of a gun from Mitchell, a whisky bottle from Betty, and another gun from Goble (a roughneck peeper from Kansas). A succession of almost episodic encounters takes him to a posh hotel where, Betty tells him, Larry the lizard lies dead on her balcony. The circumstances could scarcely favour her less. Blackmailed by Mitchell, she had the motive and the opportunity, and the report of the victim's broken neck makes it look like a nasty case of déjà vu.

Himself running from solitude, Marlowe goes to bed with Umney's expensive secretary in a tender one-night stand. The morning after he's back to shielding Betty, who tries to buy his loyalty with a retainer: first cash, then flesh. Between Brandon, a major-league gangster from Kansas, and Harvest, a tough guy with a gun, Marlowe has his hands full even before another body turns up: Ceferino Chang, a junked-out watchman hangs in his slum bedsit. Meantime the detective runs into one of Chandler's most enigmatic characters: an elderly gent with a cane in his gloved hands, mordant, observant, and full of discourse on God, existentialism, and art. There is also an old resident who, with the plot in complete abeyance, mulls over the social drift of Esmeralda in a chapter-length monologue.

Then the curtain falls. Marlowe fingers Brandon as the prime suspect but, lacking evidence, lets him go, turning down a $5,000 bribe. Goble and Harvest, beaten into pulp, fade away. Cumberland, snubbed and apoplectic, goes home. Betty, tired of running, gambles on Brandon. Umney is told to kiss a duck. And Marlowe? Closing the case with all the verve of a timeworn Sisyphus, staving off the solitaire without and within, he takes a call from Paris and pledges himself to love and marriage.

All this may strike the reader as too crazy and recherché for a plot of a mystery, and for a legion of critics this is the one book they love to hate. William Marling is typical when he berates *Playback* as a "disheartening performance" and "the least of Chandler's novels," before appealing for succor to Harold Orel, whose "It is a dreary trash" is said to speak for most readers.[9] Generally speaking, blanket dismissals make for dubious scholarship, but especially so when accompanied by interpretive myopia. To take only one example, Marling's supporting claim – "Beyond the semi-satiric portrait of the wealthy retirees of Esmeralda, there is little social criticism or insight" (150) – is plain wrong. Fred Pope's mini-treatise on Esmeralda, which takes up the entire Chapter 20, is only one of several passages where Chandler's social criticism hits home with the assurance of Jackie Robinson. A little further down, in a self-refuting gesture, Marling approvingly cites Bernard Schopen who extols Chandler's social criticism and insight. In fact, "so effective was his [Chandler's] commentary on the America he observed," concludes Schopen, "that social criticism has become a major function of the form" (152)![10]

Even Jerry Speir, widely regarded as sympathetic to Chandler, is hard to tell from those who trash *Playback* as undistinguished, forgettable, and hoked-up. His protestations that it furnishes "certain insights into the author and his attitude towards his work in his later years," damn with proverbial faint praise.[11] Worse, his otherwise discerning semi-chapter on the book contends, with no supporting evidence, that Betty becomes involved in a "vague struggle for power within the mob" (78). This too is wrong. Even though at least one critic drubbed the plot of *Playback* as a dog looking for a lamppost, whether this deprecation is true or not is debatable. It may take readers a while to figure out that the real target of blackmail is not Betty but Brandon, making Chandler a more devious plotter than allowed. After all, the better the writer, he said, "the more subtly he will disguise that which cannot be told."[12]

The point is that he is devious enough for Speir, who mistakes the bloody punishment of petty hustlers like Goble as a struggle within the mob, even though there is no struggle in the West Egg of Esmeralda – only Clark Brandon and his brand of American justice. Brandon won't be pushed around by a peeper from Kansas who threatens to talk about his past, and Goble gets a taste of discipline, while Larry Mitchell disappears on a permanent leave of absence.[13] As for Betty, she may be a deluxe gold-digger à la Hammett's Dinah Brand; but becoming the big boss's squeeze doesn't make her a player in a power struggle that just isn't there.

When even seasoned critics flounder, it is necessary to take a fresh look at the source of their interpretive confusion. Revisiting *Playback* means, of course, revisiting the multiple clues left as narrative signposts to suggest that it is a different literary species than a vintage Marlowe adventure. From the title down, *Playback* spells out an invitation to a novel kind of detective game, and literary detectives who miss the clues run the risk of misjudging the book altogether. And, indeed, many of its harshest critics take a straightforward view of Chandler's last mystery that overlooks its ironic playfulness and its complex valedictory to the hardboiled era.

THE NOVEL'S CENTRAL SYMBOL

A sin is a certain bad state of the soul, whereas crime is a certain bad course of things. There are deadly sins which are not deadly crimes, and vice versa.

Karel Čapek

Much as he admired Hemingway's titles, Chandler dallied over his own. Some he contemplated but never used are: *The Corpse Came in Person, A Few May Remember, The Man with the Shredded Ear, Zone of Twilight, Parting Before Danger, The Is to Was Man, All Guns Are Loaded, Return From Ruin, Lament But No Tears, Too Late to Sleep, The Cool-Off.* Conspicuous as the novel's central symbol, on the first pass the title of *Playback* seems to pose little interpretive difficulty. Robert Parker, who would go on to write about Philip Marlowe himself, reflects the consensus by seeing in it a replay of tragedy from which Betty flees at all costs. Barely cleared of her husband's death, the events in Esmeralda restage the nightmare of being accused of murder, with circumstantial evidence pointing the finger at her.

If that were all, of course, the wordplay would not be worth the paper it's printed on. But it isn't, partly because the 1958 novel is itself an intertextual playback of a screenplay Chandler wrote when in Hollywood.[14] After the triumph of his scripts for *Double Indemnity* (1944; co-credited with Billy Wilder) and *Blue Dahlia* (1946), Universal coughed up an unheard of contract – $4,000 a week, percentage of profits, and minimum supervision – for an original screenplay. Chandler completed the job in 1948, calling it *Playback*. Knee-deep in postwar recession, the studio never got around to shooting the picture. Yet, even as it stands, Gay Brewer judges it Chandler's "finest work for film" – no mean praise with two previous scripts being Academy Award nominees.[15] Even more to the point, the normally reticent writer openly agreed, in 1953 taking the first stab (of several) at making it over into a Marlowe novel.

Chandler's outline for the screenplay reveals remarkable structural parallels between the script and the novel. Here it is: a "crucial week in the life of a girl who decides to spend it in a tower suite in a hotel, under an assumed name, her identity concealed with great care ... During this week the frustrations and tragedies of her life are repeated in capsule form, so that it almost appears that she had brought her destiny with her ... So Betty arrives at the hotel and her name is now, let us say, Elizabeth Mayfield."[16] Apart from inevitable narrative details, the novel strays from the screenplay mostly in scenery and the endgame. The original is set in Vancouver, British Columbia, where the investigation into Mitchell's death is led by a *sympathique* Canadian lawman, Killaine, who falls for the heroine after clearing her of blame. Although the leading players step almost unedited from the stage onto the page, they are flanked by a new supporting cast. Like other Chandler novels, *Playback* delivers a cross-section of society, from hyperbolic power figures to everyday joes in everyday jobs. Buffeted across all walks of life without being of any, Marlowe comes in contact with cabbies, hotel guests, cops, night guards, motel clerks, and other anonymous people who make up a small town.

Yet, adding still another layer of metatextual complexity, the screenplay itself is a partial playback of Chandler's early *Black Mask* stories, "Guns at Cyrano's" (1936) and "I'll be Waiting" (1939). From a sultry redhead beached in a California hotel to Marlowe's "I'll always be waiting" (749), relics of such narrative cannibalization survive in the novel.[17] The number of playbacks, allusions, and outright references is thus much greater than Parker's words might lead one to believe. While even in 1948 the title already signified more than a simple mirror of events before and after Betty's flight, by 1958 it was supercharged with double meanings by harking also to the Paramount script. With the title as the symbolic gatekeeper to the garden of forking contexts, *Playback* appears to caution literary interpreters: look ye not for an old-fashioned murder case.

Taking Auden's praise as a starting point, one can better appreciate what kind of book it is by looking at what's wrong in Chandler's Great Wrong Place. Published in the 1950s, when every TV commercial implicitly reassured Americans that they lived in the best of countries and the best of times, *Playback* is closer in sensibility to the racketeering 1930s and the wartime 1940s. Nobody is outraged by corruption and vice because they are so common-place. With a fat wallet to buy friends in high places, every fat cat lands on his silk-stockinged feet. When Marlowe Y-sects the sleepy-dog resort of Esmeralda, he does it without fanfare or righteous indignation. After a lifetime of sifting through society's garbage, Chandler's hero has seen it all. His tired, almost complacent view of evil is one sign that the line between high crime and high society is about as real as a lawyer's promise. After all, California is where tier-one bandits like Brandon shop for social acceptance with the chutzpah of a real-life Jay Gould or a fictional James Gatz.

Chandler's gallery of crooked cops, corrupt judges, criminal (in all senses of the word) lawyers, untouchable bootleggers, or tycoons big enough to operate outside the law sum up his view of the United States of America. For those who would doubt his fictions, there are the facts. As early as 1895 a police commissioner by the soon-to-be-famous name of Teddy Roosevelt pontificated: "I have the most corrupt department in New York on my hands."[18] In 1929 the president of the Chicago Crime Commission actually went to Al Capone to ask for help in holding an *honest* city election. That same year the National Commission on Law Observance and Enforcement met for the first time. Its verdict? "The general failure of the police to deter and arrest criminals guilty of many murders, spectacular bank, payroll, and other hold-ups and sensational robberies with guns, frequently resulting in the death of the robbed victim, has caused a loss of public confidence in the police in our country" (Panek, 100).

In this climate, which has only gotten worse since the OJ farce, the Rodney King fiasco, and the War on Drugs fraud, it is small wonder that Chandler's cops and detectives nourish such a jaded attitude towards law enforcement.[19] The real criminals never see their day in court because graft and corruption are everywhere. Power to the people means, in practice, power to the people who can buy immunity from even the most tenacious investigators. Although Marlowe will usually get the man who pulls the trigger, there's nothing to cheer about. The corrupt system remains intact. In the last scene of "Smart-Alec Kill", a *Black Mask* story from 1934, the PI and a police captain go to celebrate after closing the case. "What'll we drink to?" asks the cop. "Let's just drink," replies the hero.

Playback lacks the type of a sadistic cop that appeared regularly in earlier novels. But the fact that Marlowe actually thanks the fuzz for not working him over hints at the enmity between the two sides of the blue line. The very existence of private detectives and private security personnel, who nowadays vastly outnumber uniformed police, is an implied censure of the latter's efficacy. With a mogul like Cumberland above the law because he owns the town in which the law is dispensed, and an ex-gangster like Brandon living it up like Howard Hughes instead of enjoying R&B with the Department of Corrections, who is to talk about justice? Whether Mitchell suffers a genuine or a planned accident, no one – not even Marlowe – can touch the Kansas kingpin.

Although justice in *Playback* is as perverted and powerless as it is in Faulkner's *Sanctuary*, in many ways the novel situates itself closer to another American crime classic, *The Great Gatsby*.[20] This is not a surprise: normally stingy with praise, on several occasions Chandler endorsed Fitzgerald's novella as a little pure art. A Midwestern Gatsby whose verbal tic, "old man," rings as phoney as his counterpart's "old sport," Brandon too is a former racketeer who buys respectability by the billfold. Acquiring lavish property, phasing out former cronies, and throwing tainted dough around, like Gatsby he hopes to con the establishment of Esmeralda. The similarities hold up until the end for the Kansas gangster's success is as genuine as is that of the New York racketeer. In Goble's inimitable words: "He's just a nigger to them" (815).

Like *The Great Gatsby*, *Playback* is at once cynical and melodramatic, a story of moral and social decay embedded in blackmail and death. Browbeaten by the prestige of the canon, we like to forget that Fitzgerald's masterpiece is a crime story set in the harddrinking, hard-partying, hard-nosed days of the speakeasies. The reason why it is not deprecated as a pre-RICO gangster fiction decked out in the jazz beat of the era is its uncompromising audit of America's soul for sale. But then it is hardly different from *Playback*, which tosses out its own audit of America's disposable soul on the heap of wrappers from TV dinners of the era.

THE DISMAL REALITY OF ANYTOWN, USA

By the way, do you ever read Raymond Chandler? I have just devoured a proof of his last story. He fascinates me, chiefly, I think, because he offers me the unusual and pleasing spectacle of a man trying to turn a cheap, popular formula into something much better. He does it, too.

J.B. Priestley

Chandler takes many potshots at guns and lawyers, two icons of the uneasy relationship between America and American justice. Guns, drawls Marlowe, "are just a fast curtain to a bad second act" (756). The third act is played out today in real time, punctuated with daily reports of firearm massacres in living rooms or school-yards. The judiciary system is another quagmire, tailored to profit lawyers at the expense of everyone else. Not that the public is above reproof: if you believe one of the unforgettable characters in Joseph Wambaugh's *Glitter Dome*, these days the next word a child learns after "mom" is "sue." True to form, Betty makes no distinction between lawyers and blackmailers when told she may need a good attorney. "That's a contradiction in terms," she sneers. "If he was good, he wouldn't be a lawyer" (808).

But as before, Chandler's top villain is America's urban sprawl rendered through his unvaryingly melancholy cityscapes. Driving around, Marlowe beholds the dismal reality of Anytown, USA: tawdry, littered, with a parade of false fronts, giant billboards, smoky poolrooms, street toughs, and fast food joints serving paper food on paper plates. Interminable miles of "divided six-lane super-highway dotted at intervals with the carcasses of wrecked, striped and abandoned cars tossed against the high bank to rust" (800) belch him out in Esmeralda, where postcard-pretty storefronts hide "broken crates, piles of cartons, trash drums, dusty parking spaces, the back yard of elegance" (834).

All this forms a fitting prelude to Chapter 20, reminiscent of Faulkner's historical digressions in *Requiem for a Nun*, when the plot takes a back seat while an inconsequential motel owner broods over Esmeralda's facelift from a lifeless village to a soulless resort in the hands of a second-generation robber baroness. This type of

131

social tableau, rare in a genre typically driven by murder mystery, is not so rare in a writer who has always deemed plots superfluous to the spirit of urban realism. Chandler's dramatic monologue, all the more effective in the mouth of an average nobody, conjures up the decline in social cohesion, the splintering of communities, the rise of the me-first ethic. "They'll take your last dollar from you between your teeth and look at you like you stole it from them" (842), warns Fred Pope.

Pictures of roadside wreckage, urban blight, and poverty are Marlowe's retinue as he makes his way through the sunlit resort's dark side to the den of Ceferino Chang. In the days before *Needle Park* and *Gridlock'd*, before dope became a middle-class problem, this is one of Chandler's most squalid and forlorn postcards from the edge. The kitchen, where the garage watchman ODs before ending strung up on an electric wire, has lino worn through to the boards. A single window jammed shut, a light bulb hangs from the cracked and leak-stained ceiling for illumination. Not fit for a pig, the junk pad is exactly what Marlowe says it is: a rich man's improvement on a rich man's property – a one-unit slum.

Nor are the divisions between the haves and the have-nots that much different from the divisions between men and women. Gazing at Betty's photo, Marlowe remarks the absence of a wedding band with the small print glaring: in her late twenties a girl ought to have a husband, or else there's something wrong with her – wrong enough to cue the investigator. Later, in the house of Helen Vermilyea, the hero states flatly: "You've been married, of course." Capturing the precariousness of a woman's economics, the syllogism is simple. Since she owns property, and property can only be acquired by men, it must have been from her marriage/husband, a conjecture confirmed in the next line.

These days we figure on social commentary in crime novels – in fact, we frequently read them for precisely that reason. Urban proceduralists like McBain or Sjöwall and Wahlöö, or else the heirs of the private eye tradition like Ross Macdonald or Walter Mosley, routinely instruct readers on how much (or how little) the urban zoo has changed since Chandler's times. But all learned their social chops from this classics-trained Californian, who, with the zest of a modern-day Michael Moore, tells us where we took the wrong turn. Paul Skenazy underscored this in 1996 when he lauded Chandler's "abundant skills" not only as a critic and formal theorist but also as a "social analyst" ("Introduction" 4).

With a Technicolor eye for image and a Panasonic ear for language, the writer follows losers in life, drifters, grifters, drunks, and washouts, lonely people coming together for a brief moment of sex or love during which even their togetherness is tinged with the certainty of solitude. People who saw too much of the wrong side of life, cynical people who lost their ideals, so that even their dreams are only in black and white. Who is to say that *Playback* is not as fresh and topical today as it was in the days when we liked Ike? Who is to say – William Marling excepted – that the novel lacks in social dimension?

PIRANDELLO MINUS THE BRAGGADOCIO

The one thing that really disturbs me about America is that people don't like to read. The last author I read was Dostoevsky. I like Dashiell Hammett and Raymond Chandler. I read, like, four books at once. I read everything.

Keith Richards (The Rolling Stones)

As is evident from his 1950 correspondence to Carl Brandt, the older Chandler was losing patience with hardboiled conventions. "From now on I am going to write what I want to write as I want to write it. Some of it may flop. There are always going to be people who will say I have lost the pace I had once, that I take too long to say things now, and don't care enough about tight active plots. But I'm not writing for those people now."[21]

Indeed he was not. In his last Marlowe adventure, with a high-aesthetic wink and an intertextual nudge, *Playback* bids adieu to an entire literary school. "I am not satisfied that ... a novel cannot be written which, ostensibly a mystery and keeping the spice of mystery, will actually be a novel of character and atmosphere with an overtone of violence and fear," confessed the author in the years before his death. Utterances like these reflect the artist's ambition to exceed the formula by leaving a lasting emotional effect on the reader, wherein a controlled half-poetic emotion should combine with a lingering aura of the places and people described.

The Long Goodbye (1953), Chandler's penultimate and arguably most accomplished work, was already a far cry from the shoot-first, ask-questions-later formula plied contemporarily by Mickey Spillane. A psychological drama, a character study, and a novel of manners, it solidified Chandler's reputation in England as an American novelist of importance. This poignant, at times almost meditative, story deals with double murder in order to deal with friendship, solitude, and middle-age compromises. All in all, it is an apt stage-setter for the perplexing, over-the-top performance at times bordering on a pastiche of the genre – *Playback*.

Having grafted contemporary drama onto the crime mystery (or was it the other way round?), Chandler would apologize for his early stories, which honoured the genre code by luxuriating in death. Not that he was ever as prone to violence as were other Black Maske-teers. Much of his early writing seems muted, almost cerebral, next to Hammett's Continental Op opus. Even before *Red Harvest*, in the days of "House Dick" (aka "Bodies Piled Up"), Hammett was wont to dish it out with both fists. "I stepped past the maid and tried the door. It was unlocked. I opened it. Slowly, rigidly, a man pitched out into my arms – pitched out backwards – and there was a six-inch slit down the back of his coat, and his coat was wet and sticky. That wasn't altogether a surprise: the blood on the floor had prepared me for something of the sort. But when another followed him – facing me, this one, with a dark, distorted face – I dropped the one I had caught and jumped back. And as I jumped a third man came tumbling out after the others." Exit realism. Enter pulp fiction at its hyperbolic and hilarious best.

Even as it traffics in hardboiled goods, *Playback* displays a flamboyantly self-reflexive attitude to the genre and its clichés. To begin, in a tribute as ironic as it is deferential, the novel swarms with allusions to Hammett's prototypal *Red Harvest*. One of the most obvious is the squat and thickset Kansas Op, Goble, whose manners and mannerisms make him a dead ringer for the squat and thickset Continental Op. The operative from *Red Harvest* is, in Dinah Brand's curt *blazon*, "a fat, middle aged, hard-boiled, pig headed guy" (85). The operative from *Playback* is "a middle sized fat man and the fat didn't look flabby" (762). Dropping hints like Cinderella slippers, Chandler is ready with another one. Asked whether Goble is a close friend of his, without batting an eye Marlowe replies: "The operative word is close" (817).

In the context, the really funny part occurs when Goble, the reincarnated Op from *Red Harvest*, gets beaten to a pulp by a red-haired gangster, Richard "Red" Harvest. Red Harvest is himself a throwback to the Hammett-era hoods with gorilla biceps and IQ stuck at room temperature level. Henry Cumberland, Betty's father-in-law? A spitting image of Hammett's Elihu Willsson, irascible and disdainful of the law in the city he owns. The red-haired knockout Betty Mayfield, alias Eleanor King? The red-haired knockout Brigid O'Shaughnessy, alias Miss Wonderly. Good girl gone bad, cold manipulator with the hots for the private eye, arrant actress who plays men like pawns for her ends, runaway whose past always catches up with her plans to start a new life, she's a carbon copy of Hammett's femme fatale. So is her propensity for lying, with the copycat refrain a dead giveaway. "I am a liar," purrs Brigid. "I have always been a liar" (88). "All right, I'm a liar," shrugs Betty. "I've always been a liar" (807).

Another character that must be singled out from these self-reflexive bows is Henry Clarendon IV. Just as Hammett cameoed in *Red Harvest* as Dan Rolff, the thin man with TB, Chandler stages his own appearance as an aging hotel-lobby philosopher.[22] This little stunt may have germinated in his mind since the 1950 collaboration with Hitchcock (who put in a cameo in all his films) on the script for Patricia Highsmith's *Strangers on a Train*. Playful and irreverent, Chandler insinuates himself into Marlowe's investigation as a wizened, snobbish, cynical hotel patron. His hair neatly parted, hands in white gloves (in later years the writer was plagued by a skin condition), his eye is as sharp as ever and as enamoured of the female form. Hardboiled Pirandello minus the braggadocio, Chandler will even sit down with his own creation, Philip Marlowe, to a conversation rife with ironic innuendoes and intimations of death.

Although some critics prefer to believe that *Playback* is, in effect, a book-long slip of an errant pen, trotting out hardboiled clichés with self-reflexive gusto it takes the simple art of murder to another level. Marlowe runs into a smart-aleck cabbie who remonstrates that car-tailing is something from crime books, mister. Helen Vermilyea mocks him as Mr Hard Guy in person. The hero himself ricochets from one throat-clearing moment to another, wisecracking about TV detectives who never take their hats off and pulp fiction sleuths who always drive in dark inconspicuous vehicles. In Chapter 3 I showed how reflexive intentions work, with the writer's moves intended to be recognized as having been meant to be recognized. The copious allusions to Hammett and the tongue-in-cheek playbacks of the hardboiled clichés are evidence that this intricate design is anything but haphazard or coincidental.

It's possible, of course, to fall victim to the interpretive game known as who-is-the-cleverest-dude-around-this-text.[23] If I caution against it, it is because the next round of allusions is somewhat more conjectural than the last. And yet, with countless echoes of the hardboiled classics setting the tone, Chandler-as-Clarendon may be only waiting to kick the playful, self-reflexive mockery into higher gear. With Hammett's ghost lurking in the wings, is it Margo West or the hardboiled style about which he lectures Marlowe? "She had an overblown style and she looked just a little hardboiled." Or three lines down: "she can't hold a man. She tries too hard" (827).

As Freud conceded, sometimes a cigar is just a cigar, and the parley between Chandler's fictive spokesmen, Clarendon and Marlowe, might be as innocent of doubles entendres as is a dissertation on Longinus. But in the wake of so many instances of exuberant play, it's hard to shake off the impression of another inside joke. A touch snide, perhaps, but who can quarrel with the perfect lowdown on the *Black Mask* school – overblown, hardboiled, and trying too hard to hold the reader's attention? Chandler was aware that holding attention was a matter of aesthetics, not body pile-ups, theorizing as much after completing *Playback* for film. The readers "just *thought* they cared nothing about anything but the action," but really, "although they didn't know it, they cared very little about the action" (2:1034).

Coincidence? Perhaps not, for little else could explain what follows. In a passage at stark odds with the canons of the genre, the action cools its heels while, with startling emotional candour, Clarendon meditates on dying. His existential anguish accentuated by clinical detachment, the old man confesses to the horror of having no other companions on his last journey but the white-starched hospital staff. Yet the moment the exorcism is over, puckish to the end, he pinpricks it with a self-reflexive wink: "I talk too much" (827). Seconds later, he brings down the theatrical fourth wall, chiding Marlowe: "You should have come to me for information. But of course you couldn't know that." Indeed!

Marlowe humours the hotel philosopher, just like he humoured another tired old man in *The Big Sleep*. But the latter is not done yet. An aficionado of mystery may be excused for thinking she opened the wrong book when, instead of a whodunit, she is detoured through a lecture in philosophy. What else to call Clarendon's ramble from the complex patterns on a strellitzia bud to the deity behind all creation? "Is he omnipotent? How could he be? There's so much suffering and almost always by the innocent. Why will a mother rabbit trapped in a burrow by a ferret put her babies behind and allow her throat to be torn out? Why? In two weeks more she would not even recognize them. Do you believe in God, young man?"

The mute howl gathers force:

> How can I imagine a hell in which a baby that died before baptism occupies the same degraded position as a hired killer or a Nazi death-camp commandant or a member of the Politburo? How strange it is that man's finest aspirations, dirty little animal that he is, his finest actions also,

his great and unselfish heroism, his constant daily courage in a harsh world – how strange that these things should be so much finer than his fate on this earth. That has to be somehow made reasonable. Don't tell me that honor is merely a chemical reaction or that a man who deliberately gives his life for another is merely following a behavior pattern. Is God happy with a poisoned cat dying in convulsions behind a billboard? Is God happy that life is cruel and that only the fittest survive? (829–30)

TRASHY, OPPRESSIVE, AND DIMWIT-FRIENDLY

Those who love *Ulysses* find new wonders in it every time they read. To which I say, cool. Read it again and again, you lucky Smart People; you really have it over the rest of us poor peasants who find it to be one long tedious joke, which isn't very funny because it has to be explained.

Orson Scott Card

If it is hard to square this monologue with the stereotype of action-driven pulps, it's because the deeper concerns of genre prose can be as profound as are those of high art, even if expressed through different narrative means. Nor is Chandler's design any less apparent when he draws parallels between God and the artist. An omniscient and omnipotent Creator, he observes, wouldn't have bothered to make the universe at all. "There is no success where there is no possibility of failure, no art without the resistance of the medium." Little wonder why, in a tête-à-tête with his own creator, Marlowe calls him a wise man before bringing up the matter of reversing the pattern.

Playback reverses the pattern whereby only highbrow fiction is said to reflect on serious matters fit for serious artists. Suffering and death, the sociobiology of the soul, Art's role in negotiating a truce with thermodynamic chaos: there is enough intellectual content here to belie the picture of genre fiction as lite entertainment and to befuddle the loyal fans of Marlowe's hardboiled antics. As if on cue, one of them complained: "I missed ... in *Playback* the climate of malevolence and danger, the exotic characterizations, the driving pace and the imaginative mayhem that made Chandler's earlier books masterpieces of that kind."[24]

For the writer, dissent from readers expecting another installment of *Murder, He Wrote* may have been a small price to pay. It is hard, he remarked, "to keep your characters and your story operating on a level which is understandable to the semi-literate public, and at the same time give them some intellectual and artistic overtones which the public does not seek or demand." But there is "a vast difference between writing down to the public ... and doing what you want to do in a form which the public has learned to accept" (Gardiner and Walker 61). What the public had learned to accept was Marlowe at his hardboiled best. What Chandler was after may have had more to do with capping his career with a work that would measure up to his self-image as an artist.

In *Something More Than Night* (1985) Peter Wolfe came up with a draconian interpretation of the multiple ironies that drive the novel's nobrow aesthetics. Accordingly, the countless playbacks of themes and motifs from Chandler's career are mere anomalies, and, because there are so many of them, the novel is an artistic failure. No matter that the consistency and the sheer multiplicity of such "anomalies" indicates that something other than a straight-laced mystery may be afoot. The playbacks so far are, after all, only the beginning. Like Chandler's first books, *Playback* opens with a missing persons case and revives his arch scoundrel, the blackmailer. Like *Farewell, My Lovely*, *The Lady in the Lake*, and *The Long Goodbye*, it features a runaway who changes names as she flees from her old self and life. The place names are familiarly ironic: Rancho Descansado (Relaxo) is as fraught with strife as are the Stillwood Heights in *Farewell, My Lovely* and Idle Valley in *The Long Goodbye*. The see-no-evil, hear-no-evil armistice between the cops and robbers also gives *Playback* the feel of an early Chandler, with strings of power in the hands of Clark Brandon, as they were in Eddie Mars's in *The Big Sleep* and Laird Brunette's in *Farewell, My Lovely*. And if Mitchell is slain by his victim, so were Lindsey Marriott of *Farewell, My Lovely*, Louis Vannier of *The High Window*, and Chris Lavery of *The Lady in the Lake*.

In *The Long Goodbye* Marlowe returns to Terry Lennox the $5,000 bill meant to buy his silence. In *Playback* he turns down a similar $5,000 gift from Betty – then its twin from Brandon. Again in *The Long Goodbye* he shares the night with Linda Loring, who, at the end of *Playback*, resurfaces as his wife-to-be. Throw in the Hammett connection, with Betty lip-synching Brigid and with Spade's lines behind some of Marlowe's, and ask yourself: What are these playbacks all about?[25]

In 1950 Hammett had this to say to the *Los Angeles Times*. "This hard-boiled stuff – it is a menace ... It went all right in the Terrible 20s. The bootlegger days. The racketeering days. There are racketeers now, to be sure, but they are nice, refined people. They belong to country clubs."[26] He was right, of course. The 1950s did mark the twilight of the hardboiled tradition. The difference is that, created in the twilight of the hardboiled tradition, *Playback* was designed to read like it was created in the twilight of the hardboiled tradition. Playing back his own script from the halcyon days of noir, playing back the classics of the genre, playing back his own oeuvre, out of a farewell Marlowe book its author fashioned a farewell bookend to the tough guy school.

With the hardboiled decades drawing to an end, with Prohibition, the Depression, and the Second World War already gone, James Bond and Dr Strangelove made the lone gumshoe in a rumpled fedora look old hat. A half-nostalgic, half-ironic farewell may have appealed to a nobrow artist set to reclaim the middle ground between literary pretentiousness and its lowbrow counterpart. The "mystery story as an art form has been so thoroughly explored," he explained, "that the real problem for a writer now is to avoid writing a mystery story while appearing to do so" (Gardiner and Walker 48). Far from a brainchild of a talent in decline, *Playback* may in fact be so far ahead of the pack that, coming full circle, it only seems like it's lagging behind.

MELODRAMA IS GOOD BUSINESS

Chandler wrote like a slumming angel and invested the sun-blinded streets of Los Angeles with a romantic presence.

Ross Macdonald

In "The Simple Art of Murder" Chandler laid down the law: in crime fiction the hero is everything. In his private notebooks, since released as "Twelve Notes on the Mystery Story," he was equally resolute: the hero of a mystery story is the detective. Everything hangs on his personality: if he hasn't one, you have very little. In Philip Marlowe, a private eye who broke free of the hardboiled type, he created one of the most famous and memorable characters of the twentieth century. The creation proved so vibrant that even its off-stage life become the subject of speculation, eventually leading the author to flesh it out for the public. From a 1951 letter to D.J. Ibberson, catalogued as "The Facts of Philip Marlowe's Life," we learn that the detective is around forty, has no living relatives, did a couple of years of college, was an investigator for an insurance company and for the Los Angeles county DA, is over six feet, and tips the scales at 210 pounds.

More to the point, he is a sensitive, nuanced, and romanticized composite who has precious little in common with real-life gumshoes. Just as his creator scoffed, a real-life PI is a drudge with no more personality than a blackjack and no more moral stature than a stop sign. In contrast, Marlowe has been cast as an urban knight from the first scene on the first page of the first book. Ogling the Sternwood mansion in *The Big Sleep*, the detective pauses before a panel where a knight is rescuing a lady tied to a tree. "I stood there and thought that if I lived in the house, I would sooner or later have to climb up there and help him," he sighs.[27] Questing for truth, Chandler's white knight enacts a pattern common to the detective genre and to what Auden considered its mirror image, the Grail Quest (indeed, in Chandler's second novel the detective searches for Mrs Grayle). Quite a ways, it seems, from Fiedler's women-punching caricature.

Case after case reveals Marlowe to be a sentimentalist with a complex inner life. By the time of *The Long Goodbye* he even admits: "I'm a romantic. I hear voices crying in the night and I go see what's the matter. You don't make a dime that way" (2:651). Crusading for a nominal fee plus expenses, the PI rebuffs all golden handshakes in a test of integrity that forms one of Chandler's perennial motifs. By everyday standards, of course, he is an anachronism. As Parker's Marlowe tells his wife in *Poodle Springs*, "I'm a failure. I don't have any money. In this great Republic that's how the judgement is made, darling" (208).

Bending the rules of the tough guy genre, turning Marlowe into a knight errant sculpted out of a shopworn dick and a redeemer of our urban sins, Chandler was heeding rules of a more pragmatic kind. Melodrama is good business, he owned, "not because I am crazy about melodrama for its own sake but because I am realistic enough to know the rules of the game" (2:1034). For all the hardboiled veneer in *Playback*, the rules of the game demand that crime be investigated by a pure and romantic hero who will triumph in the end – if only after a fashion. The same game rules demands that a couple of durable women, Betty and Helen, flicker with gold underneath the platinum facade. The same rules demand that sex be handled with almost periphrastic delicacy and wrapped up to the sound of music – none other than a march by Mendelssohn.

By the time of *Playback* Chandler was ready to take on another convention, this time one of his own making. In the Addenda to "Twelve Notes" he originally jotted: "Love interest nearly always weakens a mystery," and – assuming Marlowe is a good detective – "A really good detective never gets married." How transgressive to see Marlowe pledge himself to Linda Loring before *Poodle Springs*, a book that was to dwell on the highs and lows of their wedded life. And yet, even as flouting expectations and defying formula are said to be the hallmarks of art, critical opinion shrugs off this unique ending as a narrative misstep, chalking it up to Chandler's dotage and wish fulfillment. Writer gets old, writer gets maudlin, writer himself wants to get married, writer obliges character with a wife – simple enough if you buy this biographical fallacy. Correspondence shows, however, that it was not Chandler but Maurice Guinness who fancied the marriage, lobbying hard to put Marlowe in a situation where he could be wed.[28] The picture of diminishing intellect and creeping sentimentality is further contradicted by the author's doubts about the whole enterprise. "I think I may have misunderstood your desire that Marlowe should get married," he wrote to Guinness in 1959. "A fellow of Marlowe's type shouldn't get married."

Aware of what an unusual book he was crafting, Chandler wrote in 1953 in mock exasperation: "I have 36,000 words of doodling and not yet a stiff. This is terrible" (Gardiner and Walker 236). In fact, *Playback* deviates from crime novel conventions in so many ways that it threatens to become an anti-mystery. There are plenty of guns around, but nobody fires one. With Mitchell presumed dead, there is no formal inquest, and no one is brought to trial. The hero does not uphold the law by nabbing the bad guy – worse, he doesn't even report his findings to the police. Justice is not meted out, either in the legal or even in the poetic sense. Someone, it seems, gets away with murder.

Taking for granted that every crime mystery must have a murder, some interpreters lay Mitchell's disappearance on Brandon, others on Betty. Either way, it would mean that Chandler breaks the rules because either way the presumed murderer goes free. But few notice that, in an ultimate twist for a murder mystery, we don't even get a clear-cut case of murder, although no less than three people – Betty's husband, Mitchell, and Chang – die a sudden death. Although not unheard of, this particular break with the formula is exceedingly rare because, as Chandler himself noted, it leaves a discordant effect not unlike an unresolved chord in music. What might have been a false note in a routine whodunit, however, makes perfect sense in a book that, though "not a traditional parody," sets out to "topple all the fundamental conventions of the genre" (129). Tellingly, even though Peter Rabinowitz's words are actually aimed at the first of Chandler's novels, they apply equally well to the last. Evidence of another playback, perhaps? Possibly, inasmuch as *Big Sleep* and *Playback* are the only books that omit to punish the criminal.

Everything hinges, if course, on what happened to Mitchell. Is Betty a double murderess or a victim of bad luck? Is Brandon the killer or only Betty's gallant saviour? Did he have Mitchell taken care of or did he only take care of his corpse? Here, Chandler's stipulation from "Twelve Notes," that the most effective way to hide a mystery is to place it behind another mystery, is worth a second glance. For, even though Larry's penny-ante grift and blackmail of Betty is a smokescreen for a more lucrative scam to milk the boss gangster, Brandon does not murder Mitchell. Chandler is explicit on this point: the ex-racketeer's only crimes are disposing of a body and hiring a gunman, precluding even a scenario in which Brandon kills Mitchell inadvertently, as in the screenplay.[29]

There seems no escaping it: *Playback* is an anti-mystery, an artertainment whodunit without a dunit. This raises another set of questions. How did Mitchell get into Betty's balcony chair without crossing her room? Why did she see no injuries on him? Does the corpse disappear from the terrace or was it not there in the first place? As speculation mounts, so does the sense that this interpretive limbo is not an accident. When Marlowe asks Betty whether she saw Mitchell dead or whether she made it all up, instead of providing the answer, the next line reads: "The road forked" (806). Appropriately enough, the forking ambiguity will not be resolved. No one will actually see Mitchell – or his body – again. During the showdown with Brandon, Marlowe's reconstruction is purely circumstantial, corroborated by his authority as detective-cum-narrator alone.

Mitchell's death may have been set in motion by drink, misstep, Betty, or a combination thereof. People do, after all, fall over balustrades sometimes. But the timing and *cui prodest* are too convenient not to implicate Brandon, and if the death of the lounge lizard removes an inconvenient problem, then Chang's death removes an inconvenient witness to the removal of the problem's body. Thus if Mitchell's accident is of the premeditated variety, it puts a different spin on the rest of the plot for, if his vanishing act is a murder, it casts a sinister shadow over Chang's death. Mitchell's drunken misstep, on the other hand, bolsters the odds on the watchman's overdose being self-inflicted. In the end, we may never know who killed Larry Mitchell and Ceferino Chang. The more one looks for a solution, the more it appears that Chandler leaves Brandon's hands clean this time, while casting enough lingering suspicion to provoke an endless round of speculation for readers and scholars alike.

PLAYING FOR DIFFERENT STAKES

To be caught with a Raymond Chandler whodunit in hand is a fate that no highbrow reader need dread.

Time (1949)

Is Chandler's fiction art? As always in the case of genre literature, the answer is complicated by ingrained prejudice. In "Chandler and the Reviewers" (1995) J.K. Van Dover distills a quarter century of heat-of-the-moment criticism into the following sober appraisal: "He was defiantly proud of his commitment to the detective story and of his achievement in transforming it to serve his artistic vision, but ironically, public recognition of that achievement evidently depended upon denying its basis" (20). Dover's compilation is useful in documenting how even friendly critics felt obliged to justify Chandler's penchant for hardboiled mystery. Deploring a waste of talent, they beseeched him to leave his gumshoes in the foyer before entering the literary salons.

Knocking genre art for lack of literary mettle is like knocking a diamond for being only a compact lump of carbon. Not that Chandler harboured any illusions. "Once in a long while a detective story writer is treated as a writer, but very seldom," he growled to James Sandoe, crime-lit critic for the *New York Herald-Tribune*. However expertly he writes a mystery story, "it will be treated in one paragraph, while a column and a half of respectful attention will be given to any fourth-rate, ill-constructed, mock-serious account of the life of a bunch of cotton pickers in the deep south" (Gardiner and Walker 48). Today Chandler is slowly gaining recognition for his hardboiled lyricism. But he deserves as much, if not more, recog nition as a cream-of-the-crop regionalist and master of the dialogue and the simile, perhaps unequalled since the days of the metaphysical school of poetry. The Library of America's decision to reprint and shelve him spine to spine with Emerson, James, and Faulkner is only the first step in this direction.

In narrative terms, of course, his genre-busting elements of the hardboiled formula – such as the marriage of a hard-core bachelor – are experiments fraught with dramatic potential. As such they fit with all other unconventional aspects of this unconventional mystery: cross-genre adaptations, intertextual borrowings, self-reflexive asides, metafictional references, playfully deconstructed clichés, authorial intrusions, ironic wordplay, and passages of sociological and existential discourse. In the end Chandler was right to insist that the artistic differences between the canon and the best of popular art are "hardly measurable compared with the gap between the serious novel and any representative piece of Attic literature from the Fourth Century B.C." (Gardiner and Walker 58). For much the same reason, his hero may be a distinct fixture on the hardboiled horizon, but his roots belong to the literary tradition stretching from Natty Bumppo to Huck Finn. Poor, solitary, distrustful of phoney intellectualism, with fistfuls of common sense, a flair for the vernacular, and a heart of gold, he is a literary representative of the race – an American.

Whether his hardboiled classics are art depends ultimately on one's definition of art. In some ways it is hard to call *Playback* a masterpiece. It boasts lines that sound phoney and contrived. It cranks out jack-in-the-box characters who pop in only to disappear without a trace. It shows stitches in the plot, some as big as the helicopter said to spirit Mitchell's carcass away. In the face of these flaws in the diamond, Jerry Speir's eulogy – it is "obviously the product of age and hard work rather than of the facility of youthful talent" (79) – begins to sound a bit like an obituary. No one disputes, of course, that the novel was composed by a mature artist, sure of his craft and his medium. The question is not how much Chandler toiled to whip his screenplay into a novel but, rather, to what effect and with what degree of success. Taking up this question, George N. Dove applies the precepts of formalist aesthetics to the analysis of the structural complexity and innovative plotting from *The Big Sleep* to *Playback*. His conclusion? "Whatever else he did well, Raymond Chandler was a master in the craft of construction" (107).

On balance evidence suggests that, not content merely to relive past glories, the Old Master was playing for different stakes. The proof is in the novel. Look for social commentary, transcendent themes, self-parody, and aesthetic irony, and you'll find them. Look for the criminal jungle, hardboiled attitudes, fast blondes, and hired snoopers, and you'll find them too. But if the latter is all you look for, you'll go home let down by this nobrow neither-fish-nor-fowl. That is why, with its artertaining turn to irony and parody, *Playback* slipped through the fingers of Chandler loyalists and the sophisticates like Fiedler who went slumming to confirm their bias. Perhaps they should have listened to Auden, who, likely with Chandler in mind, wrote: "I must be careful not to get hold of a detective story for, once I begin one, I cannot work or sleep till I have finished it."[30]

A thrilling ride it is, especially for those whose hearts beat faster when the *Scientific American* arrives each month. Lem has learned the formulae of fictional suspense almost too well ... his love of sheer compilation (reflected here in his thoroughly worked-out portraits of the numerous middle-aged victims of "The Chain of Chance"), or the selfless enthusiasm long ascribed to the scientifically-minded communicates an Olympian playfulness.

John Updike, "Lem and Pym"

Would a farmer kill the goose that lays golden eggs? Would a fiction writer divorce himself from fiction? If you take these truths to be self-evident, then the strange cases of Arthur Conan Doyle, Karel Čapek, John McDonald, Thomas M. Dish, Nelson DeMille, and countless others prove that some creators care less for filling their coffers with gold than for the opportunity to pursue their artistic ambitions. And Stanislaw Lem may be the strangest case of all. In 1986, at the peak of his popularity, he released *Fiasco*, a novel chock full of echoes and outright references to a googolplex of themes and motifs from his career. Then, overnight, he stopped writing fiction of any kind and has maintained that self-imposed moratorium ever since.

There is something baffling and defiant about breaking away from literature after decades of popular and critical accolades. After all, Lem commands front-page spreads in the *New York Times Book Review* and feature reviews in the *New Yorker*. The *New York Times* hails him as a modern version of Swift or Voltaire, as one of the deep spirits of our age, and the London *Times* insists his novels should carry a government health warning: "The Reading of this Book is Good for You." Critics laud him as the Borges of scientific culture and, even more remarkably, a science fiction Bach. National and international institutions shower him with honorary doctorates, and his books are required school reading in his native Poland. Scholars from the United States to the United Kingdom, from Russia to Germany, from Japan to Canada declare him a literary movement in himself, compiling dissertations as well as bibliographies that run into hundreds of pages in all the major and dozens of minor languages of Europe, Asia, and the Americas.

Yet such extravagant tributes to this literary genius conceal the full extent of his intellectual legacy, for Lem is more than just a literary phenomenon. A Renaissance polymath, he is also a social critic par excellence, a respected philosopher of science, and a much sought-after futurologist. Many European and American scientists, including Carl Sagan and Douglas Hofstadter, and philosophers from Daniel Dennett to Nicolas Rescher, have professed their respect for Lem's writings. His cyber-evolutionary scenarios have been debated at the interdisciplinary INSTRAT workshop, with philosophers, sociologists, linguists, and cognitive scientists in attendance. In 1971 he was the only non-scientist invited to join the Soviet-American Conference on Extra-Terrestrial Intelligence (CETI).

Recipient of various European state prizes, Lem is the bestselling author in Germany and Russia, where his status is legendary. With worldwide sales pushing thirty five million and translations in more than forty languages, he is one of the most successful writers of the twentieth century. Praised in the United States by John Updike, Kurt Vonnegut, and Joyce Carol Oates, Lem's art attracts equal plaudits from East Coast critics like Ted Solotaroff and Leslie Fiedler (the same who spared Chandler no tar and feathers). Just about the only form of international acclaim that has eluded him is the Nobel Prize, although for years now he has been short-listed for this honour. All the same, the transatlantic consensus that he *ought* to get it is an open secret. The *New York Times* has long ago pronounced him "worthy of a Nobel Prize," and the *Philadelphia Inquirer* insists that, "If he isn't considered for a Nobel Prize ... it will be because somebody told the judges that he writes science fiction."[1]

A long-time member of the Commission Poland 2000, a think tank division of the Polish Academy of Sciences, Lem has hosted dozens of TV series as a national spokesman on contemporary culture and science. There are German, Polish, Czech, Russian, and French adaptations of his novels for the cinema, not counting the Soderbergh/Clooney "thirty years later" remake of the 1972 Cannes-prized film by Andrei Tarkovsky, itself based on Lem's best known novel, *Solaris* (1961).[2] Although typecast in North America as a sci-fi maven, Lem has written contemporary novels, poetry, detective fiction, fantasy, experimental prose, literary theory and criticism, scientific treatises, sociological and cultural analyses, philosophy, futurology, autobiography, television and radio plays, film scripts, and multiple volumes of polemical writings. Fame, renown, editions of collected works in Russia, Germany, Poland, Japan – and then, suddenly, nothing.

In 1984, when asked to sum up his own early hit, *The Moviegoer*, Walker Percy answered without hesitation: "a novel of ideas as well as, I hope, a good novel in its own right."[3] No words could better describe Lem's *The Chain of Chance*. As gripping today as when it first appeared in print, the recipe for its longevity is deceptively simple: a blend of cliff-hanger narration and sophisticated, science-smart philosophy. Given the acclaim and respect Lem commands worldwide, this major novel from his mature period should by now have received its share of critical nods and learned debates, but such is not the case. When I put it to him, Lem only shook his head, equally mystified by his nobrow masterpiece's limited circulation. What is it about this bloody page-turner – one that happens to be a perfect vehicle for an experimental and cerebral novel of ideas – that makes the *apocalittici* and the *integrati* alike ignore it altogether?

HEART OF THIS ARCHITECTURAL LABYRINTH

This labyrinthine way to public recognition is itself a good illustration of one of the recurring themes in Lem's work: the irreducible role of chance in every complex development...

Bernd Gräfrath

Towards the end of the 1960s, roughly around the time of Lem's *His Master's Voice* (1968) and *A Perfect Vacuum* (1971), a significant mutation began to take effect. Until then the author still peopled his fictions with relatively conventional agents – if one can call mortal engines or clouds of cybernetic micro-symbionts conventional – and charted their combinatorial potential within relatively linear plots. Now his stories would undergo transformations of a twofold variety. In the variant maximum, individual heroes would more and more often cede the spotlight to that belligerent and self-destructive species, Homo sapiens.[4] In the variant minimum, wholly hero-less narratives would become vehicles for ideas, paradoxes, and theories often of a decidedly non-literary bent. The plots, too, would diverge on either side of conventional, becoming baroquely (if not cosmically) playful or else radically thinned out, sometimes straight into non-existence.

A Perfect Vacuum, Lem's book of ungranted narrative wishes, is arguably his most daring literary experiment in a career driven by experimentation. It is also a textbook example of the new Lem: a metafiction sampler of imaginary reviews, narrative précis, plot treatments, and whatnot. It includes the minimalistic "Rien du tout, ou la conséquence," a made-up review of a non-existent *nouveau roman* – the first "ever to reach the limit of what writing can do" (69) – by a made-up French romancier, Mme Solange Marriot. Plotless, heroless, and narrativeless, just like the plotless, heroless, and narrativeless new "novel" under review, Lem's story is word become flesh: a metafictional critique of a fictive avant-garde fiction. In contrast, projected onto a canvas the size of the Metagalaxy, the final piece in the collection, "The New Cosmogony," represents the variant maximum.[5] In the guise of a Nobel acceptance speech, this story-as-theory unveils a cosmological model in which multiple Player civilizations shape the physical laws of the universe in an eons-old game of "Sim-Cosmos."

The Chain of Chance, experimental in its own write, lies outside this metafictional vein, which, in addition to *A Perfect Vacuum*, comprises *Imaginary Magnitude* (1973), *Golem XIV* (1973), *Prowokacja* (1984), and *One Human Minute* (1986).[6] This short novel seems to have all the elements of a quintessential genre fare, framed as it is around a resonant mystery, a linear structure that builds up to a cliff-hanging climax, and a clear resolution. It boasts a conventional, if not typical, hero, who, in the course of events, distinguishes himself with feats of courage, perseverance, and self-sacrifice. Its central theme, albeit scientific and brainy, brings the sundry elements of its mystery thrillethon into a nail-biting focus. It's hard to predict which elements will only bring the reader to the edge of the seat and which will send him over the edge. The nerve-racking simulation of a dead man? The suicide bombing? The post-mortem of a series of bizarre deaths? The hallucinatory psychosis climaxing in a suicidal seizure?

The action is set in the present, around the time of publication in 1976 (first English edition 1978). The discrepancies that reveal that it is an alternative present are few and far between. We learn only in passing that the United States has sent manned missions to Mars; the Eiffel Tower, amid a forest of high-rises, is about to be scrapped; and Rome boasts a new airport equipped with a state-of-the-art architectural anti-terrorist design. The common thread between the locations in Naples, Rome, and Paris is the investigation that gradually – until Paris, almost guardedly – unveils the details of the case, with the haunting effect of Poe on laudanum. From page one there's something unnerving about the story that goes beyond the protagonist wearing the clothes of a dead man or looking over his shoulder in the hope of forcing a rendezvous with death. Yet, if his behavior in Naples makes little sense, it makes even less en route to Rome. Driving tubeless, he insists on buying an inner tube; armed with a reservation, he checks a dozen hotels for a vacancy; a page for someone named Adams sends him into a tizzy.

Before he can board the plane to Paris, John (we never learn his last name) nearly loses his life in a terrorist attack. Although the revamped Rome airport is believed impregnable to assault, a Japanese suicide bomber detonates a corundum grenade in the heart of this architectural labyrinth. As the blast mangles passengers into a hail of flesh and blood, John saves the life of a young girl, diving over the balustrade to avoid the shock wave. Much later, in Paris, the hero sits down with Dr Barth to recount the chain of deaths that brought him to Naples in the first place. In the hope that the French computer expert can help salvage the investigation, John itemizes, in almost archival detail, the psychotic episodes that have reduced eleven men to self-mutilation and suicide. One of them drank iodine and died of internal burns. Another slashed himself with a razor; yet another with a chunk of glass. Someone hurled himself out of the window, another shot himself in the mouth, another (a champion swimmer) drowned. Still another, a car-lover, wandered head-on into busy highway traffic ...

During the conference in Barth's study a pattern begins to emerge, consistent but impenetrable. All victims are male, single, around fifty, tall, burly, balding, allergic, and non-diabetic. In short, they are just like John, an ex-NASA astronaut from the Mars program, whose Naples mission was to retrace the last steps of the last victim in the series, a fellow American by the name of Adams. But John's gun-for-hire trials are only beginning. Ahead of him are a brush with traffic death on the nighttime streets of Paris, a Byzantine testimony at the Sûreté that blows the cover off France's WMD research, and a suicidal hallucinatory trip triggered by a chain of chance as elusive as that which had killed the previous victims.

A WHODUNIT WITH PROBABILITY AS THE BUTLER

The intermixing of genres so typical of postwar literature can also be seen in [Lem's] science fiction, which is sometimes difficult to distinguish from philosophical treatises.

Czesław Miłosz

In under 200 slender pages, Lem takes the reader through a mosaic of styles and genres that would have buried a lesser artist. *The Chain of Chance* is at once a medical thriller, one of the best in this exacting subgenre; a private eye mystery, understated in the obligatory first-person vernacular; and a taut investigative drama, developed with the unpredictability that has become the author's hallmark. It is also a provocative and thought-provoking philosophical *roman* to be pondered long after the last goose bump has vanished.

For a connoisseur of mysteries there is something incongruous about a whodunit with probability as the butler. No matter how intricate the plot-line or how sly the denouement, some genre rules are just inviolable. With Holmes on the case – whether dressed up as Brother William of Baskerville, Inspector Treviranus, or Lucas Corso – murder must "out." Even police procedurals, the most naturalistic of crime fictions, don't let the bad guys slip free. Although the success rate of real-life homicide investigations has dipped of late to only about two out of three, even the most street-savvy writers like Ed McBain bow to this sacrosanct rule of the game. To catch readers off guard, most artists cast least suspect individuals as perps in an anti-convention by now no less entrenched than the original. As a result, ground-breaking shows like *Prime Suspect* take advantage of the secondary convention by bucking *its* premise.

But Lem is something else again. Not content with simply bending the rules, he stands the genre on its head by dispensing with the culprit altogether. Even as he trots out the standard moves and countermoves of a police inquiry, he casts chance, intrinsic in the laws of thermodynamics, as the antagonist, subverting not only the structural but the moral imperative of detective literature: the meting out of justice. There is no criminal justice to be administered when dead men are victims of random events rather than foul play.

Hard as it is to classify *The Chain of Chance* as a crime story, or at least a conventional crime story, it is harder still to classify it as science fiction – a quarter century of publishing inertia notwithstanding. Lem has frequently complained of marketers who lump his books with science fiction even when they have little in common with the space opera lampooned so enthusiastically by *Mystery Science Theatre 3000*. His protagonist is, of course, given to reminiscing about his role in the Mars mission. However, ex-astronauts are not science fiction but science fact. After the Apollo 11 moon shot, for example, Michael Collins left NASA to become director of the National Air and Space Museum, while Buzz Aldrin became president of Starcraft Enterprises in Laguna Beach, California.[7] In fact, the Mars landing excepted, the book is so realistic and contemporary that Lem himself avowed he is "ready to accept it on face value."[8]

Its nobrow novelty is equally apparent if you approach *The Chain of Chance* as an action thriller or, conversely, as a philosophical *conte*. Even as it doles out menace and violence by the bucketful, Lem's probabilistic plot rewrites the book on the action genre, standing out like Long John Silver on the dance floor amid the latter's threadbare menu of espionage conspiracies and high-level cabals. Its raison d'être is a socio-scientific thesis, a philosophical thought experiment, and a model of a civilization that functions in the manner of Brownian molecules. Governed by implacable statistical laws we dwell, reflects the author, in a "world of random chance, in a molecular and chaotic gas whose 'improbabilities' are amazing only to the individual human atoms. It's a world where yesterday's rarity becomes today's cliché, and where today's exception becomes tomorrow's rule" (188–9). With not a line of dialogue until a quarter of the way through, and only a few pages of speech in the first hundred, it may indeed be the most highbrow thriller in history.

Next to a typical *roman philosophique*, with its anaemic plot, cardboard characters, and leisurely narration, *Chain* again proves its singularity. Its unique brand of statistical philosophy feeds on gruesome and bizarre deaths, drug-induced psychoses, mutilated corpses, a spooky impersonation of a dead victim, and the brooding peril of chemical warfare research. The action races like a sprinter's heartbeat, the plot is relentless, the locations worthy of a James Cook guide, and the first-person voice-over gives it an immediacy more typical of Chandler's noir. Though more cerebral, the hero is immediately identifiable as a space-age Marlowe. The HBJ translation obscures some of the jitterbug pacing and the hard-nosed flavour of the original, but in the Polish text John's report of the

Naples mission is as hardboiled as they come. Barebones exposition, colloquial diction, lines whittled to a want-ad minimum, and the deadpan, unflappable attitude roll from the page like the devil's parody of the movies (to quote Edmund Wilson's grudging tribute to James Cain). If Rome was not too hot for a trench coat, you could almost hear John's side-of-the-mouth drawl from behind a raised collar.

With a likeable hero, hardboiled narration, and enough carnage to hook the generation raised on *American Psycho*, Lem's book is a commercial publisher's dream and a philosopher's envy. His touch is unerring, perhaps nowhere more so than during John's counsel with Barth on the interim status of the investigation. What in the hands of a lesser artist might have become a plodding chronology inundated by archival detail, in Lem's hands is a thirty-page heart-stopper. It is clear that, had he devoted his life to crime literature, he would have been as successful as he was in science fiction, at least according to the verdict of the French littèrateurs. While American booksellers barcoded *Chain of Chance* as science fiction, France honoured this nobrow thriller with the national prize for the best *detective* novel of 1975–78.

A BOOK ABOUT OTHER BOOKS

There are few masterpieces even in English and French literature. A great part of the "classics" in these literatures is second or perhaps even third rate stuff.

D.W. Brogan

"I do not consider myself an SF writer. The question of genres is simply unimportant to me" (3), shrugged Lem when interviewed by Raymond Federman in 1981. It is a safe bet, however, that you'll find *The Chain of Chance* discussed as science fiction, when discussed at all. It's not difficult to understand why Milton scholars would balk at reading sci-fi thrillers. Satan may be an arch villain and an archetypal conspirator, but he has the good aesthetic sense to stay away from time cops, galactic fleet shootouts, or aliens with pointy ears and Beverly Hills accents. On the other hand, miscued by the publisher's sci-fi blurb, genre enthusiasts will think twice before reaching for a scientific mind-twister in a market overrun by clones of Star Wars empires and x-Files pseudo-mysteries.

The ingredients should by now be familiar: a writer who deliberately positions himself outside the highbrow/lowbrow rhetoric, a book that refuses to comply with convention and formula, and artistic novelty obscured by genre prejudice. Read worldwide for his science fiction, revered among academics for his metaliterary innovation, Lem denies both groups of admirers their fill. Even in Poland discussions of *The Chain of Chance* rarely venture outside the "second-helping" comparison with its significant other, *The Investigation* (see Chapter 3). If one does not count plot synopses dressed up as analyses, then no one outside Europe has come close to giving it a fair critical shake, either. Too pulpy for the intellectuals, too intellectual for the masses, Lem's philosophy as artertainment falls through the cracks in the literary system to rest on top of *War with the Newts* and *Playback*.

With the motley of modes and genres forming the outer layer of this aesthetic onion, within lies an experiment spanning sixteen years: an intertextual dialogue with its older literary twin. Like Eco's *Name of the Rose* or Pérez-Reverte's *Club Dumas*, Lem's nobrow parable on statistical order in chaos is a book about other books, a fiction that comments on another fiction. "The first version does not satisfy me completely, even though it is quite decently constructed and generates a great deal of suspense ... *The Chain of Chance* is better because it is plausible," he wrote.[9] With these words the author describes perhaps the most remarkable episode of his career, wherein, after sixteen years of reflection, he returned to the philosophy of chance first fleshed out in *The Investigation*. Lem has repeatedly avowed that he does not write with a ready-made outline in hand. The disconcerting opening of *Solaris*, for instance, came without advance knowledge of what would befall Kelvin on board the station. But, as in many other respects, *Chain* breaks with the pattern. Revealed the writer in a 1979 questionnaire: "I knew from the start precisely what I was after: a 'rational' variant of *The Investigation*."[10]

This is not to say that even the rational variant was planned out from A to Z. Having completed Part 1 (the simulation in Naples) and Part 3 (the Paris inquiry), the author searched for years for a bridge between them, finally settling on the suicide bombing in Rome. All the same, it's not hard to recognize in *The Chain of Chance* the same brain-teaser that drove the plot of *The Investigation*, with the ghoulish intervention of indeterminacy – not on the subatomic scale but on the macro-level of workaday lives – as the narrative frame. The complex aesthetics of this cross-novelistic experiment could have come from Borges's "Pierre Menard," with either text changing the interpretive context of its twin, back and forth and back again. Underscoring the sequential and cumulative nature of this creative process, in *Lem i inni* (1990) Andrzej Stoff even coined a name for this type of intertextuality: "anthologism" (86).

Are the two novels really one, then – a literary calf with two heads? According to the familiar reduction, genre fictions, and thus crime mysteries, are all alike: you've read one, you've read them all. Were that true, as quasi-detective mysteries – based on the same narrative premise to boot – Lem's literary "twins" ought to be practically indistinguishable. The fallacy of the conclusion attests once again to the fallacy of the premise. From the fact that neither thriller could exist without the detective formula, it does not follow that they are nothing but formula.

An old-fashioned mystery, especially with ancestry as distinguished as that found in *The Chain of Chance*, is, in fact, a perfect vehicle for intellectual thrust and parry. Like an artistic yin and an entertainment yang, the stochastic philosophy behind the book's premise may, in fact, have determined the choice of literary genre. In an emblematic nobrow fashion, Lem's philosophy of statistic fluctuations is developed in terms of a classic mystery subgenre – the "locked chamber" mystery – insofar as neither appears to have a rational solution. With Poe's "Murders in the Rue Morgue," Leroux's *Le Mystère de la Chambre Jaune*, and Sjöwall and Wahlöö's *The Locked Room* defining the parameters of locked-room crime, placing John in Adams's death bed, with the door "locked from the inside and the windows hermetically sealed" (29), Lem proves he is no stranger to the formula.

At the same time, as he reiterated to me in a recent e-mail, the end result sabotages the very same formula. Where other writers display their chops by spiriting malfeasers out of locked rooms, Lem machines the walls out of probability, turning the genre (of which he admits to being an avid reader) inside out. Other nobrow creators have also been drawn to mystery of this apparently insoluble, because apparently irrational, type. But not even John Fowles's "The Enigma" can match the scientific precision of Lem's double take, in which astronomical odds ignite a macabre chain of chance.[11] Murder cannot out where there is no murder; a criminal mastermind cannot be caught where there's no mind, only happenstance.

TERRORISM IS NOT A HARDWARE ISSUE

More than any time in history, mankind faces a crossroads. One path leads to despair and utter hopelessness. The other, to total extinction. Let us pray we have the wisdom to choose correctly.

Woody Allen

Far from dying out, terrorism AD 2005 is more bloody, media-tailored, and wanton then ever. Nor, as I pointed out several years before the 9/11, Madrid, and London bombings, is there a quick "instrumental" fix for its menace. This is because terrorism is not a hardware issue.[12] The facile and self-serving doctrine that the threat will vanish if only more money is pumped into security measures has no basis in reality. As widespread as this type of thinking is in political and military circles, throwing truckloads of cash after a problem does not guarantee a solution. After all, according to the same Bigger-is-Better mindset, since one infantryman digs a foxhole in two hours, 200 should do the job in a minute.

Right up to the 1960s, for example, airport security was laughably lax by our standards. Visitors could walk up to planes sitting on the tarmac, often popping inside for a last minute hug. The fact that such a permissive attitude bred relatively few terrorist assaults strongly indicates that it is the ideological "software" programmed and educated over at least a generation that controls the behavior of suicide bombers – not escalating security measures. Terrorism will always inflict casualties as long as there are people ready to kill and die for a cause. The kamikaze attack in *The Chain of Chance* is no different. The latest security technology protecting Rome's state-of-the-art terminal proves utterly inadequate to preventing mayhem.

But things will only get worse. In our world, rocked increasingly often by terrorist explosions, be it the sun-baked streets of the Middle East or downtown USA, it is taken for granted that there must exist a connection between the target and the reason for the attack. Israel knows what the blood of its innocent civilians is payment for: military occupation in contempt of UN resolutions. But things will not stay so clear-cut for long. Violence is bound to turn even more wanton and indiscriminate because, following the law of diminishing returns, each terrorist strike must surpass the last in horror and outrage in order to steal the media spotlight. But what can be more horrendous than carnage that's wholly gratuitous, detached from any political goals the attackers might hope to win?

That's why in the topsy-turvy world of *The Chain of Chance*, and increasingly in our own, anybody can be made to pay for anything. That's why no one in the novel claims responsibility for the Rome bombing, and that's why the Japanese suicide seems to have had no particular motive for striking at this particular airport. Not crazy enough, asks Lem? How about a "New Zealand tourist [who] had tried to protest the kidnapping of an Australian diplomat in Bolivia by hijacking a charter plane in Helsinki that was carrying pilgrims bound for the Vatican" (135). Senseless? Irrational? Perhaps.

Rationality, of course, is usually modelled on a one-dimensional axis, with perfect rationality and irrationality at either pole. In truth, rationality is a much more complex and heterogeneous attribute than is usually imagined, and departures from it may scatter in many directions. Irrationality can indicate, for example, an inconsistent value system, faulty reasoning, inability to communicate, or simply inability to communicate efficiently. It may imply arbitrary decisions or merely reflect the collective nature of decision making among individuals who do not have identical value systems and whose organizational structure and communication system make them act with less than perfect unity.[13]

Bizarre and counter-intuitive as it may seem, it can be quite rational to desire to be irrational in order to gain tactical leverage over one's adversary. That's why, during the Paris talks to determine the face-saving exit from Vietnam – roughly contemporary with the genesis of Lem's novel – Kissinger-as-the-voice-of-reason and Nixon-as-the-madman played the diplomatic version of Good Cop, Bad Cop. You may not like the secretary of state or the treaty in his briefcase, until you face the alternative: "irrational" president looking for a pretext for more carpet bombing of your country. Generalized to most threat situations, many standard attributes of rationality can become disabilities against an opponent who is impervious to punitive threats by virtue of real or feigned inability to function rationally. This is why children, madmen, fanatics, and doomsday machines cannot be bullied as effectively as can agents with a certifiable ability to hear, comprehend, and act freely. On the other hand, threat efficacy increases proportionately to perceived irrationality. Far from being an inherent quality, rationality is really a function of one's ability to make decisions, and, as such, it can to a degree be manipulated. Iraqi kidnappers who threaten to slay the hostages unless their demands are met, then cut communications, render themselves impervious to counter-threats, shifting the burden for the victim's life onto the recipients of the ultimatum.

Today's fictional chains of events could be tomorrow's newsreels, as headline-grabbing violence, fanned by the victim mentality of its perpetrators, continues to spin out of control. The escalating culture of victimization, manifest across the social spectrum from crass terrorism to militant political correctness (often in the name of academic ideologies) is one of the chronic ills of our times. It is this mentality that forms the biggest threat to our future because it arms people with a will to wreak vengeance, and where there's a will, there's a way. That's why pilots in bandoliers and metal detectors in every school will not put an end to hatred, bigotry, and violence. The sooner governments and security czars accept this, the sooner we can start tackling the real reasons why, in the words of one perplexed citizen, "they all hate us so much."

So much for the sole form of terrorism that makes its way into the media. But the picture would not be complete without a mention of state terrorism, which today is as rampant as ever. It needn't even mean sponsoring acts of violence or invading sovereign states in the name of fighting communism or world terror. Crass or subtle, the purpose is the same: intimidation. Just as post-Second World War Finland dared not breathe too hard for fear of the Russian bear, so these days no one makes a move without reckoning with the American grizzly. After the dissolution of the USSR, overnight Ukraine found itself a nuclear power, brazenly willing to negotiate – in effect blackmail – for itself a better deal in the Crimea and in the Black Sea fleet. Terror, after all, can be sown by simply raising the possibility of an act, or even "inadvertently" revealing one's capacity for attack or retaliation to the other side.

YOU, ME, PULSARS, AND THE PAGE YOU'RE READING

[Lem] is one of the most intelligent, erudite, and comic writers working today.

Anthony Burgess

Whatever else good literature is, it is also a trip-wire system sensitive enough to detect social problems before they reach crisis proportions. Lem's thriller proves just that, prescient with regard to the spectre of the war industry and militarized science. It is true that most of the novel's victims perish owing to a chance combination of innocuous chemicals catalyzed by cyanide in roasted almonds. Yet their lethal synergy is more than a forensic curiosum: it's a matter of life and death for all – that much becomes apparent from the hush-hush testimony about developed nations' chemical WMDs. Vetted by a high ranking Sûreté functionary, this labyrinthine piece of intelligence is released in a pre-recorded statement, absolving anyone of responsibility for its incendiary contents. As the reels turn, John and Barth learn how far along France is in the international race to fabricate new technologies of battlefield murder.

We do not refer to wartime killings as murder because national propaganda justifies the taking of human lives as a patriotic necessity. But what if patriotic necessity arises in times of peace and brooks the murder of civilians? Even Bosch's Garden of Earthly Delights pales next to this vision of mass murder cooked up in weapon laboratories. Armed with the conscience-cleansing, "It's a well-known fact that every nation loves peace and makes plans for war" (152), the world is scrambling to perfect the Satan bug. Obsessed with refining Compound X, the book's Dr Dunant personifies modern science funded by five-star generals. According to the police report, the French researcher sent an innocent man to his death, hoping to obtain a million times more deadly form of the drug. The killing is technically a suicide since the local optician keeps maiming himself until he expires. But the macabre signature of the compound, which propels people towards paranoid dementia and suicide, is unmistakable.

The research into chemical and biological weapons of mass destruction is, of course, no secret. The extent of the hypocrisy is. With the Cold War won squarely by the West – or so we're told – funding for the military is rocketing sky high: annually more than four-tenths of a *trillion* dollars for the United States versus a mere forty billion for Russia. Seems the war was hardly worth winning. Prescient to a fault, Lem hangs a giant question mark after two things most of us take for granted: access to information and civil rights. Prominently, this includes information about scientific experiments that may impinge upon the population at large. This is not paranoia – or, if you think it is, remember that sometimes even paranoiacs are targets of conspiracies. After Watergate, Irangate, and Iraqi WMD-gate, with renegades in control of the highest echelons of policy making, no one doubts that they can operate with almost blanket impunity. After the H-bombing of Bikini and the mass murder of the indigenes downwind from the fallout; after programs in which army personnel were covertly infected with syphilis to monitor the pace of the disease; after illegal experiments on civilian groups with hallucinogens, radiation exposure, pathogens-like nerve gases, and the like; who can blame the distrustful?

Lem is too seasoned an artist, of course, to reduce these complex issues to a high-noon standoff between the forces of good (i.e., innocent citizenry) and the devilry of military technocrats. Civilization's malfunctions can manifest themselves as deliberate "rips" in the societal fabric – terrorism, kidnapping, no-holds-barred weapons research, even all-out war. But they can assume other forms – more insidious because chronic in nature – that can prove equally tough to remedy. We may find ourselves as much at the mercy of terrorist cells as we are at the mercy of the cumulative effects of everyday events, innocuous and almost unnoticed until they are upon us. Greenhouse effect, ozone depletion, mercury or pesticides in the food chain, estrogen from contraceptives infiltrating the water system, disrupting reproductive cycles and even gender in fish ...

Globalization means more than Hollywood blockbusters playing in theatres from Kinshasa to Hong Kong or a hemisphere-spanning network of trade treaties. It means a World Wide Web of interconnections between causes and effects, sometimes so indirect as to be outside anyone's grasp. Decades back who would have believed that a fiscal meltdown in Mexico would one day panic the G-8 group into an international bailout? Or that a bear market in Tokyo could trigger sell-offs and layoffs from Canada to Madagascar? Or that a hike in crude futures could race around the world leaving stalled economies, tumbling investments, and teeming bankruptcies in its wake? These days the news of such precarious interdependence is no longer news. World civilization crawls all over the surface of the planet, complexified beyond anyone's ability to track or control. And like a parasite that grows with its host, the probability of statistical exceptions recombining in a deadly chain of chance grows, as the Polish writer cautions, into mathematical certainty.

As a philosopher Lem is intrigued by social phenomena (including terrorist pathology) that emerge when society reaches a certain stage of complexity. Specifically he examines what may happen when society exceeds a certain *quantitative* threshold. The simple rise in numbers of human ants can produce regularities that transcend geographic, ideological, or economic specifics. Unobtrusively, with no fireworks or commemorative T-shirts, our technological civilization has crossed the brink of complexity beyond which its coping strategies begin to look increasingly impotent. Planned by none, hated by all, wretched results of numerical explosion turn, for example, the ideals of urban development into concrete playgrounds, snarled traffic, air-quality alerts, crime waves, pothole slaloms, toxic rivers, and toxic 'hoods. Crawling alongside other Rome-bound cars, John absorbs news flashes that mirror the chaos on the autostrada. Demonstrations, buildings on fire, terrorist threats, and the underground's vows of more unrest is how we, evolved beings, pass the days in our ever more crowded hives. John's gesture is familiar to all city commuters: "I shut off the radio as if slamming shut a garbage chute" (11).

Stripped of Enlightenment oratory, civilization means bumper-to-bumper traffic, din and pollution, a deregulated climate, and a succession of fiscal crises. A steady diet of traffic chaos and urban anarchy confirm a simple socio-statistical thesis: the more complex the social machine, the more prone to malfunction. Artfully weaving chance and probability into the murder-mystery plot, *The Chain of Chance* models the novel ways in which stochastic (i.e., those involving huge numbers) regularities stalk us in the third millennium. They arise spontaneously out of the individually indeterminate behavior of human atoms purely by virtue of the system having passed a numerically critical mass. If your barbecue tank has measurable properties, such as pressure or temperature, it is because they also arise out of the chaotic Brownian movements of propane (hydrocarbon) molecules. Lem, one might say, is a social scientist looking at civilization as a Brownian system.

Children of causality, we cannot but inquire into the reasons behind events around us. Answers to the perennial "Why?" give us a sense of understanding and control. We seek causality in our private and social lives and, not least, in scientific theories. After all, to understand something has always meant to account for the causes that brought it into existence.[14] And yet, only decades ago, this picture of the world at its most basic level began a swift journey to the scrap heap. The elementary "design" of reality, reported experiment after experiment, was far more counterintuitive than anyone imagined. Quantum physics, an assembly of some of the most successful theories ever formulated and put into practice, instructs us that at some VERY small level causal questions cease to be meaningful.

Einstein's noble duel with Bohr notwithstanding, the world – including you, me, pulsars, and the page you're reading – is at bottom unpredictable and indeterministic. Knowing it, of course, is one thing; accepting it, another. On the evidence of our senses the world of human beings *is* different from the world of quantum packets, where unpredictability comes out of the woods so dramatically. After all, the world as we know it, full of human-scale objects like cabbages and crocodiles, works in terms of cause and effect. Stubborn in the face of defeat, gut-level anthropocentrism insists that we lie beyond the pale of statistical fluctuations.

Lem's point is simple and startling: just like uranium isotopes, we are governed by atomic laws in which probability and statistical macro-effects can forge macabre chains of chance. For a scientist or philosopher this gut-level disquietude (if not full-scale disbelief) has been settled with $\Delta x \Delta p \geq h/2\pi$. Better known as the Uncertainty Principle, this cornerstone of quantum lore states that, no matter how keen the observer and how sophisticated the apparatus, some things are forever unknowable – in this case the simultaneous position and momentum of a particle. But in literature Lem's one-of-a-kind thriller is the first to investigate seriously what this might portend on the human scale. The deathly chain of chance indicates how our fates may be governed not by individual decisions but by much less obvious statistical coincidences. Next time you go to a seaside resort to take mineral baths, rub ointments in your scalp, and munch on roasted almonds, you could be signing your death warrant. But there is no point in staying away from seaside spas or light snacks. Ever the breezy Cassandra, Lem makes it plain that, if this chain of events doesn't get you, sooner or later an even less probable one will.

A BOOK DESIGNED AS A CATEGORY-SMASHER

I speak of the whole *habitus* of the intellectual and its agents, which ... results in the fact that serious aesthetic attention is not given to works of popular art; so that even when such works have significant aesthetic quality, it tends to go unnoticed or minimalized, which only reinforces the basic dismissive attitude toward such art and its artists.

Richard Shusterman

If most pulp thriller heroes are athletic gun-toting lady-killers, then John – fifty something, balding, gaining weight, and without a female lead swooning on his arm – is as remote from the stereotype as the stereotype is remote from reality.[15] A calculated reversal of the formula? Lem disingenuously disavowed any design to subvert it: "I have no idea what a thriller hero looks like so I couldn't have had it in mind writing *Katar*."[16] Yet the question is open in the face of a whole row of such departures from the genre. A man without a name until two-thirds into the book, John Doe is an anonymous cog in the series of odds-busting events without a mind or reason. The author's reticence about his protagonist is wholly in accordance with his theme. Stripped of names and identities, you and I, John, and John's creator are no more than society's atoms. At the beck of forces larger than us, like atoms we are interchangeable and expendable, acting out social roles scripted by the chaotic if often deterministic whirl of events around us.

Try as John does to check the vexing property of the best laid plans to go awry, his chances of success are zero. Chaos and delays slip into the meticulously laid out timetable in Naples; there is chaos on the approach road to Rome, chaos at the airport ... Amid this bedlam a life may even be saved in a heroic fashion, if chance were to toss out snake eyes for a couple of social atoms. Luckily for Anabelle, John's arm sweeps her into safety, but, as the hero maintains during the debriefing, someone else could have been in her (and his) place. Another time, another hero would be saving another lucky survivor from the blast. Lem's Olympian detachment fits a writer-as-social-scientist who studies the movements of his characters under the narrative microscope. For all his personable traits John is, after all, little more than a Brownian particle or a billiard ball set in motion, bouncing off others. Just as a billiard ball is unaware of forces that make it carom this or that way, so John is subject to forces that, improbable to the extreme, arise all the same simply because they are not impossible.

If all this makes John look like not much of a thriller hero, then *The Chain of Chance* looks like not much of a thriller. And if thrillers are paraliterature, then Lem's paraliterature is pressed into the service of a philosophy in which every burst of violence fortifies the supremacy of accident and chance. Adapting the action genre format, *The Chain of Chance* flouts its formulae even on the last page, where, in a classic highbrow artifice, it draws metanarrative attention to itself as a book written by the narrator as a post facto record of the events. And what a record it is. It's not for nothing that theorists of the hardboiled genre get so much mileage out of the word-play on "I" and "eye." It's par for the course that, in the heat of action, the private eye will stay cool and watchful; but John is something else again. Where other PIs are observant, he is nothing short of hyper-analytical, a private eye objectified into a camera-eye recording even the most trifling trivia in the hope of aiding the mission.

Considering his focal position in what is, after all, a first-person account, it is striking that in many ways the narrator remains an enigma even after the book has been returned to the shelf. True, we know something of his physical makeup inasmuch as he is selected for the simulation precisely because he matches the victims in appearance. But his hero quotient is something else. Belying his middle age, an equatorial bulge, and a generally anti-heroic physique, this NASA alumnus displays many traits of a classic action figure. He is smart, resourceful, courageous, and able to operate in moments of intense stress and danger, as when he saves a girl during the bombing. Or does he? "Whether I'd put my arm around her deliberately or because she just happened to be standing there, I couldn't say," recollects John with brutal candour. "It was a lucky coincidence, that's all" (56–7). Behind his self-effacing account lies scientific savvy, which dictates that, in one sense at least, his fate does hinge on pure luck. But does it mean John is no more than a lucky victim of chance when he solves the final riddle? Straining to kill himself under the spell of the psychedelic compound, he doesn't plunge to his death only because the radiator to which he had handcuffed himself is made of cast iron. Are we to conclude that the mission succeeds thanks to pure chance or, even worse, to the radiator? Not quite.

Amid the myriad potholes of chaos and chance on his way to the solution, John demonstrates a solid pattern of design and forethought. Cuffing himself to the radiator in a fit of suicidal frenzy so as not to jump out of the window is a deliberate, even if not premeditated, action. Struggling to surface from the psychotic blackout (in order to scatter clues about the constituents of the lethal compound) is another. If one goes farther back, his selection for the mission is not a fluke, either. There is nothing chancy about his NASA background. Its rigorous conditioning enables him to function under duress and provides him with experience of the effects of psychemicals. At the end of the day, Lem feels no need to resolve whether the hero is a hero by accident or design because the disjunction between heroism and chance is really a conjunction. In one sense John does owe his triumph to a string of coincidences that simply converge on his person during the mission. That said, he is also an exceptional investigator who, before he solves the mystery, survives a terrorist bombing, a brush with death on the streets of Paris, and a near fatal run-in with Compound X.

To underline this point, Lem reactivates a parabolic technique from his bestselling *The Invincible* (1964) and "The Inquest" (from *Pirx the Pilot*, 1968). In *The Invincible* an unarmed crew member steps in to lead a search-and-rescue mission where armoured goliaths fail; in "The Inquest," bumbling inefficiency proves Pirx's winning card in a confrontation with a superior breed of robots.[17] In *The Chain of Chance*, John's apparent disability again combines inextricably with eventual success. Where Achilles had his heel, Lem's hero is hyperallergic to pollen, which, from Naples to Paris, plagues him with a runny nose and fits of sneezing. It even costs him the greatest setback of his space career: the exclusion from the mission to Mars. Yet the same allergy – by his own admission, defect – is a decisive link in the chain of chance that leads him to the solution of the bizarre deaths. "Hero or not?" may just be the wrong categories to apply to a book designed as a nobrow category smasher.

Bearing the imprint of the same design, others characters never evolve beyond the minimum dictated by the book's philosophical parameters. Drawn with equal aptness and sparseness, even the scientists at Barth's party are spokesmen for conflicting points of view rather than fleshed-out individuals. In a macabre twist, the "characters" that come closest to being alive are the corpses. During his protracted presentation John unveils so many aspects of the dead men's backgrounds that theirs become the most thoroughly developed life stories in the book. Not that this database of information fosters sympathy or identification. In fact, only Dieudonné Proque, the victim of the French connection, comes across as more than just a case study. The distinction is poignant for, where all others are victims of blind chance, Proque falls victim to a morally blind killer.

KNOWING IS THE HERO OF MY BOOKS

Novel writing is a rather humble vocation, that is, making up stories to give people pleasure. That's the main business a novelist is doing – he's making up a story to divert the reader.

Walker Percy

Just like *The Chain of Chance*, Walker Percy's *Thanatos Syndrome* is an exhilarating specimen of a beachbook for intellectuals. It combines existentialism and semiotics with an amateur-sleuth hero and a covert investigation, and it runs them through the spin cycle of conspiracy, surveillance, run-ins with cops, and a race to beat the clock to rescue the abused children of Belle Ame. Just like in Lem, Čapek, and Chandler, this mélange of high IQ with high adventure is a deliberate creative stance aimed at both ends of the literary spectrum. In the media blitz and glitz that attended this philosophical thriller's ascent to a national bestseller, Percy even owned to patterning it after *The Invasion of the Body Snatchers*, a classic horror/thriller starring another besieged hero who must investigate eerie changes in the local folk. In an intertextual dig at the original horror flick, Percy's amateur sleuth, Tom More, MD, is suspected of delusion and paranoia, of imagining "a conspiracy, a stealing of people's selves, an invasion of body snatchers" (35).

Consistent with the popular tone is Percy's instant imagery and photo-flash characterization, driven by references to mass-media icons of American public life and cinema. Household names like John Wayne, George Hamilton, Tom Selleck, Harold Lloyd, Clint Eastwood, Maximilian Schell, Howard Cosell, Walter Cronkite, and so on lend their instant, one penstroke recognition to Percy's gallery of rogues and regulars. Whence this effort to render one of the most philosophical-cum-religious books of the last decades in the idiom of a medical thriller? "There is nothing wrong with the adjectives 'philosophical' and 'religious,' but when you apply them to a novel, it is enough to make the novelist turn pale," rationalized Percy.[18] To be sure, he continued, people would rather read a novel than a serious article, on top of the fact that the writer's first and most important task is to tell a gripping tale.

Maintaining in "The State of the Novel: Dying Art or New Science" that art can be as cognitive as science and that the novelist is just as concerned with discovering reality as is the physicist, Percy indeed sounds like Lem's literary doppelgänger. And yet the symmetry between them breaks right down the middle, for the American alone enjoys the hospitality of the canon. Even before his death in 1990, Percy had received imprimatur as a serious writer and a distinct voice in the Southern literary tradition (no matter that he affirmed his affinity with Malraux, not Faulkner). His prose was, of course, often philosophical, Christian, and semiotic in nature. More to the point, it was often popular, genreflecting the mass culture of the media and the movies. But how is it different from Lem?

Ever thoughtful in his investigation of scientific philosophy and existential ethics, the Polish writer repackages them as that same nobrow category: beachbooks for intellectuals. On the way he dips with gusto into popular genres to stoke his suspenseful, on occasion even sensational, plots. "One structural device has always been my favourite," owned Lem in a rare glimpse into his creative process, "treating a puzzle as if it were in a network of contradictory hypotheses and suggestions" (64). The fact that it fits *The Chain of Chance* perfectly is as revealing as is the source – a 1979 interview with Andrzej Ziembiecki, whose title sums up the Polish writer better than any other slogan: "...Knowing Is the Hero of My Books..."

Among nobrow artists who write literature in the idiom of popular thrillers, or who practise philosophy under the mantle of violent conspiracy and social studies under the cloak of a detective brain teaser, Lem stands out. "I simply never think whether what I write can be published here or not" (8), protested the author during the 1981 interview with Raymond Federman. "I never think about ... whether or not someone will be particularly interested in what I write" (11). Hardly the stereotype of a sci-fi hack, remarks like these suggest, rather, a single-minded artist in pursuit of his vision. That Lem is as readable as his sales attest, despite the intellectual admission price he charges to his followers, is a testimony to the white-knuckle power of his storytelling, all the more remarkable in that he comes to North America second-hand, as it were, filtered through the linguistic resources of his translators.

Katar, meaning *Allergy* or *Runny Nose*, but translated by Louis Iribarne as *The Chain of Chance*, is a case in point. Though serviceable, the English version falls short of the original. Not to look too far for an illustration, the Polish "So far, all that danger meant that I put on weight" (9) reads "It was always the same: the greater the danger, the more weight I'd put on" (10). The original packs a comically rueful and deprecating commentary on the futility of the mission, during which John must put away all the dishes Adams had. Hammett's middle-aged Op, with a fatty exterior and iron constitution, could have dead-panned this line, but not the English confession to a chronic problem with handling weight and danger. It's no different with the Polish "I shook my head in pity over myself" (25), which becomes "I shook the self-pity out of my head" (29): close but no cigar. Worse still, the Jove/HBJ edition is studded with typographical errors: "gnowing" for knowing, "had" for bad, "*cui podest*" for *cui prodest*, "todays" for today's. No self-respecting critic would tolerate such carelessness with the legacy of Apollinaire or Conrad, yet no efforts are made to rectify the picture when it comes to Lem, perhaps because his work is, after all, only genre fiction.

But does *The Chain of Chance* fit the bill? Is it lowbrow or nobrow, a gory thriller or a detective mystery with a twist, a social-science *Gedankenexperiment* or a philosophical primer on applied forensic statistics? Considering its puzzling character, it is no accident how little attention it got from American scholars, including science fiction scholars, given that Lem defies not only the parameters of science fiction but also the division of literature into art and entertainment. On the other hand, considering the embarrassing faux pas from even the best meaning critics, it may be for the better. After all, with friends like J. Madison Davis, author of *Starmont Reader's Guide to Stanislaw Lem* (1990), who needs critical adversaries? Few interpretive miscues can match Davis's short section on *The Chain of Chance*, in which he pins on John the name of an Italian airport security expert, Torcelli.[19]

For the most part it is Polish scholarship that renders a measure of justice to the sweeping nature of Lem's nobrow experiment. Once the discussion moves beyond the structural resemblances with *The Investigation* it becomes clear that there is more to the story than sci-fi. In fact, Andrzej Stoff insists that this crime thriller is more rewarding when interpreted as narrative philosophy than as popular entertainment. With a flair for the dramatic, he encapsulates the gist of Lem's story in a couple of koan-like questions: "Would Antigone's destiny seem as tragic with its higher emotions transcribed in the language of neural biochemistry? How tragic would be Hamlet's vagaries of fate if perceived solely as a result of the deterioration of his nervous system, itself caused by random accident?"[20]

Extrapolating even farther, Jerzy Jarzębski applies the stochastic outlook to the hallowed picture of scientific genius and scientific discovery, with startling conclusions. In our crowded times, he argues in the afterword to the Polish 1998 Collected Works edition of *Katar*, we owe our instrumental successes "no longer to a single genius's insight into the chaotic tumble of raw data, but because we lay siege to scientific problems with armies a hundred-thousand strong" (170). Statistically speaking, "one of them is bound to eventually hit on the right answer to the same, forever repeated question." Demoting an individual scientist's role in the process of discovery may sound odd but it's actually close to the truth. It is our cultural practices that may be out of date – showering project leaders with Nobel Prizes, even when they are backed by research establishments with phalanxes of supporting staff run along corporate, if not military, lines.

In the end, whatever else, *The Chain of Chance* is Lem at his entartaining best. With mouth-drying terror on every odd page, and intellectual adventure on every even page, it demonstrates that he is a writer for all reasons – and for all readers.

Conclusion: Whose Art?

There are many good reasons for studying popular fiction. The best, though, is that it matters. In the many and varied forms in which they are produced and circulated – by the cinema, broadcasting institutions and the publishing industry – popular fictions saturate the rhythms of everyday life. In doing so, they help to define our sense of ourselves, shaping our desires, fantasies, imagined past and projected futures.

Tony Bennett and Graham Martin, *Popular Fiction*

We live in the midst of one of the most vibrant eras in literary history, on par with Periclean Athens, Elizabethan England, nineteenth-century Russia, fin de siècle France, Jazz Age USA, or post-Second World War America del Sur. The volume of fiction produced daily exceeds anything witnessed in the days of yore. And even as curricular bias continues to equate literature with its highbrow margins, a popular fiction renaissance inundates the world with genre art that in some cases rivals the great masters.

War with the Newts, *Playback*, and *The Chain of Chance* raise far-reaching questions about the disjunction between art literature and genre fiction, and about artertainment as a late twentieth-century development. At once mass entertainment and high art, they prove that nobrow is a transcontinental aesthetic phenomenon of older heritage than heretofore allowed, and that no satisfactory answers will come forth until literature ceases to be divided institutionally into high and low. There are gems of genre fiction that can stand proud next to Menander, Chaucer, or Sienkiewicz, all popular writers themselves. There are classics that pale next to genre stylists like Walter Miller Jr, Larry McMurtry, or Trevanian. Literature is too precious a resource to give it up to canonical aesthetics that endorses the exile of 97 percent of the books that flow through the arteries of twenty-first-century civilization. These are hardly revisionist claims, or if they are, equally guilty are some of our most refined taste-makers. In *Evgenii Oniegin*, this fine book of literary criticism, Nabokov – himself vilified for the nymphet eroticism of *Lolita*, which now routinely makes college curricula – documented for the ages how Pushkin, the writers' writer, drew on pulpy French romances for inspiration.

In this context it is particularly disappointing that even those who would defend genre art all too often perpetuate the stereotype of its aesthetic shortcomings. This takes the form of apologias for mass fiction's literary demerits, typically vis-à-vis the avant-garde. These are attributed to extenuating circumstances of the socio-economic variety: market pressures, tight publishing schedules, lack of academic training, and so on. Unfortunately, by claiming special status for genre literature ("it's really not that bad if you keep in mind where it comes from"), the defenders buy into the value system of their opponents, shopping for justification and aesthetic upgrade in the wrong places. But there is little need for such affirmative action of the "poor cousin" variety. Popular fiction has never had any intention of doing the job of the avant-garde and, thus, is faulted for being a bird of a different feather.

Nor is it true that, in these days of postmodernism and aesthetic irony, pulp fiction does not make it into classroom. Some popular bestsellers are, after all, a socio-cultural phenomenon too potent (*Catch 22*) or too exemplary of genre fiction's sensational tendencies (*The Postman Always Rings Twice*) to ignore. Some are useful to the extent that they can be exposed as vehicles for any number of oppressive ideologies (*Valley of the Dolls*); others praised for emancipating readers from any number of oppressive social regimes (*Fear of Flying*). Conservatives exemplify the literary immaturity of genre fiction vis-à-vis timeless classics (*Jaws* versus *Moby Dick*), and just about everyone rationalizes the canon whereby popular entartainment of sufficient vintage, its pulp roots trimmed with much aesthetic dexterity, is inducted into the pantheon (*Frankenstein*). The above list makes no claim to being complete or perfectly illustrative. But one would have to look far and wide to find a curriculum abundant with genre novels which are honoured as works of art with analyses of aesthetic nuance, art-historical context, and symbolic and socio-ethical content. Theory aside, we perpetuate the myth of a categorical disunity between serious literature and genre entertainment through curricular practice. When the latter enters the picture, it is mostly in case studies that buttress the same hierarchical system which can accept the literature of entertainment from the past but not the present.

But, even if one were to take these attitudes at face value, what is wrong with the study of literature of entertainment? When has providing pleasure and diversion become as suspect as Homer in Plato's ideal republic? What is wrong with providing an imaginative refuge and a world of thrilling fun for a weary mind? Why is it bad to educate through entertainment or even simply to colour a colourless day? Intellectual taste-makers are hardly an authority on pleasure and the good life, especially when they rewrite literary history in the name of artistic purity and aesthetic ideals. Ever since Dostoevsky became the poster-boy for the intellectual elite, no one cares to remember that, in "Book Learning and Literacy," he campaigned on behalf of giving the public "as much understandable and captivating reading as possible" (44). True to his word, the Russian grandmaster revelled in plots of a sensational nature, juicing up his most famous classic with the blood of old women chopped up with an axe.

Institutional rhetoric is, of course, one thing and reality another. "Claiming to be avant-garde and wanting to discover and embrace the new and different, [intellectual critics] often are terrified of anything new and different. For example at the first presentation of Tchaikovsky's ballet *Nutcracker Suite*, the critics were aghast at the concept and presentation, vowing that the work would never live."[1] The truth is that the consumption of high culture has never been more than a minor pursuit for the majority of the culturati. So, if you find opera boring in the extreme, take heart: so did Leo Tolstoy and Mark Twain.

A LITERARY PHENOMENON THAT ENDURES

Fiction is an art, and the purpose of art is not to instruct but to please.

Somerset Maugham

It is a wonder why literature is often regarded as bad just because untutored readers can relate to it without the need for learned footnotes. Would the great writers in history be upset if someone told them their books were being merely enjoyed rather than studied with a view to scholastic nit-picking? Some perhaps. All the same, the experience of this genre fiction consumer and professor of literature prompts that non-academics frequently get books right, sometimes more so than the professional literary inquisitors in the line of duty. Curricula, it must be said, are often collections of prejudices that dictate that, unless a novel is unpopular with the public or denounced by a bishop or two, it will never make the syllabus. In the final analysis, either the institutional predilection to continue looking for art among highbrow avant-garde is arbitrary or there are persuasive reasons for doing so. If the latter, then it would be nice to see them spelled out for the benefit of those who, having examined what's been put forth so far (see Chapter 2), remain underwhelmed.

Not all that is liked by many people is good fiction. Some popular books, much as some parts of the canon, are stupid, bad, boring, or even dangerous. But the ivory tower can all too easily become the white elephant, and for every open-minded intellectual there is a William Emrys Williams, whose *Penguin Story* plugs Penguin classics in a familiar smear campaign: "they do not deal in those products which aim to excite and contaminate the mind with sensation and which could be more aptly listed in a register of poisons than in a library" (22). Shakespeare's hyper-violent *Titus Andronicus* or Chaucer's raunchy Miller's Tale should never, it seems, make the august Penguin canon.

One may wonder how the avant-garde, this breeding ground for tomorrow's classics cultivated for today's cultivated consumer, is living up to Emrys's superior standards. As headlined in the London *Daily Telegraph* under "Tate Gallery Faces Feces Furor over Art," it heeds the calling by literally affording a load of crap. In 2002, for a bargain price of US$40,000, the illustrious Tate purchased at Sotheby's a tin can containing the feces of Piero Manzoni (so did the New York Museum of Modern Art and the Pompidou Museum in Paris). Can 004, with 30 grams of excrement sold at the price of gold, is from a 1961 "edition" that was, ironically, created as an ironic statement on the art market. "In a letter to a friend," reports the *Edmonton Journal*, Manzoni "explained that his motivation was to expose the gullible nature of the art-buying public."[2] "The Manzoni was a very important purchase," countered the spokeswoman for the Tate Gallery, adding without batting an eyelid: "It was a seminal work."

While on the subject, at the peak of the 2001/2002 art season the wrath of the taxpaying public made the president of Canada's Banff Centre (subsidized by the federal and provincial governments) issue a rare apology. As reported in the Canadian media, a centre-sponsored Mexican "artist" sparked controversy "by privately masturbating into seven glass vials and calling it art," prior to loading them in a cooler and wheeling them around Banff in a cart with a message detailing the nature of the creation.[3] In the service of culture and society, the Canada Council routinely funds avant-art said to represent the most creative spirits in today's artworld. What it gets are rabbit carcasses hung in the woods until infested by maggots to celebrate "the gloriousness of putrefaction" or flesh dresses from flank steak hang in the National Gallery.

For every popular artist trying to connect with his audience there is a Donald Judd with rows of concrete boxes, a Walter de Maria with 400 steel poles embedded in the New Mexico desert, a Joseph Benys with piles of felt, a Robert Ryman with all-white "paintings," or a Dan Flavin whose gift to art are arrays of fluorescent light tubes. Defenders of conceptualism perceive in buildings wrapped in cellophane or various types of viewrinals and scatalogues tactical artistic experiments. Anyone else sees them as evidence of postmodern rigor mortis and abdication of the creative realm to popular culture. Asking on behalf of anyone else, "Is modern art – art at all?" Tsion Avital argues compellingly that the twentieth century's nonrepresentational works are only the debris of the visual tradition they superseded.[4]

In "Society and Culture" Hanna Arendt lectured memorably that an object is cultural to the extent that it endures. Hundreds of years of fruition in all corners of the world legitimates popular literature as a *literary* phenomenon that endures (even if many of its products may be fleeting) rather than as a cultural nuisance. In this view I find an unlikely ally in T.S. Eliot who, albeit with alarm, has also concluded that "it is just the literature that we read for 'amusement,' or 'purely for pleasure' that may have the greatest and least suspected influence upon us" ("Religion and Literature," 350).

Today the avant-garde, historically isolated from the experience of most people, has vanished in the postmodern Forbidden City. Its sperm and feces art or self-consciously narrativeless literature is a calculated slap on the cheek of people keen to find in art something to fill lives lost in corporate frenzy and prepackaged conformity. If what I argued in this book is right, popular literature is by now the master currency for cultural transactions as well as a new constellation of myths and metaphors capable of helping us negotiate the experience of the (post)industrial age.[5] And as such – and here Eliot and I are once more in agreement – it "requires to be scrutinized most closely" (350).

INTRODUCTION

1 Bennett, "Marxism and Popular Fiction," 141.
2 Althusser, "A Letter on Art," 204. For more on Adorno's elitism, see Brown, "Adorno's Critique of Popular Culture."
3 Although I discuss many of them as I go along, one can single out Nye, *Unembarrassed Muse*; Browne, *Against Academia*; Fulcher, "American Conspiracy"; Bennett, *Popular Fiction*; Roberts, *An Aesthetics*; Anderson, *Calliope's Sisters*; Shusterman, *Pragmatic Aesthetics*; Hayes, *Popular Fiction*; Raub, *Yesterday's Stories*; Delamater, *The Detective*; Andrew Macdonald et al., *Shape-Shifting*; or Paula Rabinowitz, *Black and White and Noir*.
4 For a good introduction to this subject, see Hawkins, *Classics and Trash*.
5 In this context, Pawling's *Popular Fiction* and Clive Bloom's *Cult Fiction* are especially valuable comprehensive studies.

CHAPTER ONE

1 For a trenchant critique of their views, see Livingston, "From Text to Work." An early version of this part of my research has appeared in "Popular and Highbrow Literature: A Comparative Look."
2 Babiak, "A Nation of 'Aliterates,'" A9.

3 Mighty Words Inc., a digital provider and Internet publisher of King's e-novella, *Riding the Bullet*, joined the ranks of other e-publishing ventures by folding in January 2002. "I thought electronic publishing was going to be big," bewailed its founder and CEO. "What a rude awakening I got" (Associated Press, "Stephen King's E-Novella Not Enough," E1).

4 Cited in Tebbel, "The History of Book Publishing," 155.

5 In a tangential though not marginal aside, during the same three decades the global literacy level has risen from 1.2 billion to 2.5 billion, which, although praiseworthy in itself, puts it (regrettably) at a rate far below that of book production.

6 Steinberg, *Five Hundred Years of Printing*, 243.

7 Associated Press, Chicago, "Book Sales Edge up in US Market."

8 *Bowker's Annual*, 530–4. Data for France, Japan, the Netherlands, and Russia was incomplete and thus omitted. Largely it conforms to the trend: although France reports a drop, and Russia holds steady, Japan chalks up a Godzilla-size upswing from 35K to 56K between 1992 and 1996, while Holland rockets from 14K to 34K between 1990 and 1993.

9 Canadian Culture, Tourism and the Centre for Education's own estimate of 11,400 is significantly at odds with UNESCO's.

10 Berelson, "Who Reads What Books and Why?" 8. See also Dutscher, "The Book Business in America."

11 In Whiteside, "Onward and Upward in the Arts," part 3, 132. A similar point is made by Dessauer in "Some Hard Facts."

12 Dessauer, *Book Publishing*, 133.

13 *Bowker's American Book Publishing Record* gives a breakdown by the number of titles, with "literature" sitting at 4 percent and "fiction" at 13 percent of all titles published in 1997 in the US (*Statistical Abstract of the United States*, 587). Without an indication of what is subsumed under either rubric, these figures are of little value.

14 Balkin, *A Writer's Guide*, 6.

15 Lynes, *Taste-Makers*.

16 An early reading of this against-the-grain type is Rabinowitz's "The Click of the Spring."

17 Van den Haag offers a brief pragmatic insight into this process in "A Dissent from the Consensual Society," 86. For a useful and more extensive philosophical perspective on the issue, see Olsen, "The Canon and Artistic Failure."

18 Levine's *Highbrow/Lowbrow* describes this process tracing the sanctification of the bard in nineteenth-century America.

19 In *Calliope's Sisters*, Anderson applies this schema to popular music.

20 Pulkhritudova, "Popular Fiction as Journalism." See also Swirski, "A Is for American."

21 Porter, *The Pursuit of Crime*, 121.

22 Tebbel, *International Book Publishing.*

23 The valuable social service and visibility provided by popular literature continued in the twentieth century, as recorded by Baker, "From Apartheid to Invisibility." A good introduction to popular culture studies from a feminist perspective is Modleski's *Studies in Entertainment.*

24 A noted case of reverse piracy was Beecher Stowe's *Uncle Tom's Cabin*; within weeks of publication, 1.5+ million pirated copies flooded England. One can speculate about the social resonance of 1.5+ million readers responding to this "pulp" novel.

25 Quoted in Tebbel, "A History of Book Publishing," 151. A chilling insider's account of these Senate hearings from one of its outspoken participants can be found in Zappa's *The Real Frank Zappa Book* and on the "Porn Wars" track from *Frank Zappa Meets the Mothers of Prevention.*

26 In "Nietzsche in the Nursery," Rasula provides a superb analysis of the witch hunt on the comic books, led in the 1950s by the notorious Fredric Wertham, MD.

27 For further discussion, see Lowenthal and Fiske's early "The Debate over Art."

28 A notorious example of such myopic forecasts was Fukuyama's *The End of History and the Last Man.*

29 Trend forecasting is, of course, notorious for its blend of descriptive and normative roles, and the present effort is no exception. Parts of this section have previously appeared in my "Place and Function of Literature in the Next Millennium."

30 Cited in Macdonald, *Discriminations*, 254.

CHAPTER TWO

1 The reader may begin with the already mentioned studies by Fulcher ("American Conspiracy"); Bennett (*Popular Fiction*); Anderson, "Popular Art and Aesthetic Theory; Shusterman (*Pragmatic Aesthetics*); Hayes (*Popular Fiction and Middle-Brow Taste*); Raub (*Yester-*

day's Stories); Delamater (*The Detective*); Andrew Macdonald (Shape-Shifting); or Paula Rabinowitz (*Black and White and Noir*).

2 An alternative definition and approach to taste cultures is developed by Bourdieu in "The Aristocracy of Culture."

3 Partial syntheses-cum-refutations attempted for popular culture by Ray Browne in "Up from Elitism" and for popular music by Richard Shusterman in *Pragmatic Aesthetics* (Chapter 7) suggest that the rap sheet of charges remains fairly stable over time, an important point in view of counter-charges that the more egregious critiques have been displaced by postmodernism and its flaunted debt to popular forms.

4 A good analysis of Spiegelman's early work in the context of the popular/highbrow debate is Roberts, "Popular Fiction in the Old Dispensation and New." See Witek's *Comics Books as History* for a general overview.

5 Hardly a defence of popular aesthetics, Bourdieu's *Distinction: A Social Critique of the Judgment of Taste* is all the same a good primer on the economic pressures and self-serving contradictions of the allegedly autotelic aesthetics of high art.

6 Gans, *Popular Culture and High Culture*, 22.

7 Stuckey, *The Pulitzer Prize Novels*. In what follows I borrow the terms "invention" and "convention" from Cawelti's classic *The Six-Gun Mystique*.

8 Kaplan, "The Aesthetics of the Popular Arts," 353.

9 "On Popular Music," 38.

10 James Fulcher, "American Conspiracy."

11 An early classic on the subject is Bauer, "The Communicator and His Audience."

12 Chandler, *Later Novels and Other Writings*, 1024.

13 For more discussion, see Kenneth Davis, *Two-Bit Culture*.

14 For further discussion and illustrations, see for example Hawkins, *Classics and Trash*; Swirski, "Stanislaw Lem."

15 Two valuable studies of this process are Dorfles (*Kitsch*) and de Campos, "Vanguarda e Kitsch."

16 Calinescu, "The Benevolent Monster," 3. The distinction between "integrated" and "apocalyptic" academics is developed by Eco in *Apocalypse Postponed*.

17 Dwight Macdonald chooses to draw a different moral from James's story; his "On Selling Out" (*Discriminations*, 171–3) is a good

example of a viciously circular attempt to defend the practices identified above.

18 See Shelden, *Orwell*, especially Chapters 19 and 22.

19 The reader may begin with Gans's *Urban Villagers*, especially Chapter 9, and Tötösy de Zepetnek and Kreisel's pilot study, "Urban English-Speaking Canadian Literary Readership."

20 This point is indirectly confirmed by Hubbard in "Magic and Transformation." For background and additional analysis, see also Miner (*Insatiable Appetites*), Mussell (*Fantasy and Reconciliation*), and Rose ("Is Romance Dysfunctional?").

21 See Fiske, *Television Culture*.

22 The data are consistent over the decades, from Katz and Lazarsfeld's *Personal Influence* to Zuidervaart and Luttikhuizen's *The Arts, Community, and Cultural Democracy*. Spradley ("The Revitalization of American Culture") also offers a pertinent, if more indirect and global, corrective.

23 In *Philosophy of Horror*, "The Nature of Mass Art," and "The Paradox of Junk Fiction." See also Chapter 3.

24 In White, "Mass Culture in America," 13.

25 An informative study of this problem is Dalziel, *Popular Fiction 100 Years Ago*.

26 Shafer, "Non-Adversarial Criticism," 10.

27 White's companion piece to Rosenberg's, "Mass Culture Revisited 2," contains not only a careful response to the mass culture critic but also a more balanced assessment of the menace and the positive contributions of TV and mass (popular) media. This view is echoed in Mardsen's "Television Viewing as Ritual," which acknowledges the power of TV while questioning its demonization.

28 Anderson, "Popular Art and Aesthetic Theory," 38.

29 Chandler, "Raymond Chandler Introduces The Simple Art of Murder," 3.

30 Witness the ridiculous amount of litigation in the entertainment industry, of which the Eddie Murphy-Art Buchwald multimillion-dollar dogfight over the story line of *Coming to America* (resolved in Buchwald's favour) may be just one example.

31 Knoepflmacher ("The Woman in White"); Briggs (*Night Visitors*); Hughes (*The Maniac in the Cellar*); Boyle (*Black Swine in the Sewers*).

32 For a detailed account of these metamorphoses, see Anderson's *Calliope's Sisters*.

33 The most thorough overview is Tatarkiewicz's mammoth *History of Aesthetics*.

34 Boas, "The Mona Lisa in the History of Taste."

CHAPTER THREE

1 Swirski, *Between Literature and Science*, Chapter 1.

2 Culler, *Structuralist Poetics*, 9.

3 See, for example, the results of the already mentioned study by Barsch, "Young People Reading Popular/Commercial Fiction," especially 378.

4 A rare study of the informational calculus of genres is Trzynadlowski's "Information Theory and Literary Genres."

5 Margolin, "Changing Individuals in Narrative," 30.

6 Radway, "Phenomenology, Linguistics and Popular Literature," 95.

7 An early version of this part of my research appeared in "Genres in Action."

8 Lévi-Strauss, "Les limites de la notion de structure en ethnologie," 41. For a review and assessment of causal theories of genre, see Swirski, "Critical Mass."

9 For example, Martindale, *The Clockwork Muse*; or Cupchik, "Identification as a Basic Problem."

10 Ryall, "Teaching through Genre," 33; Fowler, *Kinds of Literature*, 20; Rabinowitz, "The Turn of the Glass Key," 419. For a brief survey of early pragmatic approaches to genres, see Hernadi, *Beyond Genre*, 37–53.

11 For a thorough discussion of this problem, see Skwarczyńska, *Wstep do nauki o literaturze*.

12 In *Kinds of Literature* Fowler drives the same point home regarding tragedy.

13 For a pertinent discussion of "class" and "family" in the context of computer pattern recognition, see Dreyfus, *Computers*.

14 Sperber and Wilson's theory of communication (in *Relevance*) replaces some of the less likely features of Grice's model.

15 For more on the cooperative and competitive aspects of literary games, see Swirski, *Criticism* and *Between Literature and Science*; and Hjort, *Strategy of Letters*.

16 For a more comprehensive discussion, see my "Role of Game Theory in Literary Studies" and *Between Literature and Science*, Chapter 1.

17 This type of analysis can be far from inconsequential; for an early application in agriculture, see Moglower, "A Game Theory Model for Agricultural Crop Selection."

18 On environmental framing, see Shubik *The Uses and Methods of Gaming*, esp. 8–10. Kahneman, Slovik, and Tverski, *Judgment*; and Kahneman and Tverski, *Choices* also stress the role of framing in decision-making processes. A thorough application of matrix analysis to literature can be found in Swirski, "Game Theory."

19 "Why Fantasy?" in Malamud, *Talking Horse*, 47.

20 Blanchot, *Le livre á venir*, 243; and Blanchot, *The Space of Literature*, 220; a similar view is also expressed in Blanchot, *L'Entretien infini*.

21 Todorov, *Genres in Discourse*, 13–5; Todorov, *The Fantastic*, 8.

22 Awarding the Pulitzer Prize, the committee had to invent a special category, as *Maus 2* fit neither the formula for fiction or nonfiction. Its predecessor, *Maus*, was up for the Book Critic's Circle Award in the nonfiction category of biography.

23 Both quotes in Clemons, "The Joyously Versatile Thomas Disch," 66.

24 Livingston's "Justifying the Canon" offers a useful summary of the basic problems of canon formation and maintenance.

CHAPTER FOUR

1 Čapek, "Proletarian Art," 130; second quote from Čapek, "Holmesiana, or About Detective Stories," 122.

2 Čapek, "Proletarian Art," 129.

3 Mann, "A Last Talk with Karel Čapek," 68.

4 Harkins, *Karel Čapek*, 96. Whenever possible, I reference quotations using widely available English sources, such as Harkins (*Karel Čapek*) or Matuška (*Karel Čapek: An Essay*). An alternative translation of this important passage can be found in Bradbrook, "Karel Čapek and English Writers," 103.

5 Levin, in *The Nation*, 482.

6 Harkins, *Karel Čapek*, 20.

7 In Bradbrook, "Karel Čapek," 108. Bradbrook's short review of critical commentaries on page 109 reinforces this nobrow picture.

8 All references are to the readily available 1999 Northwestern University Press edition, which follows the original 1937 translation.

9   Suvin's "Introduction" also documents several other historical allusions.
10 In Matuška, *Karel Čapek*, 254.
11 Startling parallels in style, plot, character, and even phrasing between "Mountain" from Čapek and Čapek's *Wayside Crosses*, and Wells's *The Invisible Man*, are the earliest example of this transcontinental literary dialogue; see also Matuška, *Karel Čapek*, 35-6.
12 Harkins, *Karel Čapek*, 11.
13 Čapek, *In Praise of Newspapers*, 13.
14 In Matuška, *Karel Čapek*, 141.
15 Kussi, "Introduction," 13.
16 In Matuška, *Karel Čapek*, 146.
17 Elsewhere translated as *The Absolute at Large* or even *The Manufacture of the Absolute*. For a compact and apt discussion of the novel, see Bradbrook, *Karel Čapek*, 77–83.
18 Matuška, *Karel Čapek*, 305.
19 Elizabeth Maslen usefully reviews the linguistic and satirical aspects of Čapek's book in "Proper Words."
20 For forty years it remained the only biography in the English lang-uage, until Ivan Klima's *Karel Čapek: Life and Work*.
21 Daly's review of *Newts*, in the light of contemporary colonialism and the Arab-Israeli conflict, suggests one answer to this question.
22 In Harkins, *Karel Čapek*, 12.
23 Miller, "Foreword," 10; Kussi, "Introduction," 13; Doležel, "A Modern Storyteller," 27; Gannett, "Introduction," ix.
24 This argument was first developed by Robert Wechsler in "Karel Čapek in America," 121.
25 Harkins, *Karel Čapek*, 112.
26 In Matuška, *Karel Čapek*, 117.
27 Ibid., 320.
28 Ibid., 117.
29 Spielberg's *AI*, which falls outside this pattern, was conceived and developed by Kubrick, the film's producer.
30 Booth, "Sultan of Science Fiction," E13.
31 In "Karel Čapek: Overview," Suvin is more generous, calling him the most significant writer between the world wars.
32 Confirming my general point above, in 1963 Wyndham's book was made into a B-horror film (alternative title, *Invasion of the Triffids*). In 1975 Robert E. Johnson wrote a screenplay based on *War with the Newts*; it was, however, never produced.

CHAPTER FIVE

1 The interest in and the production of detective stories grew so fast that in no time the genre became a separate class in the magazine industry, getting its own heading in *The Reader's Guide to Periodical Literature* as early as 1905. Hubin's excellent *Crime Fiction 2: A Comprehensive Bibliography, 1749–1990* attests to the unflagging supremacy of this literary category.

2 Josef Skvorecky's *The Sins of Father Knox* was written in playful contravenience of Monsignor's postulates.

3 In Čapek, *In Praise of Newspapers* (see also Chapter 4). Contemporary studies, such as Mullen and O'Beirne's *Crime Scenes: Detective Narratives in European Culture since 1945*, foreground the diversity and malleability of the genre patterns rather than trying to "freeze" certain aspects of the crime story.

4 *Poodle Springs* was completed in 1989 by Robert B. Parker and appeared on book stands as a co-authored Marlowe adventure. Parker returned to Marlowe in a subsequent novel of his own, a sequel to *The Big Sleep*, entitled *Perchance to Dream*.

5 Both quotes in Auden, "The Guilty Vicarage," 408. Parts of this chapter appeared in my "Raymond Chandler: *Playback*."

6 Hiney, *Raymond Chandler*, 277.

7 Throughout, references to *Playback* (Library of America edition) are given as page numbers only; references to other Library of America texts are given as volume-page (e.g., 1:74).

8 Cumberland is Lee Kinsolving in the British edition; see also Chandler's correspondence from 4 October 1958 (Gardiner and Walker, *Raymond Chandler Speaking*, 242).

9 Marling, *The American Roman Noir*, 147, 150, 151. Van Dover furnishes several other choice dismissals in "Chandler and the Reviewers," 35–7; as does Babener in "Raymond Chandler's City of Lies," 147; and Wolfe in *Something More than Night*, 235.

10 See also Webb's review, which comments on "Chandler's brilliantly suggestive reporting of the seedy side of California." Webb, "Keeping up with the Bonds," 6.

11 Speir, *Raymond Chandler*, 78.

12 Gardiner and Walker, *Raymond Chandler Speaking*, 68. For an ample analysis of deception and artifice, see Babener, "Raymond Chandler's City of Lies."

13 Wolfe misses this point entirely. See, Wolfe, *Something More Than Night*, 224. Speaking of the body removal problem, Wolfe declares that no rope (sic!) or person is capable of lowering a man's dead weight down 120 feet. For the record: I lowered a 160-pound sack sixty feet from a Montreal apartment balcony, aided by a length of rope and common hotel room items: bed and desk.

14 The only one of his novels never to become a film. Even *Poodle Springs* is now an HBO feature, starring James Caan.

15 Brewer, "Raymond Chandler without His Knight," 267.

16 MacShane, Raymond Chandler, 143. The screenplay is available as *Raymond Chandler's Unknown Thriller*.

17 Testifying to the state of Chandler criticism, J.O. Tate complained in 1993 that he had not seen the connection between "I'll Be Waiting" and the novel noted anywhere ("Double Talk, Double Play," 122), even though Marling's well known 1986 book notes it explicitly on page 147.

18 Panek, *Probable Cause*, 45; next quote also from Panek, 100.

19 One of its most explicit and compelling indictments can be found in Levine's *Deep Cover*.

20 In "The Turn of the Glass Key" Peter Rabinowitz traces links between Chandler and Conrad, especially in their narrators.

21 Gardiner and Walker, *Raymond Chandler Speaking*, 90–1. Next Chandler quote also from Gardiner and Walker, 56.

22 For more on the Chandler-Clarendon linkage, see Speir, *Raymond Chandler*, 81–3; Tate, "Double Talk," 106–10; and Wolfe, *Something More*, 234–5. If one is to believe Wolfe, the casual reference to Sergeant Green in *Playback* is also a pun, given Chandler's then engagement to Helga Greene.

23 I analyze this issue and the general problem of the validity of interpretation in "Interpreting Art, Interpreting Literature" and in "Is There a Work in This Classroom?"

24 Charles Rolo in the *Atlantic Monthly*, quoted in Van Dover, "Chandler and the Reviewers," 35.

25 Tate's "Double Talk, Double Play" lists several other examples of allusion and wordplay. Even though Betty is cleared of her husband's death, according to Babener, Mrs Murdock's murder of her husband in *High Window* may suggest another playback.

26 7 January 1950, quoted in Diane Johnson, *Dashiell Hammett*, 229.

27 *The Big Sleep* 1:589. In "Rats behind the Wainscoting" (esp. 131), Rabinowitz discusses the symbolism of knight moves in *The Big Sleep*. Chandler himself makes frequent acknowledgments of Marlowe's romantic or sentimental nature. See, for example, a letter in 2:1038–9.

28 Gardiner and Walker, *Raymond Chandler Speaking*, 247. Following quotes in Gardiner and Walker, 248, 249.

29 Letter to Marcel Duhamel, 19 May 1958 (i.e., after the completion of *Playback* [in Gardiner and Walker, *Raymond Chandler Speaking*, 241]).

30 Auden, "The Guilty Vicarage," 406.

CHAPTER SIX

1 The NYT quote cited in Engel, "An Interview with Stanislaw Lem," 219; the *Philadelphia Inquirer* citation is from a review by David Weinberger, "A Melding of Sci-Fi, Philosophy." For biographical information and a career overview, see Swirski, "Stanislaw Lem: A Stranger in a Strange Land," in *A Stanislaw Lem Reader* (1997); "The Man Behind the Giant," in *The Art and Science of Stanislaw Lem* (forthcoming).

2 Directed by Steven Soderbergh, the new *Solaris* stars George Clooney as Kris Kelvin. Germany is reported to be contemplating production of *The Chain of Chance* at some point in the as yet undefined future.

3 Gulledge, "The Reentry Option," 300.

4 The "conventions of normal, realistic literature, or whatever you call it, are insufficient for me. It is so because they usually limit one's field of vision to small groups of people, while I am interested in the fate of humanity as a whole." Stanislaw Lem in Federman, "An Interview," 3.

5 For a good discussion of this story/theory, see Foster and Morton, "God or Game Players."

6 All dates refer to the original Polish editions. In English, *Golem XIV* was issued as part of *Imaginary Magnitude*.

7 All together, there were dozens of ex-astronauts (NASA formally designates them as *former* astronauts) by the time of Lem's novel; today there are well over a hundred.

8 Bereś, Rozmowy, 55. All quotations from Polish sources are in my own translation.

9 Ibid., 55. The "first version" is, of course, *The Investigation*; see Chapter 3 for a discussion of this novel.
10 Lem, "The Profession of Science Fiction," 42.
11 For a discussion of Lem's Investigation and Fowles's "Enigma," see Occhiogrosso, "Threats to Rationalism."
12 Swirski, "Game Theory in the Third Pentagon."
13 For background, see Schelling's still invaluable *Strategy of Conflict*.
14 For analysis of this causal model as pertinent to philosophy of science, see Chapter 2, "Towards a New Epistemology," in my *Between Literature and Science*.
15 John's age is inconsistent: said to be fifty-five years old on page 11, the protagonist is only fifty on page 96.
16 Personal e-mail, 23 October 2002.
17 For a detailed analysis, see Chapter 4, "There Is Science in My Philosophy," in Swirski, *Between Literature and Science*.
18 Samway, "An Interview with Walker Percy," 129.
19 For a full critique of Davis's monograph, see my own "A Literary Monument Revisited."
20 Stoff, *Powieści fantastyczno-naukowe Stanisława Lema*, 121.

CONCLUSION

1 Browne, "Up from Elitism," 231.
2 All quotes in this paragraph from the *Daily Telegraph*, "Tate Gallery Faces Feces Furor over Art." Compounding the irony, at least half of Manzoni's original ninety cans exploded, with full blessing from the creator who "hoped that the cans explode in the vitrines of the collectors."
3 All quotes in this paragraph from the *Calgary Herald*, "Centre Red-Faced at Sperm-Sample 'Art'."
4 Avital, *Art Versus Nonart*.
5 Good analyses of the mythic dimension of popular literature and culture can be found in Slotkin, The Fatal Environment; and Stowe, "Popular Fiction as Liberal Art."

Adorno, Theodor. "On Popular Music." *Studies in Philosophy and Social Sciences* 9, 1 (1941): 17–18

A.I. (Artificial Intelligence). Dir. Steven Spielberg. Universal Studios, DVD, 2005 [2001].

Althusser, Louis. "A Letter on Art, in Reply to André Daspre." In *Lenin and Philosophy, and Other Essays*, 221–8. London: New Left Books, 1971.

Altieri, Charles. "A Procedural Definition of Literature." In *What is Literature*, ed. Paul Hernadi, 62–78. Bloomington: Indiana, 1978.

American Booksellers Association. "Category Share of Consumer Purchases of Adult Books: The US, Calendar 1991–1998." <www.bookweb.org/research/stats/387.html>.

Amis, Kingsley. *The James Bond Dossier*. London: Cape, 1965.

Anderson, Richard L. *Calliope's Sisters: A Comparative Study of Philosophies of Art*. Englewood Cliffs, NJ: Prentice Hall, 1990.

– "Popular Art and Aesthetic Theory: Why the Muse Is Unembarrassed." *Journal of Aesthetic Education* 24 (1990 Winter): 33–46.

Anonymous. "Genus Molge." *Time*, 11 October 1937, 81–2.

Anonymous, "Man and Super-Newt." *Times Literary Supplement*, 30 January 1937, 75.

Arendt, Hanna. "Society and Culture." In *Mass Culture Revisited*, ed. Bernard Rosenberg, and David Manning White, 93–101. New York: Van Nostrand Reinhold, 1971.

Associated Press, Chicago. "Book Sales Edge up in US Market."
 Edmonton Journal, 3 June 2001, C6.
– "Stephen King's E-Novella Not Enough to Keep Mighty Words
 Solvent." *Edmonton Journal*, 14 December 2001, E1.
Auden, W.H. "The Guilty Vicarage." *Harper's Magazine*, May 1948,
 406–12.
Avital, Tsion. *Art Versus Nonart: Art out of Mind*. Cambridge, UK:
 Cambridge University Press, 2003.
Babener, Liahna K. "Raymond Chandler's City of Lies." In *Los Angeles
 in Fiction*. Rev. ed., ed. David Fine, 127–49. Albuquerque: University
 of New Mexico Press, 1995.
Babiak, Todd. "A Nation of 'Aliterates': Are We Too Busy to Really
 Read?" *Edmonton Journal*, 3 June 2001, A1, A9.
Baines, Roger, W. *Inquiétude in the Work of Pierre Mac Orlan*. Amster-
 dam/Atlanta, GA: Editions Rodopi, 2000.
Baker, Donald G. "From Apartheid to Invisibility: Black Americans in
 Popular Fiction, 1900–60." *Midwest Quarterly* 13 (1982): 365–85.
Balkin, Richard. *A Writer's Guide to Book Publishing*. New York:
 Hawthorn Books, 1977.
Barrow, John. *Theories of Everything: The Quest for Ultimate Explana-
 tion*. New York: Fawcett, 1991.
Barsch, Achim. "Young People Reading Popular/Commercial Fiction."
 In *Systemic and Empirical Approach to Literature and Culture as
 Theory and Application*, ed. Steven Tötösy de Zepetnek and Irene
 Sywenky, 371–83. Edmonton and Siegen: University of Alberta RICL-
 CCS and Siegen University, 1997.
Bauer, Raymond A. "The Communicator and His Audience." In *People,
 Society and Mass Communications*, ed. Lewis A. Dexter and David
 M. White, 125–40. New York: Free Press, 1964.
Beacon, Richard L. "Let's Supersize It." *Time*, 9 June 2003, 49–50.
Bednar, Marie. "Čapek, Karel. Three Novels." *Library Journal*,
 1 June 1990, 128.
Beekman, E. M. "Raymond Chandler and an American Genre."
 Massachusetts Review 14 (1973): 149–73.
Bennett, Tony, ed. "The Bond Phenomenon: Theorising a Popular Hero."
 Southern Review 16 (July 1983): 195–225.
– "Marxism and Popular Fiction." *Literature and History* 7, 3rd ser.
 (1981): 138–65.

- "Marxism and Popular Fiction: Problems and Prospects." *Southern Review* 15 (July 1982): 218–33.
- "Marxist Cultural Politics: In Search of 'The Popular.'" *Australian Journal of Cultural Studies* 1 (1983): 2–28.
- *Popular Fiction: Technology, Ideology, Production, Reading*. London: Routledge, 1990.

Berelson, Bernard. "Who Reads What Books and Why?" *Saturday Review of Literature*, 12 May 1951, 7–8, 30–1.

Bereš, Stanisław. *Rozmowy ze Stanisławem Lemem*. Cracow: Wydawnictwo Literackie, 1987.

Berger, Arthur Asa. *Popular Culture Genres*. Newbury Park, CA: Sage, 1992.

Birch, M.J. "The Popular Fiction Industry: Market, Formula, Ideology." *Journal of Popular Culture* 21 (Winter 1987): 79–102.

Blanchot, Maurice. *Le livre á venir*. Paris: Gallimard, 1959.
- *L'Entretien infini*. Paris: Gallimard, 1969.
- *The Space of Literature*. Lincoln: University of Nebraska Press, 1982.

Bloom, Allan. *The Closing of the American Mind*. New York: Simon and Schuster, 1987.

Bloom, Clive. *Cult Fiction: Popular Reading and Pulp Theory*. New York: St Martin's, 1996.

Bloom, Harold. *How to Read and Why?* New York: Scribner, 2000.

Boas, George. "The Mona Lisa in the History of Taste." *Journal of the History of Ideas* 1, 2 (1940): 207–24.

Bonn, Thomas L. *Heavy Traffic and High Culture: New American Library as Literary Gatekeeper in the Paperback Revolution*. Carbondale: Southern Illinois University Press, 1989.

Booth, William. "Sultan of science fiction." *Edmonton Journal*, 14 January 2001, E13.

Bourdieu, Pierre. "The Aristocracy of Culture." In *Media, Culture and Society: A Critical Reader*, eds. Richard E. Collins, James Curran, Nicholas Garnham, Paddy Scannell, Philip Schlesinger, Colin Sparks, 225–54. Beverly Hills: Sage, 1986.
- *Distinction: A Social Critique of the Judgment of Taste*. Cambridge: Harvard University Press, 1984.

Bowker Publications. *Books in Print*. New Providence, NJ: Bowker, 2000.
- *Bowker Annual*. 45th ed. London: Bowker, 2000.

Boyle, Thomas. *Black Swine in the Sewers of Hampstead: Beneath the Surface of Victorian Sensationalism*. New York: Viking, 1988.

Bradbrook, Bohuslava R. "Karel Čapek and English Writers." In *Literature and Politics in Eastern Europe*, ed. Cecilia Hawksworth, 149–65. London: Macmillan, 1992.

– *Karel Čapek: In Pursuit of Truth, Tolerance and Trust*. Brighton: Sussex Academic Press, 1998.

– "Czech. Karel Čapek." *World Literature Today* (Spring 1991): 323–4.

Brantlinger, Patrick. *Bread and Circuses: Theories of Mass Culture as Social Decay*. Ithaca: Cornell University Press, 1983.

Brewer, Gay. "Raymond Chandler without His Knight: Contracting Worlds in *The Blue Dahlia* and *Playback*." *Literature and Film Quarterly* 23, 4 (1995): 273–8.

Briggs, Julia. *Night Visitors: The Rise and Fall of the English Ghost Story*. London: Faber, 1977.

Brogan, D.W. "The Problem of High Culture and Mass Culture." *Diogenes* 5 (Winter 1954): 1–13.

Brown, Lee B. "Adorno's Critique of Popular Culture: The Case of Jazz Music." *Journal of Aesthetic Education* 26 (Spring 1992): 17–31.

Browne, Ray B. *Against Academia: The History of the Popular Culture Association/American Culture Association and the Popular Culture Movement, 1967–88*. Bowling Green: Popular Press, 1989.

– *Eye on the Future: Popular Culture Scholarship into the Twenty-First Century*. Bowling Green: Popular Press, 1994.

– "Up from Elitism: The Aesthetics of Popular Fiction." *Studies in American Fiction* 9 (1981): 217–31.

Browne, Ray B., and Marshall Fishwick, eds. *Preview 2001+: Popular Culture Studies in the Future*. Bowling Green: Popular Press, 1995.

Bruccoli, Matthew J. "Raymond Chandler and Hollywood." In Raymond Chandler, *The Blue Dahlia*. Carbondale, IL: Southern Illinois University Press, 1976.

Burgess, Anthony. "The Non-Book Fame." *The Observer*, Sunday 27 May 1979, 37.

Buriánek, F. *Karel Čapek*. Prague: Melantrich, 1978.

Butler, Marian, ed. *Canadian Books in Print*. Toronto: University of Toronto Press, 2001.

Calgary Herald. "Centre Red-Faced at Sperm-Sample 'Art.'" *Edmonton Journal*, Friday, 14 December 2001, E4.

Calinescu, Matei. "The Benevolent Monster: Reflections on 'Kitsch' as an Aesthetic Concept." *Clio* 6 (Fall 1976): 3–21.

Čapek, Karel. *The Absolute At Large.* [Alternative title: *Factory of the Absolute*] New York: Macmillan, 1927.

– *The Gardener's Year.* New York, London: G.P. Putnam's Sons, 1931.

– "The Meaning of RUR." *Saturday Review* 136 (21 July 1923): 79.

– *In Praise of Newspapers, and Other Essays on the Margin of Literature.* London: G. Allen, 1951.

– "Proletarian Art." *In Praise of Newspapers, and Other Essays on the Margin of Literature*, 123–32. London: G. Allen, 1951.

– "Holmesiana, or About Detective Stories." *In Praise of Newspapers, and Other Essays on the Margin of Literature*, 101–22. London, G. Allen, 1951.

– *Tales From Two Pockets.* Trans. Norma Comrada. North Haven, CT: Catbird Press, 1994.

– *War with the Newts.* Trans. M. and R. Weatherall. Evanston, IL: Northwestern University Press, 1999 [1936].

Čapek, Karel, and Josef Čapek. *R.U.R. and The Insect Play.* London: Oxford University Press, 1966.

– *Wayside Crosses.* In English *Cross Roads.* Trans. Norma Comrada. Highland Park: Catbird Press, 2002.

Carey, John. "Revolted by the Masses." *Times Literary Supplement*, 12–18 January 1990, 34, 44–5.

Carroll, Nöel. "Mass Art, High Art, and the Avant-Garde: A Response to David Novitz." *Philosophic Exchange* 23 (1992): 51–62.

– "The Nature of Mass Art." *Philosophic Exchange* 23 (1992): 5–37.

– *The Philosophy of Horror.* New York: Routledge, 1990.

Cawelti, John. *Adventure, Mystery and Romance: Formula Stories as Art and Popular Culture.* Chicago: University of Chicago Press, 1976.

– *The Six-Gun Mystique.* Bowling Green: Popular Press, 1970.

Chandler, Raymond. *Later Novels and Other Writings.* New York: Library of America, 1995.

– *The Big Sleep.* Vintage Books, 1976 [1939].

– *The High Window.* Penguin Books, 1951 [1942].

– "I'll be Waiting." In *Five Murderers* (Avon Murder Mystery Monthly 19, 1944).

– *Playback. Later Novels and Other Writings.* New York: Library of America, 1995.

– "Raymond Chandler Introduces *The Simple Art of Murder.*" In *The Midnight Raymond Chandler.* Boston: Houghton Mifflin, 1971.
– *Raymond Chandler's Unknown Thriller: The Screenplay of Playback.* New York: Mysterious Press, 1985.
– *Stories and Early Novels.* New York: Library of America, 1995.
Chandler, Raymond, and Robert Parker. *Poodle Springs.* New York: Berkley Books, 1989.
Clark, J., and A.L. Motto. "At War With Our Roots: Karel Čapek Revisited." *Studies in Contemporary Satire* 15 (1987): 1–15.
Clemons, Walter. "The Joyously Versatile Thomas Disch." *Newsweek,* 11 July 1988, 66–7.
Coming to America. Dir. John Landis. DVD. Paramount Studios, 2004 [1998].
Cominsky, Paul, and Jennings Bryant. "Factors Involved in Generating Suspense." *Human Communications Research* 9 (Fall 1982): 49–58.
Comrada, Norma. "Karel Čapek on Science, Progress and Responsibility." *Czechoslovak and Central European Journal* (Summer 1991): 65–72.
Conrad, Peter. "The Private Dick as Dandy." *Times Literary Supplement,* 20 January 1978, 60.
Coser, Lewis A., Charles Kadushin, and Walter W. Powell. *Books: The Culture and Commerce of Publishing.* Chicago and London: University of Chicago Press, 1982.
Csicsery-Ronay, Istvan, Jr. "How Not to Write a Book About Lem." *Science-Fiction Studies* 40 (1986): 387–91.
Culler, Jonathan. *Structuralist Poetics.* Ithaca: Cornell University Press, 1975.
Cupchik, Gerald. "Identification as a Basic Problem for Aesthetic Reception." In *Systemic and Empirical Approach to Literature and Culture as Theory and Application,* ed. Steven Tötösy de Zepetnek and Irene Sywenky, 11–22. Edmonton and Siegen: University of Alberta RICL-CCS and Siegen University, 1997.
Curwen, Peter. *The World Book Industry.* New York and Oxford: Fact On File Publications, 1986.
Daily Telegraph. "Tate Gallery Faces Feces Furor over Art." *Edmonton Journal,* 30 June 2002, A2.
Daly, Macdonald. "*War with the Newts* ... Being the Science-Fiction Book That Helps Put the Gulf War in Perspective." June 2002. <http://www.oneworld.org/ni/issue226/reviews.htm>.

Dalziel, Margaret. *Popular Fiction 100 Years Ago: An Unexplored Tract of Literary History*. London: Cohen and West, 1957.

Davies, Stephen. *Definitions of Art*. Ithaca, NY: Cornell, 1991.

Davis, J. Madison. *Stanislaw Lem*. Mercer Island, WA: Starmont, 1990.

Davis, Kenneth C. *Two-Bit Culture: The Paperbacking of America*. Boston: Houghton Mifflin, 1984.

Day of the Triffids. Dir. Steve Sekely and Freddie Francis. DVD. Aae Films, 2002 [1963].

de Campos, Haroldo. "Vanguarda e Kitsch." In *A arte no horizonte de provável*. 2nd ed. Sao Paulo: Editôra Perspectiva, 1972.

Delamater, Jerome H., and Ruth Prigozy. *The Detective in American Fiction, Film and Television*. Westport, CT: Greenwood, 1998.

Dennis, Everette E., Edward C. Pease, and Craig LaMay, eds. *Publishing Books*. New Brunswick and London: Transaction Publishers, 1997.

Dessauer, John P. *Book Publishing: The Basic Introduction*. New expanded ed. New York: Continuum, 1999.

– "Some Hard Facts about the Economics of Publishing." *Publishers Weekly*, 5 August 1974, 22–5.

Dessner, Lawrence J. "Value in Popular Fiction: The Case of Raintree County." *Junction* 1 (1973): 147–52.

Dickstein, Morris. *Popular Fiction and Critical Values: The Novel as a Challenge to Literary History*. Cambridge: Harvard University Press, 1986.

Doherty, Thomas. "Toward – and Away from – an Aesthetic of Popular Culture." *Journal of Aesthetic Education* 22 (Winter 1988): 31–43.

Doležel, Lubomir. *Narrative Modes in Czech Literature*. Toronto: University of Toronto Press, 1973.

– *On Karel Čapek: A Michigan Slavic Colloqium*. Ed. Michael Makin and Jindrich Toman. Ann Arbor, MI: Michigan Slavic Publications, 1992.

Dorfles, Gillo. *Kitsch: The World of Bad Taste*. New York: Universe Books, 1969.

Dorinson, Zahava K. "Ross Macdonald: The Personal Paradigm and Popular Fiction." *Armchair Detective* 10 (1977): 43–5, 87.

Dostoevsky, Fyodor. *Polnoe sobranie sochinenia*. Vol. 19. Leningrad: Nauka, 1979.

Douglas, Ann. *The Feminization of American Culture*. New York: Knopf, 1977.

Dove, George. "The Complex Art of Raymond Chandler." *Armchair Detective* 8 (1974–75): 271–4.

– *Suspense in the Formula Story.* Bowling Green: Popular Press, 1989.

Dresler, Jaroslav. "Čapek and Communism." In *The Czechoslovak Contribution to World Culture*, ed. M. Rechcigl Jr, 68–75. The Hague: Mouton, 1964.

Dreyfus, Hubert. *What Computers Can't Do: A Critique of Artificial Reason.* New York: Harper and Row, 1972.

Druce, Robert. "An Appetite for Vulgarity: *Jaws* and the Blockbuster Complex: The 'Bestseller' Business." *Dutch Quarterly Review of Anglo-American Letters* 12 (1982): 236–43.

Dubrow, Helen. *Genre.* London: Methuen, 1982.

Duffus, R.L. "Out of the Sea to Conquer the Earth." *New York Times Book Review*, 24 October 1937, 2.

Dunlop, M.H. *Practicing Textual Theory and Teaching Formula Fiction.* Urbana: Council of Teachers of English, 1991.

Durham, Philip. *Down These Mean Streets a Man Must Go: Raymond Chandler's Knight.* Chapel Hill: University of North Carolina Press, 1963.

Dutscher, Alan. "The Book Business in America." *Contemporary Issues* 5 (April–May 1954): 38–58.

Easthope, Anthony. "Notes On Genre." *Screen Education* 32–3 (1979–80): 39–44.

Eco, Umberto. *Apocalypse Postponed.* Ed. Robert Lumley. Bloomington: Indiana University Press, 1994.

– *The Role of the Reader.* Bloomington: Indiana University Press, 1979.

Eisner, Will. *Comics and Sequential Art.* Tamarac, FL: Poorhouse Press, 1991.

Eliot, T.S. *Notes Toward the Definition of Culture.* New York: Harcourt, Brace, 1949.

– "Religion and Literature." In *Selected Essays*, 300. New York: Harcourt, 1950 [1936].

Engel, Peter. "An Interview with Stanislaw Lem." Trans. John Sigda. *The Missouri Review* 7 (1984): 218–37.

Escarpit, Robert. *Trends in Worldwide Book Development 1970–78.* New York: UNESCO, 1982.

Ewen, Stuart. *Captains of Consciousness: Advertising and the Social Roots of the Consumer Culture.* New York: McGraw-Hill, 1976.

Faulkner, William. "Introduction to the Modern Library edition of *Sanctuary*" [1932]. In *Essays, Speeches and Public Letters by William Faulkner*, ed. James B. Meriwether, 176–8. New York: Random House, 1965.

Federman, Raymond. "An Interview with Stanislaw Lem." *Science-Fiction Studies* 29 (1983): 2–14.

Fiedler, Leslie A. *The Inadvertent Epic: From Uncle Tom's Cabin to Roots*. Toronto: Canadian Broadcasting Corporation, 1979.

– *Love and Death in the American Novel*. Rev. ed. New York: Stein and Day, 1966.

– *What Was Literature? Class Culture and Mass Society*. New York: Simon and Schuster, 1982.

Fine, David, ed. *Los Angeles in Fiction*. Rev. ed. Albuquerque: University of New Mexico Press, 1995.

Fiske, John. *Television Culture*. London: Methuen, 1987.

Foster, Thomas R., and Luise H. Morton. "God or Game Players: The Cosmos, William Paley and Stanislaw Lem." *Polish Review* 32, 2 (1987): 203–9.

Foust, R.E. "Poetics, Play, and Literary Fantasy." *New Orleans Review* 9 (1982): 40–4.

Fowler, Alastair. *Kinds of Literature*. Cambridge, MA.: Harvard University Press, 1982.

Frye, Northrop. *The Secular Scripture: A Study of the Structure of Romance*. Cambridge: Harvard University Press, 1976.

Fukuyama, Francis. *The End of History and the Last Man*. New York: Free Press, 1992.

Fulcher, James. "American Conspiracy: Formula in Popular Fiction." *Midwest Quarterly* 24 (1983): 152–64.

Gannett, Lewis. "Introduction." In Karel Čapek, *War with the Newts*, trans. M. and R. Weatherall, vii–xii. New York: Bantam, 1959.

Gans, Herbert J. *Popular Culture and High Culture: An Analysis and Evaluation of Taste*. New York: Basic Books, 1974.

– *The Urban Villagers*. New York: Free Press of Glencoe, 1962.

Gardiner, Dorothy, and Kathrine Sorley Walker, eds. *Raymond Chandler Speaking*. Berkeley: University of California Press, 1997.

Geherin, David. *The American Private Eye: The Image in Fiction*. New York: Ungar, 1985.

Gibian, Peter. *Mass Culture and Everyday Life*. New York: Routledge, 1997.

Glover, David. *Vampires, Mummies and Liberals: Bram Stoker and the Politics of Popular Fiction*. Durham, NC: Duke University Press, 1996.

Greenberg, Clement. *Art and Culture*. Boston: Beacon, 1969.

– *Clement Greenberg: The Collected Essays and Criticism*. Ed. John O'Brian. Chicago: University of Chicago Press, 1986.

Greenwood, Alice. "Language Stereotypes in Mass Market Romances." *Cunyforum: Papers in Linguistics* 9 (1983): 157–73.

Grice, H.P. "Intention and Uncertainty." *Proceedings of the British Academy* 57 (1971): 263–79.

– "Meaning." *Philosophical Review* 66 (1957): 377–88.

– "Meaning Revisited." In *Mutual Knowledge*, ed. N.V. Smith, 223–43. New York: Academic, 1982.

– "Utterer's Meaning and Intentions." *Philosophical Review* 78 (1969): 147–77.

– "Utterer's Meaning, Sentence Meaning and Word Meaning." *Foundations of Language* 4 (1968): 225–42.

Gross, Miriam, ed. *The World of Raymond Chandler*. New York: A and W Publishers, 1978.

Gulledge, Jo. "The Reentry Option: An Interview with Walker Percy." In *Conversations with Walker Percy*, ed. Lewis A. Lawson and Victor A. Kramer, 284–308. Jackson: University Press of Mississippi, 1985.

Habermehl, Lawrence. *The Counterfeit Wisdom of Shallow Minds: A Critique of Some Leading Offenders of the 1980's*. New York: Lang, 1995.

Hammett, Dashiell. "Bodies Piled Up." In *The Black Mask Boys: Masters in the Hard-boiled School of Detective Fiction*, ed. William F. Nolan. New York: William Morrow, 1985 [1923].

– *Red Harvest*. New York: Vintage Crime/Black Lizard, 1992 [1929].

Harkins, William. *Karel Čapek*. New York and London: Columbia University Press, 1962.

– "The Real Legacy of Karel Čapek." In *The Czechoslovak Contribution to World Culture*, ed. M. Rechcigl Jr, 60–7. The Hague: Mouton, 1964.

Hawkins, Harriett. *Classics and Trash: Traditions and Taboos in High Literature and Popular Modern Genres*. Toronto: University of Toronto Press, 1990.

Hayes, Michael. *Popular Fiction and Middle-Brow Taste*. London: Longman, 1993.

Heath, Robert Lawrence, and Jennings Bryant. *Human Communication Theory and Research: Concepts, Contexts, and Challenges.* 2nd ed. Mahwah, NJ: Lawrence Erlbaum, 2000.

Heller, Terry. *The Delights of Terror: An Aesthetics of the Tale of Terror.* Urbana: University of Illinois Press, 1987.

Hennings, Ralf-Dirk, ed. *Informations- und Kommunikationsstrukturen der Zukunft: Bericht anlaesslich eines Workshop mit Stanislaw Lem.* Munich: Wilhelm Fink, 1983.

Herald, Diana Tixier. *Genreflecting: A Guide to Reading Interests in Genre Fiction.* Englewood, CO: Librarians Unlimited, 1995.

Hernadi, Paul, ed. *Beyond Genre.* Ithaca: Cornell, 1972.

– *What Is Literature.* Bloomington, IN: Indiana University Press, 1978.

Highet, Gilbert. "Kitsch." In *A Clerk of Oxenford.* New York: Oxford University Press, 1954.

Hiney, Tom. *Raymond Chandler: A Biography.* New York: Atlantic Monthly Press, 1997.

Hirsh, E.D. "What Isn't Literature." In *What Is Literature*, ed. Paul Hernadi, 24–34. Bloomington, IN: Indiana University Press, 1978.

Hjort, Mette. *The Strategy of Letters.* Cambridge, MA: Harvard University Press, 1993.

Holden, Jonathan. "The Case for Raymond Chandler's Fiction as Romance." *Kansas Quarterly* 10 (1979): 41–7.

Holt, Henry. "The Commercialization of Literature." *Atlantic Monthly* 96 (November 1905): 578–600.

Holt, Patricia. "Turning Best Sellers Into Movies." *Publishers Weekly*, 22 October 1979, 36–40.

Horkheimer, Max, and T.W. Adorno. *Dialectic of Enlightenment.* New York: Continuum, 1990 [1947].

Howell, Yvonne. "Karel Čapek in 1984." *Cross-Currents: A Yearbook of Central European Culture* 3 (1984): 121–30.

Hubbard, Rita C. "Magic and Transformation: Relationships in Popular Romance Novels, 1950 to the 1980s." In *Popular Culture: An Introductory Text*, ed. Jack Nachbar and Kevin Lause, 476–88. Bowling Green: Popular Press, 1992.

Hubin Allen J. *Crime Fiction 2: A Comprehensive Bibliography, 1749–1990.* New York: Garland, 1994.

Hughes, Winifred. *The Maniac in the Cellar.* Princeton: Princeton University Press, 1980.

Humm, Peter, Paul Stigant, and Peter Widdowson. *Popular Fictions: Essays in Literature and History*. London, New York: Methuen, 1986.

International Publishers Association. "Annual Book Title Production." *International Publishers Association*, 10 April 2001. <www.ipa-uie.org>.

Jacobson, Marcia. "Popular Fiction and Henry James's Unpopular Bostonians." *Modern Philology* 73 (1976): 264–75.

Jameson, Fredric. "On Raymond Chandler." *Southern Review* 6, 3 (July 1970): 624–50.

Janaszek-Ivanickova, Halina. *Karol Čapek*. Warsaw: Czytelnik, 1985.

Jarzębski, Jerzy. "Posłowie" [Afterword]. In *Katar*, 167–73. Cracow: Wydawnictwo Literackie, 1998.

Jensen, Margaret Ann. *Love's Sweet Return: The Harlequin Story*. Bowling Green: Popular Press, 1984.

Johnson, Deidre A. "Electronic Alger? Or, Popular Fiction via Modem." *Dime Novel Roundup* 63 (1994): 90–4.

Johnson, Diane. *Dashiell Hammett: A Life*. New York: Random House, 1983.

Joint Committee on the Library of Congress of the United States. *Books in Our Future*. Washington, DC: Center for the Book, 1984.

Jones, Anne Goodwyn. *Gone with the Wind and Others: Popular Fiction, 1920–50*. Baton Rouge: Louisiana State University Press, 1985.

Kahneman, Daniel, and Amos Tversky. *Choices, Values, and Frames*. New York: Russell Sage Foundation; Cambridge, UK: Cambridge University Press, 2000.

Kahneman, Daniel, Paul Slovic, and Amos Tversky. *Judgment Under Uncertainty: Heuristics and Biases*. New York: Cambridge University Press, 1982.

Kaplan, Abraham. "The Aesthetics of the Popular Arts." *Journal of Aesthetics and Art Criticism* 24 (Spring 1966): 351–64.

Katz, Bill. *Dahl's History of the Book*. Metuchen and London: Scarecrow, 1995.

Katz, Elihu, and Paul Lazarsfeld. *Personal Influence*. Glencoe, IL: Free Press, 1955.

Kaye, Howard. "Raymond Chandler's Sentimental Novel." *Western American Literature* 10 (1975): 135–45.

Klima, Ivan. "Čapek's Modern Apocalypse." In *War with the Newts*, trans. M. and R. Weatherall, i–xxi. Evanston, IL: Northwestern University Press, 1999.

– *Karel Čapek: Life and Work.* Trans. Norma Comrada. Highland Park: Catbird Press, 2002.

Knight, Stephen. "'A Hard-Boiled Gentleman': Raymond Chandler's Hero." In *Form and Ideology in Crime Fiction*, 135–67. Bloomington: Indiana University Press, 1980.

Knoepflmacher, U.C. "The Woman in White." In *Worlds of Victorian Fiction*, ed. Jerome H. Buckley, 351–70. Cambridge, MA: Harvard University Press, 1975.

Krajka, Wiesław. "The Concept of the Literary Genre." *Zagadnienia rodzajów literackich/Les Problèmes des Genres Littéraires* 28 (1985): 117–25.

Kussi, Peter. "Introduction." In *Toward the Radical Center: A Karel Čapek Reader*, ed. Peter Kussi, 11–30. Highland Park: Catbird Press, 1990.

– ed. *Toward the Radical Center: A Karel Čapek Reader.* Highland Park: Catbird Press, 1990.

Law, Graham. "'Il s'agissait peut-etre d'un roman policier': Leblanc, Mac-donald, and Robbe-Grillet." *Comparative Literature* 40 (Fall 1988): 335–57.

Leavis, F.R. *Mass Civilisation and Minority Culture.* Cambridge, UK: Minority Press, 1930.

Lem, Stanislaw. *The Chain of Chance.* Trans. Louis Iribarne. New York: Jove/HBJ, 1979 [1976].

– *The Investigation.* Trans. Adele Milch. New York: Avon, 1974 [1959].

– *Katar.* Trans. Louis Iribarne. Cracow: Wydawnictwo Literackie, 1998 [1976].

– *A Perfect Vacuum.* Trans. Michael Kandel. Evanston, IL: Northwestern University Press, 1999 [1971].

– "The Profession of Science Fiction: Answers to a Questionnaire." Trans. Maxim and Dolores Jakubowski. *Foundation* 15 (1979): 41–50.

– *Solaris.* Trans. Joanna Kilmartin and Steve Cox. San Diego: Harvest Books, 2002 [1961].

Levin, Harry. N.t. *Nation*, 20 October 1937, 482–3.

Levine, Lawrence. *Highbrow/Lowbrow: The Emergence of Cultural Hierarchy in America.* Cambridge: Harvard University Press, 1988.

Levine, Michael. *Deep Cover.* New York: Dell, 1990.

Lévi-Strauss, Claude. "Les limites de la notion de structure en ethnologie." In *Sens et usages du terme structure dans les sciences humaines et sociales*, ed. R. Bastide, 44. The Hague: Mouton, 1962.

Lewis, David. *Convention: A Philosophical Study*. Cambridge, MA: Harvard University Press, 1969.

Livingston, Paisley. "From Text to Work." In *After Poststructuralism: Interdisciplinarity and Literary Theory*, ed. Nancy Easterlin, and Barbara Riebling, 91–104. Evanston: Northwestern University Press, 1993

– "Justifying the Canon." In *In Search of a New Alphabet: Comparative Studies in Literature, Dedicated to Douwe W. Fokkema*, 145–50. Amsterdam: John Benjamins, 1996.

Livres Disponibles. Paris: Electre, 1998.

Longhurst, Derek. "A Response to Peter Rabinowitz." *Critical Inquiry* 12 (Spring 1986): 597–604.

Lowenthal, Leo. *Literature, Popular Culture, and Society*. Englewood Cliffs, NJ: Prentice Hall, 1961.

Lowenthal, Leo, and Marjorie Fiske. "The Debate over Art and Popular Culture in Eighteenth-Century England." In *Common Frontiers of the Social Sciences*, ed. Mirra Komarovsky, 33–96. Glencoe: Free Press, 1957.

Luhr, William. *Raymond Chandler and Film*. New York: Ungar, 1982.

Lynes, Russell. *The Taste-Makers*. New York: Harper and Brothers, 1954.

Macdonald, Andrew, Gina Macdonald, and MaryAnn Sheridan. *Shape-Shifting: Images of Native Americans in Recent Popular Fiction*. Westport, CT: Greenwood, 2000.

Macdonald, Dwight. *Against the American Grain*. New York: Random House, 1962.

– *Discriminations: Essays and Afterthoughts 1938–74*. New York: Grossman, 1974.

– "A Theory of Mass Culture." *Diogenes* 3 (Summer 1953): 1–17.

MacRone, Michael, and Tom Lulevitch (illustrator). *Naughty Shakespeare: The Lascivious Lines, Offensive Oaths, and Politically Incorrect Notions from the Baddest Bard of Them All*. New York: Cader Books; Kansas City: Andrews and McMeel, 1997.

MacShane, Frank. *The Life of Raymond Chandler*. New York: Dutton, 1976.

– *The Selected Letters of Raymond Chandler*. New York: Columbia Uni-versity Press, 1986.

Madden, David. "The Necessity for an Aesthetics of Popular Culture." *Journal of Popular Culture* 7 (Summer 1973): 1–13.

Mailloux, Steven. *Interpretive Conventions*. Ithaca: Cornell University Press, 1982.

Makin, Michael, and Jindrich Toman, eds. *On Karel Čapek: A Michigan Slavic Colloquium*. Ann Arbor, MI: Michigan Slavic Publications, 1992.

Malamud, Bernard. *Talking Horse. Bernard Malamud on Life and Work*. Ed. Alan Cheuse and Nicholas Delbanco. New York: Columbia University Press, 1996.

Mann, Erika. "A Last Talk with Karel Čapek." *The Nation*, 14 January 1939, 68–9.

Mardsen, Michael T. "Television Viewing as Ritual." In *Rituals and Ceremonies in Popular Culture*, ed. Ray B. Browne, 120–4. Bowling Green: Popular Press, 1980.

Margolies, Edward. *Which Way Did He Go? The Private Eye in Dashiell Hammett, Raymond Chandler, Chester Himes, and Ross Macdonald*. New York: Holmes and Meier, 1982.

Margolin, Uri. "Changing Individuals in Narrative: Science, Philosophy, Literature." *Semiotica* 107, 1–2 (1995): 5–31.

Marling, William. *The American Roman Noir: Hammett, Cain, and Chandler*. Athens: University of Georgie Press, 1995.

– *Raymond Chandler*. Boston: Twayne, 1983.

Martindale, Colin. *The Clockwork Muse: The Predictability of Artistic Change*. New York: Basic, 1990.

Maslen, Elizabeth. "Proper Words in Proper Places: The Challenge of Čapek's War with the Newts." *Science-Fiction Studies* 41, 14 (1987): 82–92.

Matuška, Alexander. *Karel Čapek: An Essay*. Trans. Cathryn Allan. Prague: Artia, 1964.

McCloud, Scott. *Understanding Comics: The Invisible Art*. Northampton, MA: Kitchen Sink Press, 1993.

Merton, Robert K. *Social Theory and Social Structure*. New York: Free Press, 1968.

Miller, Arthur. "Foreword." In *Toward the Radical Center: A Karel Čapek Reader*, ed. Peter Kussi, 9–10. Highland Park: Catbird Press, 1990.

Miner, Madonne M. *Insatiable Appetites: Twentieth-Century American Women's Bestsellers*. Westport, CT: Greenwood Press, 1984.

Modleski, Tania. *Studies in Entertainment: Critical Approaches to Mass Culture*. Bloomington: Indiana University Press, 1986.

Moglower, Sidney. "A Game Theory Model For Agricultural Crop Selection." *Econometrica* 30 (1962): 253–66.

Morson, Gary Saul. *The Boundaries of Genre.* Austin: University of Texas Press, 1981.

Mott, Frank Luther. *Golden Multitudes; The Story of Best Sellers in the United States.* New York: Macmillan, 1947.

Mullen, Anne, and Emer O'Beirne, eds. *Crime Scenes: Detective Narratives in European Culture since 1945.* Amsterdam/Atlanta, GA: Editions Rodopi, 2000.

Mussell, Kay. *Fantasy and Reconciliation: Contemporary Formulas of Women's Romance Fiction.* Westport, CT: Greenwood, 1984.

Neale, Catherine. "Desperate Remedies: The Merits and Demerits of Popular Fiction." *Critical Survey* 5 (1993): 117–22.

Nelson, Cary, and Lawrence Grossberg. *Marxism and the Interpretation of Culture.* Urbana: University of Illinois Press, 1988.

Nemoianu, Vergil, and Robert Royal. *The Hospitable Canon: Essays on Literary Play, Scholarly Choice, and Popular Pressures.* Philadelphia: J. Benjamins, 1991.

Novitz, David. "Nöel Carroll's Theory of Mass Art." *Philosophic Exchange* 23 (1992): 39–49.

Nussbaum, Martha. "The Literary Imagination of Public Life." *New Literary History* 22 (1991): 876–910.

Nye, Russell B. *The Unembarrassed Muse: The Popular Arts in America.* New York: Dial Press, 1970.

O'Brian, Geoffrey. *Hardboiled America: The Lurid Years of Paperbacks.* New York: Van Nostrand Reinhold, 1981.

Occhiogrosso, Frank. "Threats of Rationalism: John Fowles, Stanislaw Lem, and the Detective Story." *Armchair Detective* 13 (1980): 4–7.

Oliker, Michael A., and Walter P. Królikowski, eds. *Images of Youth: Popular Culture as Educational Ideology.* New York: Peter Lang, 2001.

Olsen, Stein Haugom. "The Canon and Artistic Failure." *British Journal of Aesthetics* 41, 3 (2001): 261–78.

Palmer, Jerry. *Potboilers: Methods, Concepts and Case Studies in Popular Fiction.* London: Routledge, 1991.

Panek, Leroy Lad. *Probable Cause: Crime Fiction in America.* Bowling Green: Popular Press, 1990.

Parker, Robert B. "Introduction to *Playback*." In *Raymond Chandler's Unknown Thriller: The Screenplay of Playback*, xi–xxi. New York: Mysterious Press, 1985.

– *Perchance to Dream*. New York: Berkley, 1991.

Parrott, Cecil. "Karel Čapek: Overview." In *Reference Guide to World Literature*. 2nd ed., ed. Lesley Henderson, 229–31. Detroit: St James Press, 1995.

Partridge, Ralph. "Detection and Thrillers." *The New Statesman and Nation*, 30 August 1958, 254.

Pawling, Christopher, ed. *Popular Fiction and Social Change*. New York: St Martin's, 1984.

Peer, Willie van. "But What Is Literature? Toward a Descriptive Definition of Literature." In *Literary Pragmatics*, ed. Roger D. Sell, 127–41. London: Routledge, 1991.

Percy, Walker. *The Thanatos Syndrome*. New York: Ivy Books, 1987.

– *State of the Novel: Dying Art of New Science*. New Orleans: Faust Publishing Company, 1988.

Pérez-Reverte, Arturo. *The Club Dumas*. Trans. Sonia Soto. New York: Vintage, 1998.

Philips, Deborah, and Alan Tomlinson. *Homeward Bound: Leisure, Popular Culture and Consumer Capitalism*. London: Routledge, 1992.

Phy, Allene Stuart. *The Bible and American Popular Culture: An Overview and Introduction*. Philadelphia: Fortress Scholars, 1985.

Porter, Dennis. *The Pursuit of Crime: Art and Ideology in Detective Fiction*. New Haven: Yale University Press, 1981.

Pulkhritudova, Elizaveta. "Popular Fiction as Journalism." *Journal of Communication* 41 (Spring 1991): 92–101.

Rabinowitz, Paula. *Black and White and Noir: America's Pulp Modernism*. New York: Columbia University Press, 2002.

Rabinowitz, Peter J. "The Click of the Spring: The Detective Story as Parallel Structure in Dostoyevsky and Faulkner." *Modern Philology* 76 (May 1979): 355–69.

– "Rats behind the Wainscoting: Politics, Convention and Chandler: *The Big Sleep*." *Studies in American Literature* 7, 2 (1979): 175–89.

– "The Turn of the Glass Key: Popular Fiction as Reading Strategy." *Critical Inquiry* 11 (1985 March): 418–31.

Radway, Janice A. *A Feeling for Books: The Book-of-the-Month Club, Literary Taste, and Middle-Class Desire*. Chapel Hill: University of North Carolina Press, 1997.

– "Phenomenology, Linguistics and Popular Literature." *Journal of Popular Culture* 12, 1 (1978): 88–98.

– *Reading the Romance: Women, Patriarchy, and Popular Literature*. Chapel Hill: University of North Carolina Press, 1984.

Rasula, Jed. "Nietzsche in the Nursery: Naive Classics and Surrogate Parents in Postwar American Cultural Debates." *Representations* 29 (Winter 1990): 50–77.

Raub, Patricia. *Yesterday's Stories: Popular Women's Fiction of the Twenties and Thirties*. Westport, CT: Greenwood, 1994.

Reader's Guide to Periodical Literature. Minneapolis: H.W. Wilson, 1905.

Reck, Thomas. "Raymond Chandler's Los Angeles." *The Nation*, 20 December 1975, 661–3.

Roberts, Thomas J. *An Aesthetics of Junk Fiction*. Athens: University of Georgia Press, 1990.

– "Popular Fiction in the Old Dispensation and the New." *Literature: Literature Interpretation Theory* 4 (1993): 245–59.

Rose, Suzanna. "Is Romance Dysfunctional?" *International Journal of Women's Studies* 8 (May/June 1985): 250–65.

Rosenberg, Bernard. "Mass Culture Revisited 1." In *Mass Culture Revisited*, ed. Bernard Rosenberg, and David Manning White, 3–12. New York: Van Nostrand Reinhold, 1971.

Rosenberg, Bernard, and David Manning White. *Mass Culture: The Popular Arts in America*. Glencoe: Free Press, 1957.

– *Mass Culture Revisited*. New York: Van Nostrand Reinhold, 1971.

Rosmarin, Adena. *The Power of Genre*. Minneapolis: University of Minnesota Press, 1985.

Ross, Malcolm. *The Aesthetic Impulse*. New York: Pergamon, 1984.

Ruszkowski, Marek. "Syntaktyczne ukształtowanie powieści popularnej: Na przykładzie literatury polskiej dwudziestolecia międzywojennego." *Poradnik Językowy* 3 (1993 March): 108–17.

Ryall, Tom. "Teaching Through Genre." *Screen Education* 17 (1975): 27–33.

Samway, Patrick H. "An Interview with Walker Percy." In *More Conversations with Walker Percy*, ed. Lewis A. Lawson and Victor A. Kramer, 127–33. Jackson: University Press of Mississippi, 1993.

Sarland, Charles. *Young People Reading: Culture and Response*. Philadelphia: Open University Press, 1991.

Seabrook, John. *Nobrow*. New York: Knopf, 2000.

Schelling, Thomas C. *The Strategy of Conflict*. Cambridge, MA: Harvard University Press, 1960.

Schmoller, H. "The Paperback Revolution." In *Essays in the History of Publishing*, ed. Asa Briggs, 297–8. London: Longman, 1974.

Scholes, Robert. *Stillborn Literature*. Lincoln: University of Nebraska Press, 1982.

Schubert, Peter Z. *The Narratives of Čapek and Cexov: A Typological Comparison of the Authors' World Views*. San Francisco: International Scholars Publications, 1996.

Shusterman, Richard. "Popular Art and Education." *Studies in Philosophical Education* 13 (1994–95): 203–12.

– *Pragmatic Aesthetics: Living Beauty, Rethinking Art*. Oxford: Blackwell, 1992.

– "Too Legit to Quit? Popular Art and Legitimation." *Iyyun, The Jerusalem Philosophical Quarterly* 42 (January 1993): 215–24.

Schwartz, Delmore. "Masterpieces as Cartoons." *Partisan Review* 19, 4 (1952): 461–71.

Shafer, Ingrid. "Non-Adversarial Criticism, Cross-Cultural Conversation, and Popular Literature." *Proteus* 6 (Spring 1989): 6–15.

Shelden, Michael. *Orwell: The Authorized Biography*. London: Minerva, 1991.

Showalter, Elaine. *A Literature of Their Own*. Princeton: Princeton University Press, 1977.

Shubik, Martin. *The Uses and Methods of Gaming*. New York: Elsevier, 1975.

Skenazy, Paul. "Introduction." In *Raymond Chandler Speaking*, ed. Dorothy Gardiner and Kathrine Sorley Walker, 1–7. Berkeley: University of California Press, 1997.

– *The New Wild West: The Urban Mysteries of Dashiell Hammett and Raymond Chandler*. Boise: Boise State University, 1982.

Skvorecky, Josef. *Sins for Father Knox*. Trans. Kaca Polackova Henley. Toronto: Lester and Orpen Dennys, 1988.

Skwarczyńska, Stefania. "Niedostrzeżony problem podstawowy genologii." *Wstęp do nauki o literaturze*. Vol. 3. Warsaw: Czytelnik, 1965.

Slote, Michael A. "The Objectivity of Aesthetic Value Judgements." *Journal of Philosophy* 68 (1971): 821–39.

Slotkin, Richard. *The Fatal Environment: The Myth of the Frontier in the Age of Industrialization, 1800–90*. New York: Atheneum, 1985.

Solaris. Dir. Steven Soderbergh. Twentieth Century Fox, DVD, 2004 [2002].

Speir, Jerry. *Raymond Chandler*. New York: Ungar, 1981.

Sperber, D., and D. Wilson. *Relevance: A Theory of Communication*. Cambridge, MA: Harvard University Press, 1986.

Spiegelman, Art. *Maus: A Survivor's Tale*. Vol. 1: *My Father Bleeds History*. New York: Pantheon, 1986.

– *Maus: A Survivor's Tale*. Vol. 2: *And Here My Troubles Began*. New York: Pantheon, 1991.

Spradley, James. "The Revitalization of American Culture: An Anthropological Perspective." In *Qualities of Life. Critical Choices for Americans*. Vol. 7. Lexington, MA.: Lexington Books, 1976.

Statistical Abstract of the United States. The National Data Book. 119th ed. Washington: US Census Bureau, 1999.

Statistics Canada. *Book Publishing 1992–93*. Ottawa: Minister of Industry, Science and Technology, 1995.

– *Canadian Culture in Perspective: A Statistical Overview*. Ottawa: Minister of Industry, 2000.

Stecker, Robert. "The Role of Intention and Convention in Interpreting Artworks." *Southern Journal of Philosophy* 31 (1993): 471–89.

Steinberg, S.H. *Five Hundred Years of Printing*. Rev. ed. Ed. John Trevitt. London: The British Library and Oak Knoll Press, 1996.

Stoff, Andrzej. *Lem i inni: szkice o Polskiej science fiction*. Bydgoszcz: Pomorze, 1990.

– *Powieści fantastyczno-naukowe Stanisława Lema*. Warszawa: Panstwowe Wydawnictwo Naukowe, 1983.

Stowe, Harriet B. *Uncle Tom's Cabin*. New York: Chelsea House Publishers, 1999 [1852].

Stowe, William W. "Popular Fiction as Liberal Art." *College English* 48 (November 1986): 646–63.

Stuckey, William Joseph. *The Pulitzer Prize Novels: A Critical Backward Look*. 2nd ed. Norman: University of Oklahoma Press, 1981.

Sturm, Terry. *Popular Fiction*. Auckland: Oxford University Press, 1991.

Sutherland, John. *Bestsellers: Popular Fiction of the 1970s*. London: Routledge and Kegan Paul, 1981.

Suvin, Darko. "Introduction." In Karel Čapek, *War with the Newts*. Boston: Gregg Press, 1975.

– "Karel Čapek, or the Aliens among Us." In *Metamorphoses of Science Fiction*. New Haven: Yale University Press, 1979.

– "Karel Čapek: Overview." In *St. James Guide to Science Fiction Writers*, 4th ed., ed. Jay P. Pederson, 159–61. Detroit: St James Press, 1996.

Swirski, Peter. "A is for American, B is for Bad, C is for City: The ABC of Police and Urban Procedurals." In *All Roads Lead to the American*

City, ed. Peter Swirski. Edmonton: M.V. Dimic Research Institute, 2006. Forthcoming.

– *Between Literature and Science. Poe, Lem, and Explorations in Aesthetics, Cognitive Science, and Literary Knowledge.* Montreal: McGill-Queen's University Press, 2000; Liverpool: Liverpool University Press, 2001.

– "Critical Mass: Mass Literature and Generic Criticism." *Zagadnienia rodzajów literackich/Les Problèmes des Genres Littéraires* 37 (1994): 97–107.

– "Game Theory in the Third Pentagon: A Study in Strategy and Rationality." *Criticism: A Quarterly for Literature and the Arts* 38 (1996): 303–30.

– "Genres in Action: The Pragmatics of Literary Interpretation." *Orbis Litterarum: International Review of Literary Studies* 52 (1997): 141–56.

– "Interpreting Art, Interpreting Literature." *Orbis Litterarum: International Review of Literary Studies* 56, 1 (2001): 17–36.

– "Is There a Work in This Classroom? Interpretations, Textual Readings, and American Fiction." *International Fiction Review* 32 (2005). Forthcoming.

– "Karel Čapek: *War With the Newts.*" In *Beacham's Encyclopedia of Popular Fiction.* Vol. 13, ed. Katy Maker, Alan Hedblad, Marie Lazzeri, Thomas McMahon, Deborah J. Morad, and Colleen Tavor, 411–19. Detroit: Gale Group, 2000.

– "A Literary Monument Revisited: Davis's *Stanislaw Lem* and Seven Polish Books on Lem." *Science-Fiction Studies* 58 (1992): 411–17.

– "The Man Behind the Giant." In *The Art and Science of Stanislaw Lem*, ed. P. Swirski. Montreal: McGill-Queen's University Press. Forthcoming.

– "Place and Function of Literature in the Next Millenium." *SPIEL: Siegener Periodicum zur internationalen empirischen Literaturwissenschaft* 16, 1/2 (1997): 429–32.

– "Popular and Highbrow Literature: A Comparative View." In *Comparative Literature and Comparative Cultural Studies*, ed. Steven Tötösy de Zepetnek, 183–205. West Lafayette: Purdue University Press, 2003.

– "Raymond Chandler: *Playback.*" In *Beacham's Encyclopedia of Popular Fiction.* Vol. 14, ed. Scot Peacock, 327–35. Detroit: Gale Group, 2001.

– "The Role of Game Theory in Literary Studies." In *Empirical Approaches to Literature: Proceedings of the Fourth Biannual Conference of the International Society for the Empirical Study of Literature–IGEL*, ed. Gebhard Rusch, 37–43. Siegen: Lumis Publications, 1995.

– "Stanislaw Lem." In *Science Fiction Writers*. Rev. ed., ed. Richard Bleiler, 453–66. New York: Charles Scribner's Sons, 1999.

– "Stanislaw Lem: *Fiasco*." In *Beacham's Encyclopedia of Popular Fiction*. Vol. 9, ed. Kirk Beetz, 5491–500. Osprey, Florida: Beacham Publishing, 1998.

– "Stanislaw Lem: Stranger in a Strange Land." In *A Stanislaw Lem Reader*. Evanston, IL: Northwestern University Press, 1997.

Symons, Julian. *Mortal Consequences: A History – From the Detective Story to the Crime Novel*. New York: Harper and Row, 1972.

Tatarkiewicz, Władysław. *History of Aesthetics*. Ed. J. Harrell, C. Barrett, D. Petsch. Trans. Adam and Ann Czerniawski, R.M. Montgomery, Chester Kisiel and John F. Besemeres. The Hague: Mouton, 1970, 1974.

Tate, J.O. "Double Talk, Double Play: Rewinding Raymond Chandler's *Playback*." *Clues* 14, 1 (1993): 105–34.

Tebbel, John. "The History of Book Publishing in the United States." In *International Book Publishing: An Encyclopedia*, ed. Philip G. Altbach and Edith S. Hoshino, 147–55. New York and London: Garland, 1995.

Todorov, Tzvetan. *The Fantastic: A Structural Approach to a Literary Genre*. Cleveland, OH: Case Western Reserve, 1975.

– *Genres in Discourse*. Trans. Catherine Porter. Cambridge, MA: Cambridge University Press, 1990.

Tötösy de Zepetnek, Steven, and Philip Kreisel. "Urban English-Speaking Canadian Literary Readership: Results of a Pilot Study." *Poetics* 21 (1992): 211–38.

Trzynadlowski, Jan. "Information Theory and Literary Genres." *Zagadnienia rodzajów literackich/Les Problèmes des Genres Littéraires* 4, 1–6 (1993): 31–48.

Tuchman, Barbara W. *The Book*. Washington, DC: Center for the Book, Library of Congress, 1980.

UNESCO. "Book Production: Number of Copies by UDC Classes." *UNESCO Institute for Statistics* 4, 6 (2002). <http://www.uis.unesco.org/templage/html/cult_consult.html>.

- "Book Production: Number of Titles by UDC Classes." *UNESCO Institute for Statistics* 4, 5 (2002). <http://www.uis.unesco.org/templage/html/cult_consult.html>.
- Index Translationum: Cumulative Index since 1979. CD-ROM. Paris: UNESCO, 1999.

Uspensky, Gleb and Peter B. Kaufman. "Fifty Million Agatha Christies Can Be Wrong." *Publishers Weekly* 9 (November 1992): 60–2.

Van den Haag, Ernest. "A Dissent from the Consensual Society." In *Mass Culture Revisited*, ed. Bernard Rosenberg, and David Manning White, 85–92. New York: Van Nostrand Reinhold, 1971.
- "Notes on American Popular Culture." *Diogenes* 17 (Spring 1957): 56–73.

Van Dover, J. Kenneth. "Chandler and the Reviewers: American and English Observations on a P.I.'s Progress, 1939–64." In *The Critical Response to Raymond Chandler*, 19–37. Westport, CT: Greenwood Press, 1995.
- *The Critical Response to Raymond Chandler*. Westport, CT: Greenwood Press, 1995.

Verzeichnisses Lieferbarer Bücher 1999–2000. Verlag der Buchhändler-Vereinigung: Frankfurt, 1999.

Waites, Bernard, Tony Bennett, and Graham Martin, eds. *Popular Culture: Past and Present*. London: Croom Helm, 1982.

Walton, Kendall. "Categories of Art." *Philosophical Review* 66 (1970): 334–67.

Walton, Priscilla L., and Manina Jones. *Detective Agency: Women Rewriting the Hard-Boiled Tradition*. Berkeley: University of California Press, 1999.

Webb, W.L. "Keeping up with the Bonds." *Manchester Guardian*, 11 July (1959): 6.

Wechsler, Robert. "Karel Čapek in America." In *On Karel Čapek: A Michigan Slavic Colloqium*, ed. Michael Makin and Jindrich Toman, 109–25. Ann Arbor, MI: Michigan Slavic Publications, 1992.

Weinberger, David. "A Melding of Sci-Fi, Philosophy: Review of *His Master's Voice*." *Philadelphia Inquirer* 7 May 1983, D04.

Wellek, René. *Essays on Czech Literature*. The Hague: Mouton, 1962.

Whitaker's Books in Print 2000. Whitaker and Sons: London, 2000.

White, David Manning. "Mass Culture in America: Another Point of View." In *Mass Culture: The Popular Arts in America*, ed. Bernard Rosenberg, and David Manning White. Glenco, IL: Free Press, 1957.

– "Mass Culture Revisited 2." In *Mass Culture Revisited*, ed. Bernard Rosenberg, and David Manning White. New York: Van Nostrand Reinhold, 1971.

Whiteside, Thomas. *The Blockbuster Complex: Conglomerates, Show Business, and Book Publishing*. Middletown, CT: Wesleyan University Press, 1981.

– "Onward and Upward with the Arts: The Blockbuster Complex." *The New Yorker*, 29 September 1980, 48–101; 6 October 1980, 63–146; 13 October 1980, 52–143.

Williams, William Emrys. *The Penguin Story*. London: Penguin, 1956.

Winter, Douglas E. *Faces of Fear: Encounters with the Creators of Modern Horror*. New York: Berkley, 1985.

Witek, Joseph. *Comics Books as History: The Narrative Art of Jack Jackson, Art Spiegelman, and Harvey Pekar*. Jackson, MS: University Press of Mississippi, 1989.

Wittgenstein, Ludwig. *Philosophical Investigations*. Oxford: Blackwell, 1953.

Wolfe, Peter. *Something More Than Night: The Case of Raymond Chandler*. Bowling Green: Popular Press, 1985.

Worpole, Ken. *Contemporary Publishing and Popular Fiction*. London: Comedia, 1984.

Wyndham, John. *Day of the Triffids*. Modern Library, 2003 [1951].

Yanarella, Ernest J., and Lee Sigelman. *Political Mythology and Popular Fiction*. New York: Greenwood Press, 1988.

Zappa Frank, and Peter Occiogrosso. *Frank Zappa Meets the Mothers of Prevention*. CD. Rykodisc: 1985.

– *The Real Frank Zappa Book*. New York, London, Sydney: Poseidon Press, 1989.

Ziembiecki, Andrzej. "'...Knowing Is the Hero Of My Books...'" *Polish Perspectives* 9 (1979): 64–9.

Zuidervaart, Lambert, and Henry Luttikhuizen, eds. *The Arts, Community, and Cultural Democracy*. New York: St Martin's, 2000.